Management for Professionals

More information about this series at https://link.springer.com/bookseries/10101

Marc Helmold • Ayşe Küçük Yılmaz
Tracy Dathe • Triant G. Flouris

Supply Chain Risk Management

Cases and Industry Insights

Springer

Marc Helmold
IU, International University of applied Science
Berlin, Germany

Tracy Dathe
Macromedia University
Berlin, Germany

Ayşe Küçük Yılmaz
Faculty of Aeronautics and Astronautics
Technical University 2 Eylul Campus
Eskişehir, Turkey

Triant G. Flouris
American College Greece
Athens, Greece

ISSN 2192-8096 ISSN 2192-810X (electronic)
Management for Professionals
ISBN 978-3-030-90799-0 ISBN 978-3-030-90800-3 (eBook)
https://doi.org/10.1007/978-3-030-90800-3

This Springer imprint is published by the registered company Springer Nature Switzerland AG
The registered company address is: Gewerbestrasse 11, 6330 Cham, Switzerland

Preface

Fierce competition, megatrends, the COVID-19 pandemic, the ongoing globalization, and the permanent liberalization of markets have changed the face of supply chains drastically. Companies, which want to survive in a hostile environment, must establish the optimum combination of supply, supply chains, and operations. Supply chain resilience and stability has severe impacts on the planning, design, and management of supply chains and the implementation of sustainable supply chain risk management approaches. Supply chain risk management (SCRM) is defined in this context as the implementation of strategies to manage both everyday and exceptional risks along the supply chain based on continuous risk assessment with the objective of reducing vulnerability and ensuring continuity. SCRM applies risk management process tools after consultation with risk management services, either in collaboration with supply chain partners or independently, to deal with risks and uncertainties caused by, or affecting, logistics-related activities, product availability (goods and services) or resources in the supply chain. This book provides a holistic and practical approach to SCRM and supply management. It combines operations, supply chain, and supply chain risk management best practices across the value chain. It explains comprehensively how these new paradigms enable companies to concentrate on value-adding activities and processes to achieve a long-term sustainable and competitive advantage. The book contains a variety of best practices, industry examples, and case studies. Focusing on best-in-class examples, the book offers the ideal guide for any enterprise in operations and supply in order to achieve a competitive advantage across all business functions focusing on value-adding activities.

Berlin, Germany — M. Helmold
Eskişehir, Turkey — A. Küçük Yılmaz
Berlin, Germany — T. Dathe
Athens, Greece — T. Flouris

Contents

About the Authors

Marc Helmold is full-time professor at IU Internationale Hochschule in Berlin. He teaches bachelor's, master's, and MBA courses on operations management, information management, procurement, strategic management, and supply chain management.From 1997 until 2016, he held several top management positions in the automotive and railway industry. Between 1997 and 2010, he worked in several companies like Ford, Ford-Mazda Japan, Porsche, and Panasonic Automotive in managerial supply chain management functions and executed lean workshops throughout the value chain.From 2013 until 2016, he was the general manager of Bombardier Transportation in China and led the sourcing and spare parts sales activities. Since 2016, he has been professor at IUBH and has his own consultancy. In this capacity, he improves companies' performance.

Ayşe Küçük Yılmaz is a full-time professor at Eskisehir Technical University in Eskisehir, Faculty of Aeronautics and Astronautics. She has received her PhD from Anadolu University. She has also served as vice dean of the Faculty of Aeronautics and Astronautics from February 02, 2015 to October 2020. She was airport business manager at the international Eskisehir Hasan Polatkan Airport for 6 years (between Feb, 2015 and 2020 October).She is a Master of Science in Management and Strategy. She teaches bachelor's, master's, and PhD course at aviation management and pilotage departments on management and organization, enterprise risk management, safety management systems, airport business and management, airline management, and strategic risk management. Her research interests include performance management, risk management, reputation risk, stakeholder relations, airport business management, culture, supply chain risk management, logistic management, and organizational behavior. She has authored 13 books and 5 chapters, and over 50 refereed journal articles and international conference papers. She has performed many scientific projects at the national level. She is member of the editorial boards of several international academic journals. She is a licensed aircraft engine framework maintenance technician since 2001.

Tracy Dathe is a freelance business advisor and lecturer in the fields of financial management and international communication.She owes her expertise in international cooperation not least to her practical experience in the industry. From 2012 to 2016, as CFO of an automotive spare part manufacturer, she was responsible for general commercial management at the German headquarter, as well as for the subsidiaries in China, France, Italy, Sweden, the Czech Republic, Turkey, and the USA.Her professional focus lies in financial management and intercultural communication in multinational SMEs.

Triant Flouris is vice president of academic affairs at Metropolitan College in Athens, Greece. He has over 25 years of experience as a researcher, teacher, and administrator in the USA, Canada, and Greece, half of which in executive positions. An internationally recognized aviation scholar, Triant has published numerous works on risk management, strategy, and project management applied to the aviation industry including books, refereed journal articles, and reports. Flouris' work illustrates a firm belief and commitment in the interplay between the link of theory and applied practice in academe. Triant is a member of the board of trustees of the Aviation Accreditation Board International (AABI) and a professional pilot and flight instructor with over 10,000 hours of flight time.

Abbreviations

AI	Artificial Intelligence
AM	Additive Manufacturing
AR	Augmented Reality
AviSCRM	Aviation Supply Chain Risk Management
BSC	Balanced Score Card
BME	Bundesverband Materialwirtschaft, Einkauf und Logistik
BMW	Bayerische Motorenwerke
BOS	Bombardier Operating System
CSR	Corporate Social Responsibility
DIN	Deutsche Industrienorm
DSCM	Downstream Supply Chain Management
ERP	Enterprise Resource Planning
EXW	Ex Works
IOT	Internet of Things
IOP	Internet of People
IPO	International Procurement Office
ISO	International Standardisation Organisation
IUBH	International University Bad Honnef
JIT	Just-in-Time
KPI	Key Performance Indicator
MPS	Mercedes Benz Production System
OEE	Overall Equipment Effectiveness
OKR	Objectives Key Results
PDCA	Plan, Do, Check, Act
PDSA	Plan, Do, Study, Act
PE	Physical Education
PESTEL	Political, Economic, Social, Technological, Environmental and Legal (Macro) Analysis
PPS	Production Planning System
QR	Quick Response
SFM	Shop Floor Management
SCC	Smart Cities and Communities
SCM	Supply Chain Management
SCOR	Supply Chain Operation Reference

SCRM	Supply Chain Risk Management
TIMWOOD	Seven Types of Waste in Manufacturing
TÜV	Technischer Überwachungsverein
UN	United Nations
USCM	Upstream Supply Chain Management
USP	Unique Selling Propositions
VW	Volkswagen
5S	Seiri, Seiton, Seiso, Seiketsu, Shitsuke
7R	7 Rights

Introduction to Supply Chain Risk Management (SCRM) 1

Progress cannot be generated when we are satisfied with existing situations

—*Taiichi Ohno (1912–1990)*

1.1 Supply Chain Management (SCM)

Supply chain management (SCM) can be described as the process of planning managing, executing, and improving the key business process that ensure effective delivery of products and services from suppliers through to the end customer as shown in Fig. 1.1 (Helmold & Terry, 2021). SCM involves the process of enabling the effective flow of information, materials, and services from suppliers from upstream supply chain with raw materials and materials to operation and to finally deliver products and services to end customer or the downstream supply chain. SCM allows the simultaneous integration of customer specifications, which is an important aspect that helps in enhancing better performance of the internal process that ultimately influences greater upstream supplier performance (Werner, 2020). Based on these definitions, it is evident that the common feature of SCM is to enhance end-to-end coordination as a result of effective integrating of both internal and external processes in the supply chain in order to deliver value to the end customer. Therefore, it can be argued to suggest that the potential benefits of an enhanced SCM can be considered to provide higher quality of products or services, effective cost savings, shorter and more reliable delivery times, fewer disruptions, and risk reduction. Customer satisfaction and effective service delivery can be seen to be the key factors that enable a business to survive in the highly competitive market (Bozarth & Handfield, 2013). Effective supply chain management (SCM)

M. Helmold et al., *Supply Chain Risk Management*,
Management for Professionals, https://doi.org/10.1007/978-3-030-90800-3_1

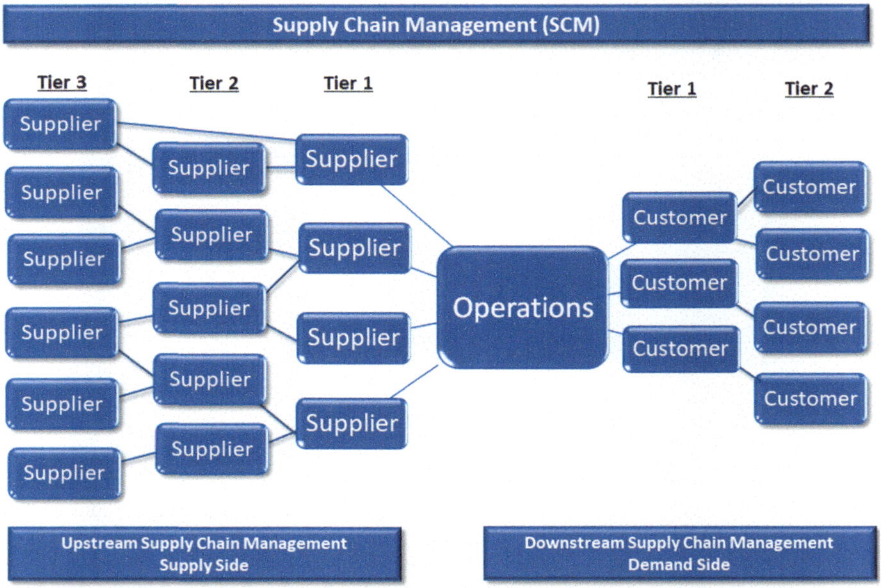

Fig. 1.1 Supply chain management. (Source: Author's source)

practices have become valuable in enhancing competitive advantage by reducing waste, increasing efficiency therefore, improving overall organizational performance and its strategy.

By concentrating on core competencies and shifting services to supplier networks that are in competition with one another, new models, strategies, and processes emerge, which lead supplier management into a central role in every company. For a long time now, the focus in the future has not only been on increasing company-internal cost advantages, but much more on the exchange of information and the exploitation of global cross-company potential. Scope of added value can no longer be handled by the manufacturer alone, but must rely on innovative, efficient, and flexible supplier structures. Increasing competition, global trends, the COVID-19 pandemic, sustainability elements, technological change, and shortened product life cycles place ever higher demands on companies and their suppliers in numerous industries. The increasing variety of products, shorter innovation cycles, and cross-sector business models with digital business processes also increase the complexity of future control of value networks. However, the planning, control, and monitoring of the upstream value creation networks, that is, the supplier networks, become more difficult, so that these tasks have to be covered by holistic, standardized, and innovative supplier management. But modern supplier structures are becoming increasingly volatile. The control of the external value-added networks must therefore also adapt to the new requirements. Risk prevention in the supply chain is therefore of central importance to every company, but only 17 percent of

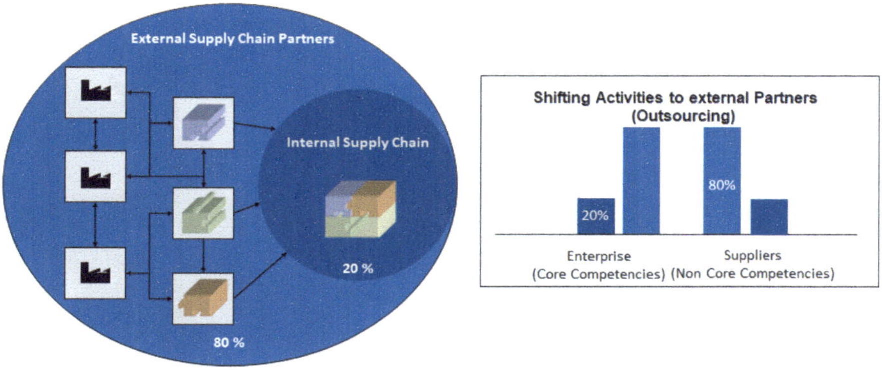

Fig. 1.2 Shifting activities to the upstream supply chain management. (Source: Author's source)

companies operate preventive supplier management with early and standardized involvement of their suppliers, and more than two-thirds only assess a selection of suppliers (Dust, 2016). These alarming figures emerge from the study "Total Supplier Management—Strategic Competitive Advantages through Risk Prevention in Supplier Management." The representative survey of 221 companies from different sectors from industry, trade, and services was carried out by the Technical University of Berlin in cooperation with the BME region Berlin-Brandenburg (Dust, 2016). Figure 1.2 shows the proportion of peripheral competencies being transferred to external suppliers to more than 80 percent (outsourcing). In contrast, own core competencies, that is, processes and skills from which competitive advantages are developed for your own company, are around 20 percent.

1.2 Globalization and Global Supply Networks

Global supply chains and supply chains cause problems due to their complexity and growing challenges. But it should also be emphasized that increasing requirements, response times and risk protection contribute to the differentiation of companies and value-added networks (Dust, 2019). Not only the own company but also its supplier networks are in constant competition in order to gain the favor of the customer. Value networks are competitive, global, and customer-relevant. They enable companies to provide services that are coordinated across the company, in which the individual partners focus on their core competencies, as Fig. 8.1 shows (Fig. 1.3).

The aim of a value-added network in supplier management (supplier network) is usually the realization of collaborative competitive advantages and the possibility of own specialization. Because each partner involved brings their specific core competencies into the network, the conflict of goals between a high degree of specialization on the one hand and a broader, more diverse range of services on the other can be resolved. In the network, the advantages of more flexible task distribution and

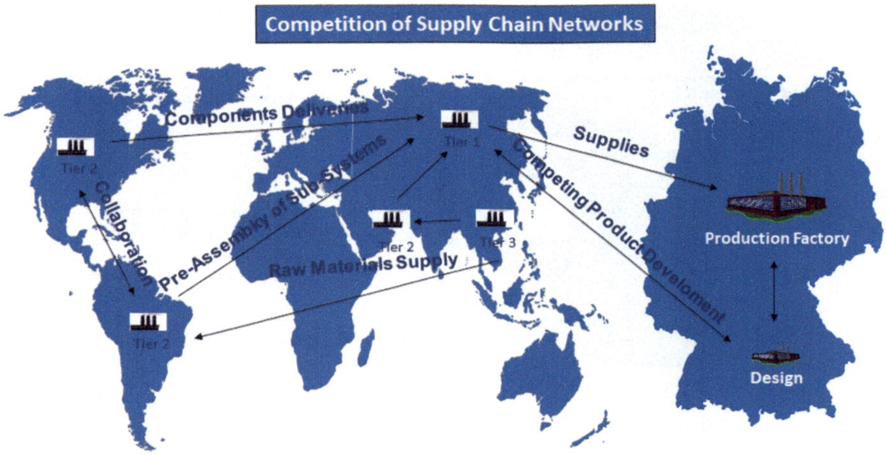

Fig. 1.3 Globalized supply and value chains. (Source: Marc Helmold)

capacity utilization at network level can be combined with specialization advantages at the level of the value-added units (economies of scale and economies of scope). This works all the better, the more the individual skills complement each other. Examples of a successful implementation of this idea are production networks, procurement networks, or knowledge and competence networks. The hybridity of the network in comparison to the market and hierarchy is particularly evident from the forms of coordination used. In general, a distinction is made between price, instruction, and trust, which are assigned to the institutions market, hierarchy, and network according to their focus of application. Figure 8.2 shows global competition and the international orientation of supplier networks. In this real example of the automotive industry, the spatially separate development and production take place in Germany. The development requires a cooperation between the two locations in southern and northern Germany. In this constellation, there are tier 1, 2, and 3 suppliers who each produce raw materials, components, or systems in their own production and provide them to the downstream level (tier 3 and tier 2 and tier 1). Raw material (e.g., steel) is supplied to the component supplier (tier 2) from China. The tier-2 suppliers are located in the Arabian Peninsula and South America, from where components are sent to the tier-1 system supplier. This supplier is located in Russia and delivers the systems to the German end customer. The system check and homologation take place at the supplier's premises before the delivery. The supplier also has employees at the end customer who ensure a smooth process and the synchronization of the supply chain. Development and tier-1 supplier collaborate in the product creation process of development (competitive development). This is how a global value chain works (Fig. 1.4).

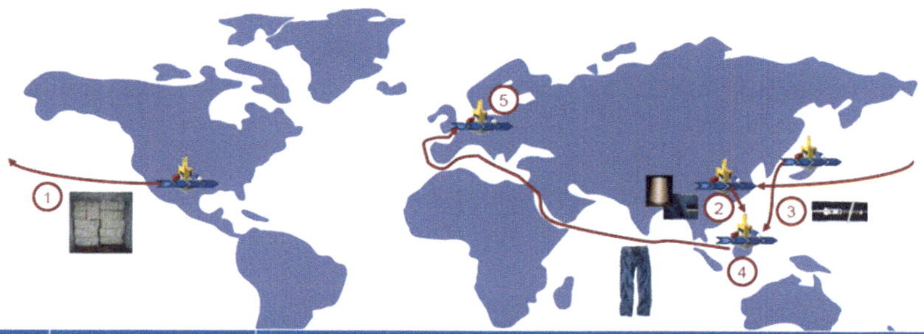

Step	Place and Material	International Value-adding Activites and Processes
1.	Cotton from Texas (U.S.A.)	Transport by truck to texas and to Los Angles. Via vessel transport to China. Container transport. Transport inside China via truck
2.	Garment from China	Consolidation. Transport per vessel to China.
3.	Fasteners from Japan	Transport via plane from Japan Osaka to Malaysia.
4.	Jeans trousers from Malaysia	Packaging and consolidation. Transport to Hamburg in Germany.
5.	Final Product	Commissioning and distribution to Europe and in Germany.

Fig. 1.4 Example of international trade and supply chains. (Source: Author's source)

1.3 Risks in the Supply Chain

Supply chain disruptions on your business by identifying the risks within your supply chain and developing ways to mitigate them. You should document this process in a risk management plan, which is part of your overall business continuity plan. There are two major types of risk to include in your risk management plan:

- External risks—those that are outside of your control
- Internal risks—those that are within your control

External risks can be driven by events either upstream or downstream in the supply chain. There are five main types of external risks:

- Demand risks—caused by unpredictable or misunderstood customer or end-customer demand
- Supply risks—caused by any interruptions to the flow of product, whether raw material or parts, within your supply chain
- Environmental risks—from outside the supply chain; usually related to economic, social, governmental, and climate factors, including the threat of terrorism

- Business risks—caused by factors such as a supplier's financial or management stability, or purchase and sale of supplier companies
- Physical plant risks—caused by the condition of a supplier's physical facility and regulatory compliance

Internal risks provide better opportunities for mitigation because they are within your business's control. There are five main types of internal risks:

- Manufacturing risks—caused by disruptions of internal operations or processes
- Business risks—caused by changes in key personnel, management, reporting structures, or business processes, such as the way purchasers communicate to suppliers and customers
- Planning and control risks—caused by inadequate assessment and planning, which amount to ineffective management
- Mitigation and contingency risks—caused by not putting contingencies (or alternative solutions) in place in case something goes wrong
- Cultural risks—caused by a business's cultural tendency to hide or delay negative information. Such businesses are generally slower to react when impacted by unexpected events

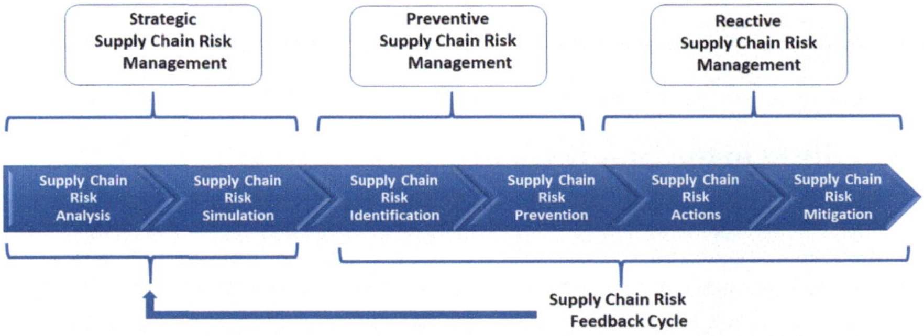

1.4 Supply Risk Prevention and Mitigation

Supply disruptions are defined as "unplanned and unanticipated events that disrupt the normal flow of goods and materials within the supply chain." They distinguish between coordination risks and disruption risks. Supply chain complexity is described as (Helmold & Terry, 2021) "the sum of the total number of nodes and the total number of forward, backward and within-tier material flows" in the upstream supply chain network. Such complexity has a huge impact on supply chain reliability and supply chain stability. The overall recommendation made in several papers is to reduce the number of suppliers, since supply chain complexity increases the risk of disruption. Highlighted the definitions of various authors, using a variety of criteria: (1) function, (2) type of risk (Ellram & Liu, 2002), (3) drivers of risks, and (4) likelihood of occurrence. While the literature on supply management and risk management is growing, there is no organized structure regarding the sources of causal factors for supply chain risks and supply disruptions. Several papers show that supply disruptions can lead to high monetary recovery cost, waste, and sharp decreases in sales as pointed out in one of the previous sections by (Helmold & Terry, 2021). As well as findings in literature other sources such as field research, internal reports, and interviews display that supply disruptions have severe impacts on companies in the analyzed European transportation industry. Supply disruptions and their associated risks have been classified in the literature using a variety of criteria, for example, function, type of risk, and drivers of risk. Pointed out that enterprises without operational slack and redundancies in their supply chains experience negative stock effects. They also revealed the tremendous impacts of supply chain disruptions on stock price performance and shareholder value. Causal factors for supply disruptions are automatically associated with risks in the supply network, as stated by (Helmold & Terry, 2021). Several authors outline incidents in which supply disruptions caused production standstill or temporary stops in manufacturing companies in the European industry. Other authors refer to capacity management in terms of supply disruptions as being a crucial risk factor for supply chain discrepancies. Due to such risks, specific measures are necessary in terms of overcoming potential supply disruptions caused by supplier capacity shortages. Mitigations and preventive measures can take the form of diverse capacity management, back-up equipment, or alternative manufacturing locations, as recommended by (Helmold & Terry, 2021).

It is useful to compare the supply chain strategies of companies and their resulting ability to cope with some of the abovementioned disruptions. Created models which can be used by managers to measure and assess the vulnerability of their company and supply chain in relation to the associated risks. Typology may also provide avenues for future research and thus guide practitioners in the management of their supply chain risk portfolio. Such a classification is a useful tool for supply chain managers in differentiating between independent and dependent variables and the mutual relationships, which would help them to focus on those key variables that are most important for effective risk minimization in a supply chain. Zsidisin typologized causal factors for supply disruptions into different categories—high, medium, and low risk—based on managerial perception. Other authors besides Zsidian have built on this typology and outlined causal factors for supply disruptions as follows, which comprise the following:

- Capacity shortages
- New product launches
- Disaster issues (e.g., earthquake, flood)
- Lack of supply chain transparency
- Labor-related issues (e.g., strike)
- Constraints on market capacity
- Pricing instabilities

- Quality discrepancies
- Transport issues
- Product transfers to sites or plants
- Inflexible production capacities

1.5 Method of Global Risk Evaluation

Once a company has decided what it is going to evaluate, the next step is to establish how it will evaluate the performance of the supplier. There are many ways to do this, and some are more costly, time consuming, and resource intensive than others. By quantifying the level of risk and the projected benefit of a method of evaluation, company personnel can determine the most appropriate method or combination of methods that should be used. Some methods that companies commonly use to evaluate and measure supplier performance include the following:

- Site visits by cross-functional teams
- Supplier audits (process, special process, or product audits)
- Paper supplier questionnaires
- Web-based supplier questionnaires
- Organizing existing data
- Internal questionnaires
- Requiring external certifications
- Developing own certifications
- Third-party reviews
- Phone call with a supplier
- Independent ratings
- Contacts with other supplier customers

1.6 Fair Trade

Fair trade is a controlled trade in which the producers receive a minimum price for their products, which is determined by a fair-trade organization. This is intended to enable producers to earn a higher and more reliable income than in conventional retail even at lower market prices. The amount of a fair price has been a topic of business ethics that has been discussed for decades. In addition, this form of trade tries to build long-term "partnership" relationships between traders and producers. In production, international environmental and social standards as well as those prescribed by the organizations should also be complied with. The very heterogeneous fair-trade movement mainly focuses on goods that are exported from developing countries to industrialized countries. Fair trade encompasses agricultural products as well as products from traditional handicrafts and industry and is increasingly expanding into new areas such as tourism under the name "fair travel." Fairly traded products are offered in natural food and world shops as well as in supermarkets and restaurants. According to the umbrella organization Fairtrade International, over 1.5 million farmers took part in such programs in 2015.

1.7 Glocal Supply Chains

With rapid advances in communications and information technologies, manufacturers are now able to truly operate globally, source their raw materials where it is cheapest and most practical, and expand their customer base internationally (Cousins et al., 2008). However, manufacturers must also adapt their offerings to local trends, predict which items will be in greater demand in a particular region, and adjust their stocks accordingly. In today's connectivity and information technology world, political, economic, and social relationships naturally tend to be global, interwoven, and interdependent. And that is exactly the fundamental characteristic of globalization. This term was first used in the 1980s in an economic context and since then has spread more and more and in other contexts.

Globalization has brought numerous advantages for the manufacturing industry, such as the possibility of easy access to technical knowledge or the opportunity to learn from countries that are pioneers in areas such as automation and digitization. In addition, in a globalized world, it is easier to communicate with business partners in real time, no matter where they are. This is a clear advantage for business transactions and helps to build trust between business partners.

However, one of the most controversial aspects of globalization is the risk of homogenization. In a globalized society, the same goods are often produced and sold in vastly different markets, with little attention paid to the preferences and habits of the different end customers. In the long run, this can have a negative impact on sales and prevent companies from really gaining a foothold in a particular region.

That is why a new term has recently been circulating that shows that companies can act globally and still target the specifics of regional markets—welcome to the age of glocalization. The transition from globalization to glocalization was driven by several factors. First of all, the recent past has shown more and more clearly that failure to observe local market conditions can have a negative impact on business and lead to problems in ongoing operations and in the supply chain. The second reason for this transformation is the increased public awareness of the need to support the national and regional economies through the local procurement of raw materials, which can also help optimize the supply chain and reduce transport costs.

But in fact glocalization is not really a new concept, because international corporations have always been forced to adapt their production to local demand. Automobile manufacturers have always had to adhere to specific regulations when diversifying their product range depending on the sales market—an obvious example of this is the side on which the steering wheel is installed and whether the speedometer shows miles or kilometers per hour.

What is new is the influence that glocal business models have on supply chain management, as manufacturers strive to establish a supply chain that operates globally and yet adapts to local demand.

1.8 IncoTerms 2020

Foreign trade between exporters and importers can only function smoothly if the exports and imports include standardized and generally recognized trade clauses in their delivery and payment conditions that regulate the transfer of risk and place of delivery, transport costs and transport risk, the obligation to take out transport insurance, and the destination. The Incoterms regulate which of the duties the seller or buyer is responsible for. If the Incoterms are the basis, only a certain abbreviation needs to be used without having to describe the distribution of costs and risks in detail.

The Incoterms are clauses that enable the contracting parties to make extensive, standardized regulations on the place of performance, other performance obligations, and the transfer of risk within the framework of a sales contract.

Incoterms, a widely used terms of sale, are a set of 11 internationally recognized rules that define the responsibilities of sellers and buyers. Incoterms specify who is responsible for paying for and managing the shipment, insurance, documentation, customs clearance, and other logistical activities. There are certain terms that have special meaning within Incoterms, and some of the more important ones are defined as follows:

- Delivery: The point in the transaction where the risk of loss or damage to the goods is transferred from the seller to the buyer.
- Arrival: The point named in the Incoterms to which carriage has been paid.
- Free: Seller has an obligation to deliver the goods to a named place for transfer to a carrier.
- Carrier: Any person who, in a contract of carriage, undertakes to perform or to procure the performance of transport by rail, road, air, sea, inland waterway, or by a combination of such modes.
- Freight forwarder: A firm that makes or assists in the making of shipping arrangements.
- Terminal: Any place, whether covered or not, such as a dock, warehouse, container yard or road, rail or air cargo terminal.
- To clear for export: To file Shipper's Export Declaration and get export permit.

1.9 Case Study: Lidl's Glocal Supply Strategy

As part of the Schwarz group of companies based in Neckarsulm, the Lidl retail company is one of the leading companies in the food retail sector in Germany and Europe. Lidl is currently present in 32 countries and operates around 10,800 branches in 29 countries worldwide. In Germany, around 83,000 employees in around 3200 branches ensure customer satisfaction every day. Dynamic in daily implementation, high performance in the result and fairness in dealing with one another characterize the work at Lidl. Since 2008, the Lidl online shop offers non-food products to various categories, wines and spirits as well as travel and other services. The range of the Lidl online shop is constantly expanding and currently comprises around 30,000 items. As a discounter, Lidl attaches great importance to an optimal price-performance ratio for its customers. Simplicity and process orientation determine daily actions. Lidl takes responsibility for society and the environment and focuses on five areas of activity in the area of sustainability: product range, employees, environment, society, and business partners. Lidl generated sales of EUR 81.2 billion in the 2018 financial year, of which EUR 22.7 billion Lidl Germany. Lidl Germany is one of the first grocery retailers to publish a list of the main suppliers for its food and non-food private label range on its website. The company is thus making a relevant contribution to greater transparency in its global supply chains. It lists independent manufacturers that Lidl commissions to manufacture its own brand products such as baked goods, beverages, cosmetics, cleaning agents, or hardware such as toys, sports equipment, or garden furniture. The list is updated regularly and supplements the main production sites in the supply chain published in 2017 for the textile and shoe range of Lidl's own brands. "In our own brand range, we can work directly with the manufacturers to promote a more responsible production method. In order to know where and how our products are made, it is important to know our business partners as well as possible. At the same time, our customers want to learn more about how our products are made. We want to meet this wish, combined with our demand for more transparency," says Jan Bock, Purchasing Manager at Lidl Germany.

Grocer with Regional and Global Supply Chains

As one of the large grocery retailers, Lidl sources its goods from suppliers in the region and all over the world. The basis of every business relationship is the "Code of Conduct" prescribed by Lidl, which guarantees basic rights for employees along the supply chain. Lidl also places a special focus on the implementation of recognized minimum standards: Independent and local experts regularly check all production sites for Lidl non-food products in accordance with the recognized amfori Business Social Compliance Initiative (BSCI) or the international standards for social accountability (SA 8000) and systematically examine potential for improvement.

References

Bozarth, C. C., & Handfield, R. B. (2013). *Introduction to operations and supply chain management* (3rd ed.). Harlow Pearson.

Cousins, P., Lawson, L. B., & Squire, B. (2008). *Strategic supply management: Principles, theories and practice*. Harlow Prentice Hall.

Dust, R. (2016). *Lieferanten–/Risikomanagement. Bislang wenig Risikoprävention in der Supply Chain*. In BME. Abgerufen am 28.9.2020. https://www.bme.de/bislang-wenig-risikopraevention-in-der-supply-chain-1468/

Dust, R. (2019). *Total supplier management*. Hanserverlag München.

Ellram, L. M., & Liu, B. (2002). The financial impact of supply management. *Supply Chain Management Review, 6*(6), 30–36.

Helmold, M. & Terry, B. (2021). *Operations and supply management 4.0. Industry insights, case studies and best practices*. Springer: Cham.

Werner, H. (2020). *Supply chain management. Grundlagen, Strategien, Instrumente und Controlling*. Springer Wiesbaden.

SCRM Strategy 2

When you're dying of thirst, it is too late to think about digging a well

—*Japanese say*

2.1 SCRM as Part of the Overall Strategy

Supply chain management (SCM) can be defined as the process of planning, controlling, executing, and optimizing the flow of materials, information, money, and people over the entire length of the internal and external value chain, that is, from the supplier of the raw materials to the end customer (Werner, 2020). This is primarily intended to improve the efficiency of the processes, increase customer benefits, and optimize the resource requirements in order to ultimately supply customers and markets with goods that are economically successful. SCM is a core function and must be integrated into the overall strategy of the enterprise (Helmold & Terry, 2021). Supply chain management operates at three levels: strategic, tactical, and operational. At the strategic level, company management makes high-level strategic supply chain decisions that are relevant to whole organizations. The appropriate supply chain strategy is a key success factor for any business and is one of the keys to sustainable success (Werner, 2020). Strategy helps organizations to maximize their resources and environment and allows them to develop new ways to stay ahead of competitors. Even with great ideas, or great products and services, you are unlikely to be successful in the long term without an appropriate strategy. A sustainable and long-term strategy must be the integral part of the corporate strategy (Helmold, Dathe & Hummel, 2019). Strategic management is a framework that is dealing with recognizing and making the important changes toward its mission and vision by using resources and assets in the most efficient way (Helmold & Samara, 2019). It is a framework which links strategic planning and decision-making with

M. Helmold et al., *Supply Chain Risk Management*,
Management for Professionals, https://doi.org/10.1007/978-3-030-90800-3_2

the everyday business of operational administration. Strategic management is very important for an organization's long-term success, which is making companies able to compete in a hostile and competitive environment (Johnson et al., 2017). Translation of strategic management plans into practice is the most important aspect of the planning itself in any organization. Strategic and lean plans can include actions like entering new markets, global sourcing, make or buy strategies, deployment of new products or services, centralization or decentralization of activities, or aligning leadership and resources as outlined by various authors (Helmold, 2021). The three levels of strategy, developed by Gerry Johnson and Kevan Scholes along with other major managerial thinkers, are a way of defining the different layers of strategy which, in tandem, orient the direction of the organization and define its success (Johnson et al., 2017). The three levels are as follows:

1. Corporate supply chain strategy level.
2. Business and tactical supply chain level.
3. Functional or operational supply chain levels.

When synchronized and coordinated, successful strategies at each of these levels will contribute to successful overall organizational strategy including right measures to prevent and avoid inefficiencies in the supply chain and other functions of an enterprise (Khojasteh, 2018). This is the top layer of strategic planning, and is often associated with the organization's mission and values, though it is developed in much more significant depth (Helmold, 2021). Corporate strategy is defined by those at the very top of the organization—managing directors and executive boards—and is an outline of the overall direction and course of the business. In effect, it defines the following:

- General, overall strategy and direction in terms of markets, supply, and supply chains.
- Which markets the organization will operate in.
- Which suppliers and supply chains to procure from.
- How the markets will be entered and the general activities of the organization.
- How to prevent risks in the upstream or downstream supply chains.
- How to apply a Supply Chain Risk Management (SCRM) measures.

2.1.1 Corporate Strategy

Corporate strategy is crucial as it will define all other decisions that are made within the organization along the line. Smaller, newer organizations which are targeting a very specific niche market, or operate with a small set of unique products/services, will find it far easier to develop a corporate strategy as there are fewer variables to consider. However, larger and more developed organizations will find the process much simpler, as they may need to diverge from activities and behaviors which define who they are in order to reach out into new markets and to take new opportunities.

2.1.2 Business Strategy

Business strategy generally emerges and evolves from the overarching corporate strategy which has been set by those at the helm. They are usually far more specific than corporate strategy and will likely be unique to different departments or subdivisions within the broader organization. In general, they use corporate strategy as an outline to:

- Define specific tactics and strategies for each market the organization is involved in.
- Define how each business unit will deliver the planned tactics.

Due to their nature, they are more common in larger firms that engage in multiple activities, than they are in small businesses. However, they can still be engaged in by smaller organizations who wish to define how they go about each different subsection of their operations, by breaking down the overall scope of the corporate strategy.

2.1.3 Functional Strategy

The functional long-term strategy, also defined as market-level strategy, refers to the day-to-day operation of the company, which will keep it functioning and moving in the correct direction. While many organizations fail because they do not have an overarching corporate strategy, others fail because they have not developed plans for how to engage in everyday activities. Even with an overall direction you wish to head in, without a plan for how to successfully operate, an organization will be unable to progress. These will be numerous and will define very specific aspects and operations within smaller departments, teams, groups, and activities. Overall, they define the following:

- Day-to-day actions which are required to deliver corporate and business strategies.
- Relationships needed between units, departments, and teams.
- How operational goals will be met, and how they will be monitored.

It is at this level, the lowest in strategic development, that leaders should define how different departments and functions will work together to achieve higher goals. There will be managers that will oversee departments (e.g., manufacturing and HR) that do not perform the same functions, but need to be synchronized in order to achieve the goals set out by the corporate and business strategies.

2.1.4 Alignment of Strategies

Though corporate strategy will get all of the attention, it is success at the bottom of the hierarchy—through day-to-day functions—which will truly define where the organization as a whole will succeed. You need to build from the ground up, in small steps, in order to keep moving forward. If operations break down, so does the organization. As mentioned previously, it is crucially important that each level of strategy is synchronized, both from top-to-bottom and horizontally across the organization. Feedback should down from both corporate strategy to functional strategy, and vice versa, in order for all three levels to ensure that they are operating in line with one another (Helmold, 2021).

Strategy itself will not define organizational success; however, it is a very good place to start. Once sound strategies are in place, an organization can move forward and begin to execute said strategies. They may need some adjustment along the way—and you should be prepared to do so, in response to feedback from different levels and from the external environment—but they should be initially developed in such a way that they will keep the organization in line with its long-term objectives.

2.2 Strategic Triangle

The process of strategic management cycle is a process with three elements as outlined in Fig. 2.1 (strategic triangle or strategic cycle) (Johnson & Scholes, 1997). The three steps are (1) the strategic analysis, (2) the strategic choice, and (3) the strategic implementation and will be described in the following sections. The triangle is raising the following questions:

1. Where are we in terms of strategy and positioning in our supply chains?
2. Where do we want to go?
3. How do we achieve this?

2.3 Strategic Analysis

2.3.1 Analyzing Important Factors

The strategic analysis of an organization is about understanding the strategic position of the organization in terms of Lean Management. This stage requires a profound analysis where the organization stands in terms of Lean Management tools and processes (Johnson & Scholes, 1997). The existing competencies and resources of the organization need to be assessed to determine if there are any opportunities to be gained from these and to determine if they need to be enhanced in order to pursue strategic objectives and goals (Johnson & Scholes, 1997). The major stakeholders which influence the organization and the opinions or viewpoints must be taken into account as the purpose of all of the strategic analysis is to define the potential future

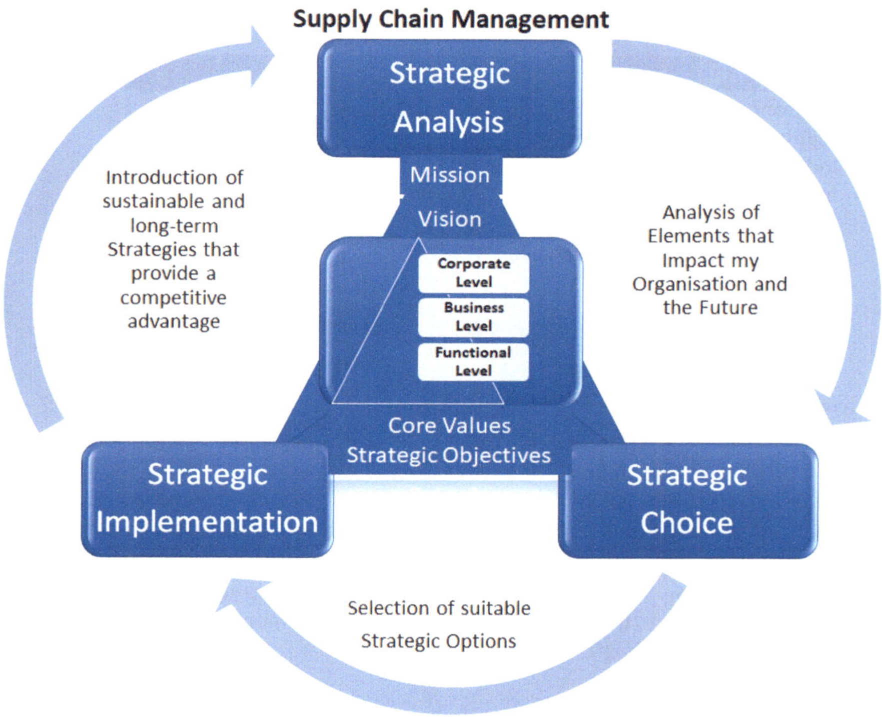

Fig. 2.1 Strategic triangle. (Source: Author's Source, adopted from Johnson et al. (2017))

direction of the organization. The purpose of this phase (strategic analysis) is to create a suitable starting position and to understand the key influences on the present and future state of the organization and what opportunities are afforded by the environment and the competencies of the organization (Johnson & Scholes, 1997). Assessing the strategic position consists of evaluating the following elements as shown in Table 2.1:

Since strategy is concerned with the position a business takes in relation to its environment, an understanding of the environment's effects on an organization is of central importance to the strategic analysis. The historical and environmental effects on the business must be considered, as well as the present effects and the expected changes in environmental variables. The analysis of the environment can be done via the macro and micro analysis (PESTEL, Porters 5 Forces). Additionally, strengths, weaknesses, opportunities, and threats complete the assessment of the environment (SWOT). This step is a major task because the range of environmental variables is so great. Another area of the strategic analysis is the evaluation of the strategic capability of an organization and where it is able to achieve a competitive advantage. Considering the resource areas of a business such as its physical plant, its management, its financial structure, and its products may identify these strengths and weaknesses (Johnson & Scholes, 1997). The expectations of stakeholders are

Table 2.1 Elements in the strategic analysis

Strategic Analysis of Elements	Strategic Tool
Environment (e.g. markets, regulations, political impacts)	PESTEL Analysis (Macro)
Industry and competition (e.g. rivalry in industry)	Industry Analysis (Micro)
Internal strengths & weaknesses, external threats & opportunities	SWOT Analysis (Internal)
Cultures and beliefs	Cultural Analysis
Strategic capabilities & competencies	Benchmarking Analysis
Expectation of stakeholders	Stakeholder Analysis

Source: Author's source

important because they will affect what will be seen as acceptable in terms of the strategies advanced by management. Stakeholders can be defined as people or groups inside or outside the organization, who have an interest in the activities of the organization. A typical list of stakeholders for a large company would include shareholders, banks, employees, managers, customers, suppliers, government, and society. Culture affects the interpretation of the environmental and resource influences (Helmold & Terry, 2021).

2.3.2 Analyzing the Environment

A PESTEL analysis or PESTLE analysis is a framework or tool used to analyze and monitor the macro-environmental factors that may have a profound impact on an organization's performance. This tool is especially useful when starting a new business or entering a foreign market. It is often used in collaboration with other analytical business tools such as the SWOT analysis and Porter's Five Forces to give a clear understanding of a situation and related internal and external factors. PESTEL is an acronym that stand for Political, Economic, Social, Technological, Environmental, and Legal factors. However, throughout the years, people have expanded the framework with factors such as Demographics, Intercultural, Ethical, and Ecological resulting in variants such as STEEPLED, DESTEP, and SLEPIT. In this chapter, we will stick simply to PESTEL since it encompasses the most relevant factors in general business. Each element will be elaborated as shown in Fig. 2.2.

2.3.3 Analyzing the Industry

Porter is best known for his strategic frameworks and concepts in his paper, which was published in 1980 (Porter, 1980). The five forces model (Industry Analysis) has five elements that can be utilized to assess the attractiveness and competitive situation of the industry as outlined in Fig. 2.3. The five elements are as follows:

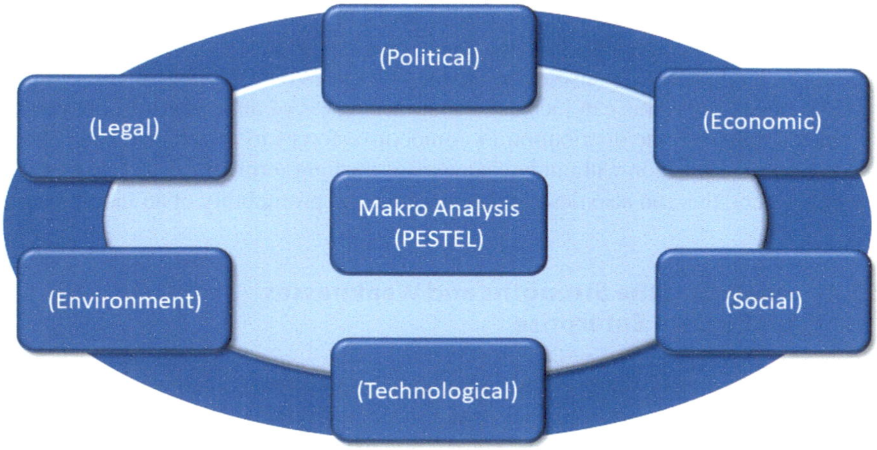

Fig. 2.2 PESTEL analysis. (Source: Author's source)

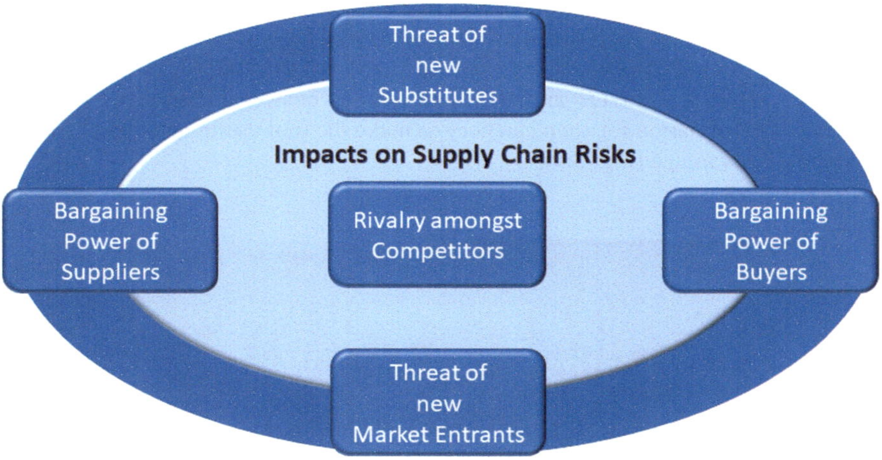

Fig. 2.3 Industry analysis. (Source: Author's source)

1. Rivalry among competitors.
2. Bargaining power of suppliers.
3. Bargaining power of buyers.
4. Threat of new market entrants.
5. Threat of new substitutes.

The stronger the threat posed by these five competitive forces, the less attractive the industry under consideration and the more difficult it is to achieve a sustainable competitive advantage. Companies should therefore try to be active in an industry with an attractive industry structure and to build up a defensible position in their industry, that is, a position in which the five competitive forces are as less threatening as possible. Companies can also influence the five forces with the help of appropriate strategic orientation. This can increase the attractiveness of an industry. If, however, companies influence the distribution of competitive forces to the advantage of their own competitive position without being aware of the long-term effects or consciously accepting them, this can also destroy the structure and profitability of an industry.

2.3.4 Analyzing the Strengths and Weaknesses of the Own Enterprise

The SWOT (strengths, weaknesses, opportunities, and threats) analysis is a framework used to evaluate a company's competitive position and to develop strategic planning. SWOT analysis assesses internal and external factors, as well as current and future potential. This technique, which operates by peeling back layers of the company is designed for use in the preliminary stages of decision-making processes and can be used as a tool for evaluation of the strategic position of organizations of many kinds (profit enterprises, local and national governments, NGOs, etc.). It is intended to specify the objectives of the business venture or project and identify the internal and external factors that are favorable and unfavorable to achieving those objectives. Users of a SWOT analysis often ask and answer questions to generate meaningful information for each category to make the tool useful and identify their competitive advantage (Fig. 2.4).

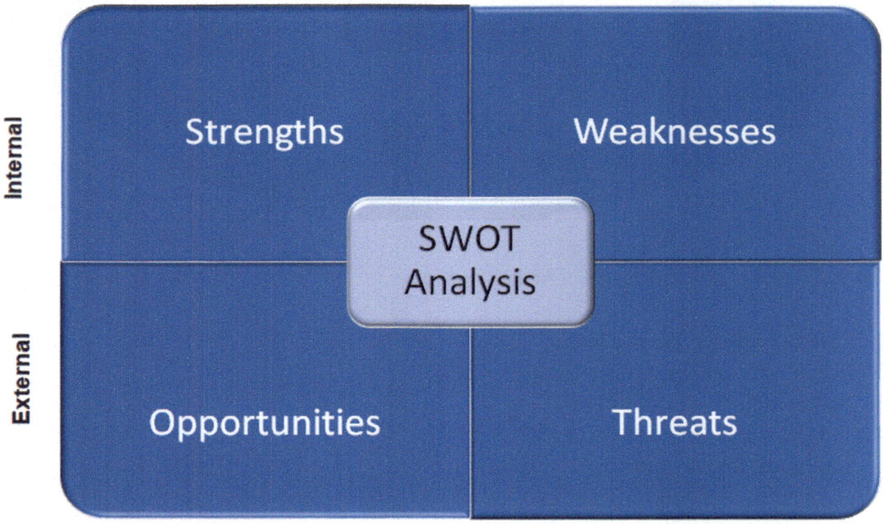

Fig. 2.4 SWOT Analysis. (Source: Author's source)

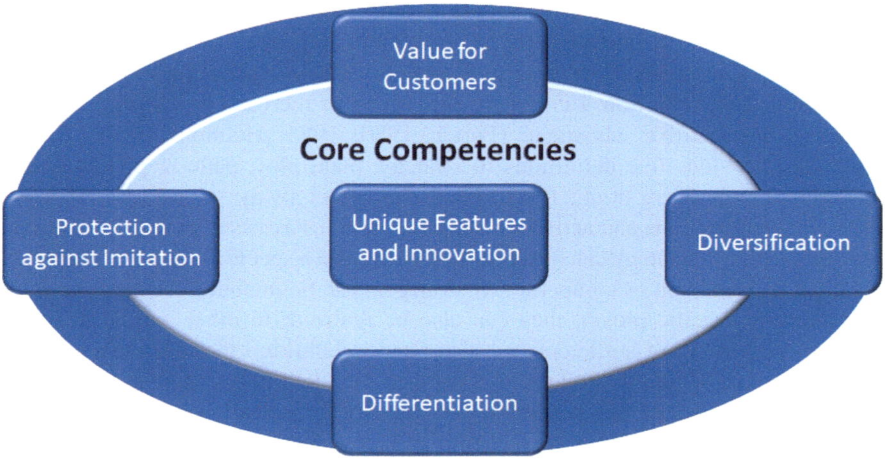

Fig. 2.5 Core competencies. (Source: Author's source)

2.3.5 Analyzing the Core Competencies

The core competency concept describes a product, feature, process, skill, brand, or activity that a company can perform better than its competitors and has thus achieved a competitive advantage. It is determined by the certain characteristics like customer value or benefits, protection against imitation, differentiation, diversification, and innovation or unique features as shown in Fig. 2.5. In business, a competitive advantage is the attribute that allows an organization to outperform its competitors.

2.4 Strategic Choice

2.4.1 Generic Strategies

Strategic choice typically follows strategic analysis. Strategic choice involves a whole process through which a decision is taken to choose a particular option from various alternatives. There can be various methods through which the final choice can be selected upon. Managers and decision-makers keep both the external and internal environment in mind before narrowing it down to one. It is based upon the following three elements. First, the generation of strategic options, for example, growth, acquisition, diversification, or concentration. Second, the evaluation of the options to assess their relative merits and feasibility. Third, the selection of the strategy or option that the organization will pursue. There could be more than one strategy chosen, but there is a chance of an inherent danger or disadvantage to any choice made. Although there are techniques for evaluating specific options, the selection is often subjective and likely to be influenced by the values of managers and other groups with an interest in the organization (Helmold, 2020).

The generic strategies, differentiation and cost leadership, are a good method to define, in which direction a company should go to increase profitability and to acquire a competitive advantage (Porter, 1980, 1985; Helmold et al., 2019). Mintzberg provides five definitions of strategy, plan, ploy, pattern, position, and perspective (Mintzberg et al., 1995). First, strategy is always a plan. A plan integrates intended actions and activities based on previous assessment of the situation. Second, as plan, a strategy can be a ploy too, really just a specific maneuver intended to outwit an opponent or competitor. If strategies can be intended (whether as general plans or specific ploys), they can also be realized. In other words, defining strategy as plan is not sufficient; we also need a definition that encompasses the resulting behavior. Third, strategy is a pattern. The definitions of strategy as plan and pattern can be quite independent of one another. Plans may go unrealized, while patterns may appear without preconception. Plans are intended strategy, whereas patterns are the realized strategy. Fourth, strategy is a perspective. A perspective is not just of a chosen position, but it consists of an ingrained way of perceiving the world (Mintzberg et al., 1995) (Fig. 2.6).

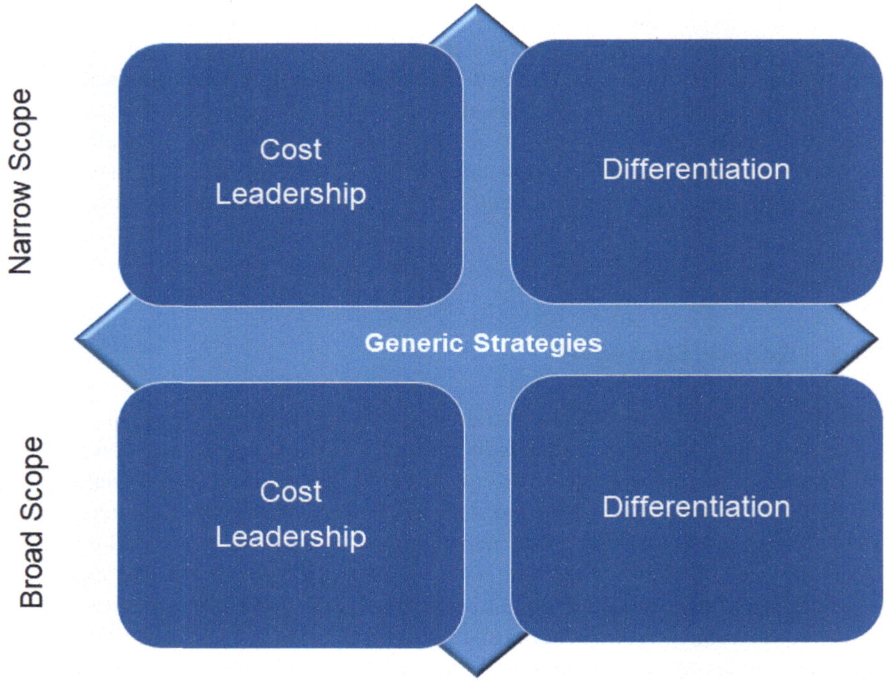

Fig. 2.6 Generic strategies. (Source: Author's own figure, adopted from Porter (1985))

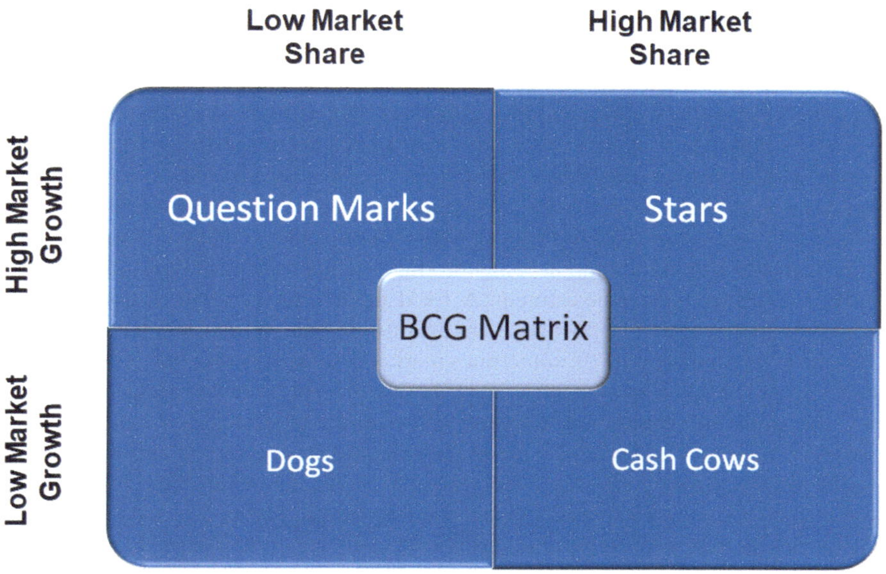

Fig. 2.7 BCG strategies. (Source: Author's source)

2.4.2 Boston Consulting Matrix (BCG Matrix)

The BCG matrix is named after the Boston Consulting Group (BCG), whose founder Bruce Henderson developed this matrix in 1970 (Fig. 2.7). This concept should clarify the connection between the product life cycle and the cost experience curve. The matrix is often visualized as a scatter or bubble diagram; the area of a circle then represents the sales of the respective product. The BCG matrix is, put simply, a portfolio management framework that helps companies decide how to prioritize their different businesses and supply chains. It is a table, split into four quadrants, each with its own unique symbol that represents a certain degree of profitability: question marks, stars, dogs, and cash cows. By assigning each business to one of these four categories, executives could then decide where to focus their resources and capital to generate the most value, as well as where to cut their losses. The products or business units of a company are assigned to one of the four areas based on their values. Each area embodies a standard strategy. It should give a good recommendation on how to proceed. The life cycle of a typical product runs from the question mark to the star and cash cow to the poor dog. There are also products that do not follow this ideal path. Many product failures and flops do not even reach the star range. An imitating product, on the other hand, may skip the question mark area. The question marks, normally young products, are the newcomers among the products. The market has growth potential, but the products only have a small relative market share. Management is faced with the decision of whether to invest or abandon the product. In the case of an investment, the product requires liquid funds, which it cannot generate itself. A typical strategy recommendation is: selection and possibly an offensive penetration strategy to increase market share. The stars are the company's most promising products. You have a high relative market share in a growth market. They already cover the investment needs resulting from market growth with their own cash flow. The strategy recommendation is: investment and possibly a skimming strategy to increase profit margins without endangering market share. The cash cows (milking cows) have a high relative market share in only slightly growing or static market. They produce stable, high cash flows and can be "milked" without further investment. A fixed price strategy or price competition strategy is appropriate. The poor dogs are the discontinued products in the company. They have low market growth, sometimes market contraction, and low relative market share. At the latest as soon as the contribution margin for these products is negative, the portfolio should be adjusted (disinvestment strategy). In addition to assessing the individual products using the standard strategies, the entire portfolio should also be considered. Pay attention to the static financial equalization—the products in the portfolio should support and finance each other a possible question can be raised if it is possible that cash cows and well-running products finance expansions and new projects. Future developments can also be seen. The products should be evenly represented in the individual areas—a company without question marks would have little chance in the future market. The matrix reveals two factors that companies should consider when deciding where to invest, company competitiveness, and market attractiveness, with relative market share and growth rate as the underlying drivers of these factors. Each of the four quadrants represents a specific combination of relative market share, and growth:

- Low growth, high share. Companies should milk these "cash cows" for cash to reinvest.
- High growth, high share. Companies should significantly invest in these "stars" as they have high future potential.
- High growth, low share. Companies should invest in or discard these "question marks," depending on their chances of becoming stars.
- Low share, low growth. Companies should liquidate, divest, or reposition these "dogs."

2.4.3 Ansoff Matrix

The Product-Market-Matrix (also Ansoff matrix, after its inventor Harry Igor Ansoff or Z-Matrix) is a tool for the strategic management of companies. It can be used by a management (= company management) who has decided on a growth strategy as an aid for planning this growth. When it comes to market penetration, the focus is on gaining additional market shares with existing products. The company is trying to sell more of its products to existing, new, and competitive customers. Existing marketing activities usually have to be adapted to achieve this goal. Although the product portfolio does not change, companies often have to experiment with new advertising concepts in order to further promote product adoption in the existing market.

However, this market penetration can only be successfully implemented up to the point at which the market has not yet been fully saturated. The focus of the market development strategy is on creating new sales markets for existing products. By entering new market segments or opening up further geographical regions, a company puts itself in the position of attracting new target groups for its existing products.

A regionally operating bakery can also offer its own products nationwide, for example by setting up digital sales channels, and thus generate growth. Of course, the implementation of this strategy is initially offset by considerable investment costs. The chances of success should therefore first be assessed by means of careful planning and a comprehensive risk analysis. If opening up new markets is not an option, it is often worth taking a look at the product development strategy. The existing range is expanded through product innovations or the creation of product variants in the existing market. The resulting added value should encourage consumers to buy. This strategy is particularly attractive for companies in niche markets in which acquiring new customers and upselling would be almost impossible with a pure market penetration strategy. The reluctance to enter new markets is reinforced by high development costs and the risk of failure of the newly developed product. The most risky quadrant of the Ansoff matrix is that of diversification. This requires the development of a new product while at the same time opening up a new market. The associated investment costs in terms of product development, business analyses, setting up local subsidiaries, etc., can quickly mean the end of a company if the corresponding ROI is not achieved. The diversification strategy can be broken down into horizontal, vertical, and lateral diversification, depending on the degree of risk tolerance of a company:

- Vertical diversification.
- Horizontal diversification.

Horizontal Diversification

Horizontal diversification describes the development of a new product that is still factually related to the product range previously offered. The existing value chain can continue to be used with minimal adjustments. With horizontal diversification, a company expands its offerings at the same economic level to reach new customers. An example of this type of diversification is the development of the iPad, which with its introduction gradually expanded Apple's existing smartphone and computer portfolio.

Vertical Diversification

With vertical diversification, a company deepens its commitment to sales-oriented activities (forward integration) and / or the actual manufacturing process of its products (backward integration). Diversification does not take place on the same level of the value chain as with horizontal diversification, but on the upstream or downstream one. With forward integration, a company takes the sales of its products and services into its own hands, for example by opening its own branches or an online shop. Backward integration describes the safeguarding of a company's reference markets, for example by taking over production processes that were previously outsourced to external companies. While horizontal diversification aims to reduce dependency on one product line, vertical diversification focuses on reducing dependence on suppliers and dealers. The acquisition of the necessary skills and know-how for the successful implementation of sales and production processes is in turn associated with high investment costs and thus increased financial risks.

Lateral Diversification

With the lateral diversification strategy, companies expand into completely new markets that have no material connection with the existing business.

The aim and purpose of this alignment is to minimize the dependence on developments in the existing market segment. Google can be mentioned as a good example in this context: In addition to the search engine core business, the company expanded early on into other market segments such as telecommunications (fiber), biotechnology (Calico), or autonomous automotive technology (Waymo). The lateral diversification strategy is used by multinational companies in particular to respond flexibly to changes and trends in the market. The necessary know-how is usually acquired through the acquisition of specialized companies that are already represented in the market of interest. Accordingly, this strategy requires enormous investment costs and harbors not only financial but also immaterial risks, such as a diluted brand image due to product offerings that are too diversified (Fig. 2.8).

2.4.4 Blue and Red Ocean Strategies

Blue ocean strategy is a method for developing permanently profitable business models from the field of strategic management: The basic idea is that only through the development of innovative and new markets, which really differentiate and relevant benefits for the broad mass of customers or non-customers, "Blue oceans" offer lasting successes. Among other things, this is to be achieved through competition that has become meaningless, new customer acquisitions and optimized cost structures.

The concept of the blue ocean strategy was developed by W. Chan Kim and Renée Mauborgne at the INSEAD Business School, where it was initially referred to as Value Innovation. Based on empirical studies over a period of 15 years and based on the analysis of more than 100 leading companies, examples of companies were found that opened up new, previously unused sub-markets and thus made the previous competition irrelevant. The term "ocean" describes a market or branch of industry in connection with the blue ocean strategy. "Blue oceans" are understood as untouched markets or branches of industry with little or no competition. Anyone who plunged into the blue ocean would find undiscovered markets or industries. "Red oceans," on

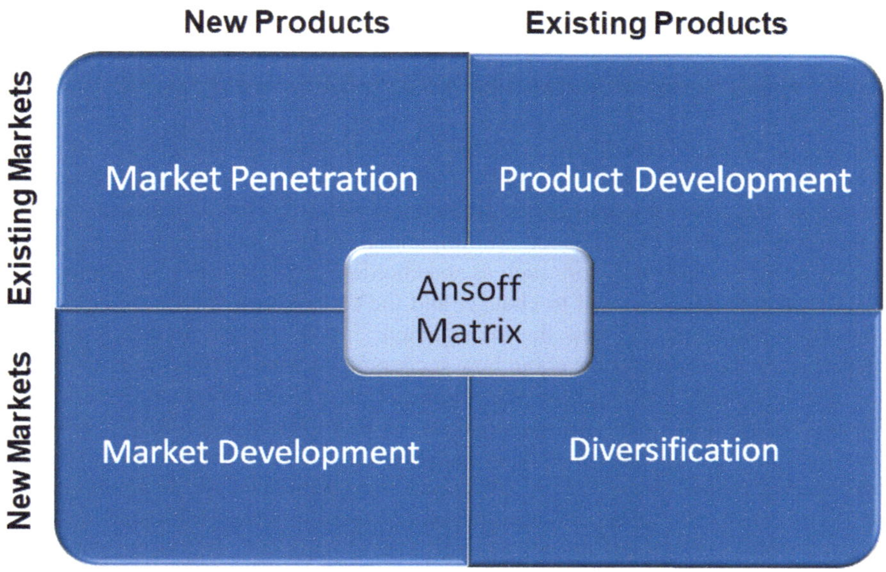

Fig. 2.8 Generic strategies. (Source: Author's source)

Table 2.2 Blue ocean strategy

Red Ocean Strategy	Blue Ocean Strategy
Compete in existing Market Spaces	Create uncontested Market Spaces
Defeat the Competition	Make the Competition irrelevant
Apply Differentiation or Cost Leadership	Apply Differentiation and Cost Leadership
Achieve a Competitive Advantage	Achieve Value Innovations
Segment smartly existing Customers	Attract new Customers
Exploit existing Demand	Create and capture new Demands

Source: Author's source, adapted from Kim and Maubourgne (2015)

the other hand, designate saturated markets, characterized by tough competition, overcrowded with competitors who all offer the same service or the same products. The term "red ocean" is based on the image of bloody fights of predatory fish (the competitors), while the "blue ocean" is free from bloody fights (Table 2.2).

2.5 Strategic Implementation

2.5.1 Assessment of Suitability, Acceptability, and Feasibility

Strategic implementation is concerned with the translation of the selected strategy into action (Johnson & Scholes, 1997). The ways in which strategies are implemented are described as the strategic architecture or framework of the organization (Johnson & Scholes, 1997). Successful implementation of the chosen strategy will be dependent on several factors such as stakeholder's expectations, the employees, the company culture, the will to change, and the cooperation within the organization. These elements and how the management and employees work together to adopt the new plan will decide about how successful the strategy implementation is. The available skills and/or the ability to develop new skills when required for the planned change and issues like the structural re-organization and resulting cultural disturbance would also affect success. Resource availability and planning for the utilization of such resources need to be addressed as part of the implementation plan. The entire process necessitates the management of strategic change and will concern handling both hard and soft factors of the organization, that is, structure and systems and culture and motivation. Implementing a strategy has three elements.

- Organizational structure and layout: Where and how should the organization is split into European, US, and Asian divisions? How autonomous should divisions be? What parenting style should be applied?
- Resources: Enabling an organization's resources should support the chosen strategy: What are the appropriate human and non-human resources? What assets need to be acquired?
- Change management: Most strategic planning and implementation will involve change, so managing change, in particular employees' fears and resistance, is crucial.

Johnson and Scholes argue that for a strategy to be successful, it must satisfy three criteria (Johnson & Scholes, 1997). These criteria can be applied to any strategy decision such as the competitive strategies, growth strategies, or development strategies:

1. Suitability—whether the options are adequate responses to the firm's assessment of its strategic position.
2. Acceptability—considers whether the options meet and are consistent with the firm's objectives and are acceptable to the stakeholders.
3. Feasibility—assesses whether the organization has the resources it needs to carry out the strategy.

2.5.2 Suitability

Suitability is a useful criterion for screening strategies, asking the following questions about strategic options:

- Does the strategy exploit the company strengths, such as providing work for skilled craftsmen or environmental opportunities, for example, helping to establish the organization in new growth sectors of the market?
- How far does the strategy overcome the difficulties identified in the analysis? For example, is the strategy likely to improve the organization's competitive position, solve the company's liquidity problems, or decrease dependence on a particular supplier?
- Does the option fit in with the organization's purposes? For example, would the strategy achieve profit targets or growth expectations, or would it retain control for an owner-manager?

2.5.3 Acceptability

Acceptability is essentially about assessing risk and return and is strongly related to expectations of stakeholders. The issue of "acceptable to whom?" thus requires the analysis to be thought through carefully. Some of the questions that will help identify the likely consequences of any strategy are as follows:

- How will the strategy impact shareholder wealth? Assessing this could involve calculations relating to profitability, for example, net present value (NPV).
- How will the organization perform in profitability terms? The parallel in the public sector would be cost/benefit assessment.
- How will the financial risk (e.g., liquidity) change?
- What effect will it have on capital structure (gearing or share ownership)?
- Will the function of any department, group, or individual change significantly?
- Will the organization's relationship with outside stakeholders, for example, suppliers, government, unions, customers need to change?
- Will the strategy be acceptable in the organization's environment, for example, higher levels of noise?

2.5.4 Feasibility

Assesses whether the organization has the resources it needs to carry out the strategy. Factors that should be considered can be summarized under the M-word model.

- Machinery. What demands will the strategy make on production? Do we have sufficient spare capacity? Do we need new production systems to give lower cost/better quality/more flexibility/etc.?

- Management. Is existing management sufficiently skilled to carry out the strategy?
- Money. How much finance is needed and when? Can we raise this? Is the cash flow feasible?
- Manpower. What demands will the strategy make on human resources? How many employees are needed, what skills will they need, and when do we need them? Do we already have the right people or is there a gap? Can the gap be filled by recruitment, retraining, etc.?
- Markets. Is our existing brand name strong enough for the strategy to work? Will new brand names have to be established? What market share is needed for success—how quickly can this be achieved?
- Materials. What demands will the strategy make on our relationships with suppliers? Are changes in quality needed?
- Make-up. Is the existing organizational structure adequate or will it have to be changed?

2.5.5 Strategic Pyramid

A useful tool for the translation of the corporate strategy and strategic objectives into negotiations is the strategic pyramid (Johnsons & Scholes, 1997). Strategy in this context is the long-term positioning as well as the decision of the enterprise, which business fields and which strategies to choose. Strategy is therefore "the fundamental, long-term direction of three to five years and organization of a company in order to gain competitive advantages in a changing environment through the use of resources and competences and to realize the long-term goals of the stakeholders" (Johnson & Scholes, 1997) (Fig. 2.9).

2.5.6 Mission and Vision

Enterprises must manifest in their strategy to strive for lean excellence (Helmold & Samara, 2019). The mission is the starting point of the strategic pyramid. The mission statement of an enterprise is the long-term purpose of the company and the strategic direction as defined by Johnson and Scholes (1997). The vision or strategic intent describes more specifically what an organization aims to achieve and the long-term aspirations (Johnson & Scholes, 1997).

Mission example: Become a Lean Enterprise of excellence on a global basis.

Vision example: Become the world-leading company in lean in the industry in the next five years.

Fig. 2.9 Strategic pyramid. (Source: Author's own figure)

2.5.7 Qualitative and Quantitative Lean Goals and Objectives

The mission and vision are followed by generic goals and specific objectives. Generic goals are not quantified and more general, but specific objectives are quantified and specific (Helmold et al., 2019). The strategists Johnson and Scholes distinguish in longer-term and generic (English: Goals) as well as shorter and quantified objectives (English: Objectives) for the company (Johnson & Scholes, 1997). Quantified goals can include sales, financial, quality, logistics, cost, and alpha goals.

Goal example: Increase and improve quality, reduce cost, and provide productivity improvements between 30 and 40 percent within the next three years.

Objectives example: Quantification of the generic aims (goals).

2.5.8 Core Competencies

The next level in the strategic pyramid is the identification of core competencies. Core competences are those competences which allow companies to gain a superior or competitive advantage and that are very difficult for your competitors to emulate (Johnson & Scholes, 1997). These describe the resources, skills, knowledge, or any other feature that lead to a competitive advantage. Core competencies must be perceived by customers and clients (Helmold, 2020).

Example: Create lean academy and lean culture.

2.5.9 Strategies

After defining mission, vision, goals, and core competencies, the elements must be translated into strategic objectives and key performance indicators (KPI). The long-term implementation of these elements is defined as the formulation of strategic objectives and important for the negotiations (Helmold et al., 2019). In implementing the strategic goals, negotiations will take place with many stakeholders (Helmold, 2020). Become a lean differentiator by answering customer demands: Reduce operating cost by 25 percent in 12 months from now, increase customer satisfaction by 10 percent.

2.5.10 Strategic Architecture

In addition to buildings, machines, plants, offices, resources, or employees, the infrastructure in the sense of strategic management also includes knowledge and innovations of the company that ensure long-term success (Helmold et al., 2019). This requires facilities, buildings, factories, or offices that represent the strategic infrastructure. In addition, however, other success criteria such as resources, knowledge, experts, name recognition, network, or innovations are of central importance.

2.5.11 Control and Execution

The final element of the strategic pyramid is the performance control (control and execution) and a target-performance comparison. A suitable tool for this step is the Balance Score Card (BSC) or an action plan. The instrument of the BSC was already developed in 1992 by the professors Norton and Kaplan. The BSC is an instrument in strategic management and includes four categories (Johnson et al., 1997):

1. Customer satisfaction.
2. Financial category.
3. Internal processes and improvements.
4. Learning organization.

In practice, it seems that companies are adapting or expanding the original four dimensions to their specific needs (Johnson et al., 1997).

Example: Establishing process and key performance indicators (KPI) of monitoring improvements and successful execution of strategy. Creating scorecard and checking running time, sequence, weight, and other elements on a daily basis.

2.6 Core Values

2.6.1 Strategies Must Focus on Value-Creation

Porter postulated three generic or broad alternative strategies which may be pursued as a response to the competitive pressures. They are termed "generic strategies" because they are broadly applicable to any industry or business. They are differentiation, cost leadership, and focus. A focus strategy may be further defined as cost focus, differentiation focus, or cost and differentiation focus. A differentiation strategy may be based on actual unique product features or the perception thereof, conveyed through the use of advertising and marketing tactics, in the eyes of the customers. Obviously, the product or service feature must be one the customer needs or desires. Moreover, such enhanced features and designs or advertising and marketing will increase costs, and customers must be price-insensitive—willing to pay for the differentiated product or service. This willingness to pay for the differentiated product of service is what provides the company relief from competitive pressure, cost pressure specifically. Firms pursuing a cost leadership strategy must make lower production and distribution costs their priority (Helmold & Terry, 2021). By keeping their cost lower than those of their competitors, firms using cost leadership can still price their products up to the level of their competitors and still maintain higher gross profit margins. Alternatively, these firms can price their products lower than those of their competitors in the hope of achieving greater market share and sales volume at the expense of gross profit margins. A focus strategy is based on a particular market, customer, product, or geographic. A focus strategy is a concentrated, narrowly focused niche strategy. Figure 2.10 shows the example of a mission statement of Bombardier Transportation in China International Procurement Office.

2.7 Case Study: Siemens Strategy

The company Siemens has outlined its mission, vision, goals, strategic objectives, core values, and cultural specifics in its strategy outline "Siemens, vision 2020" (Siemens, 2019). The president and CEO, Joe Kaeser, outlines the key elements of the Siemens strategy for the coming years. He stresses that with the positioning along the electrification value chain, Siemens has know-how that extends from power generation to power transmission, power distribution and smart grid to the efficient application of electrical energy. And with the outstanding strengths in automation, Kaeser confirms that Siemens is well equipped for the future and the age of digitalization. The "Siemens, vision 2020" defines an entrepreneurial concept that will enable the enterprise to consistently occupy attractive growth fields, sustainably strengthen our core business, and outpace our competitors in efficiency and performance. All goals are focused on a long-term success (Siemens, 2019). The mission of Siemens can be defined as "We make real what matters, by setting the benchmark, in the way we electrify, automate and digitalize the world around us. Ingenuity drives us and what we create is yours. Together we deliver" (Siemens, 2019).

Fig. 2.10 Example of mission statement and vision. (Source: Author's source)

References

Helmold, M., Dathe, T., & Hummel, F. (2019). Erfolgreiche Verhandlungen. Best-in-Class Empfehlungen für den Verhandlungsdurchbruch. Springer Gabler Wiesbaden.

Helmold, M., & Samara, W. (2019). Progress in Performance Management. Springer Cham.

Helmold, M. (2020). Lean Management and Kaizen Fundamentals from Cases and Examples in Operations and Supply Chain Management. Springer Cham.

Helmold, M. (2021). *Innovatives Lieferantenmanagement. Wertschöpfung in globalen Lieferketten*. Springer Wiesbaden.

Helmold, M. & Terry, B. (2021). *Operations and supply management 4.0. Industry insights, case studies and best practices*. Springer: Cham

Johnson, G., et al. (1997). Exploring Strategy. FT Prentice Hall London.

Johnson, G., et al. (2017). *Exploring strategy* (11th ed.). FT Prentice Hall.

Khojasteh, Y. (2018). Supply chain risk management. Advanced tools, models, and developments.

Kim, C., & Maubourgne, R. A. (2015). *Blue Ocean strategy, expanded edition: How to create uncontested market space and make the competition irrelevant*. Harvard Business Press.

Mintzberg, H., Quinn, J. B., & Ghoshal, S. (1995). *The strategy process*. Revised Euro-pean edition. Prentice Hall.

Porter, M. E. (1980). *Competitive strategy: Techniques for Analyzing industries and competitors*. Free Press.

Porter, M. E. (1985). *Competitive advantage. Creating and sustaining superior performance*. Free Press.

Siemens (2019). Siemens Strategy. www.siemens.de.

Werner, H. (2020). *Supply chain management. Grundlagen, Strategien, Instrumente und controlling*. Springer Wiesbaden.

Digitalization in Air Transportation and Reflections on SCRM

3

The supply chain stuff is really tricky.

– Elon Musk

3.1 Supply Chain Management (SCM) Digitization

Digitalization, which is the absolute necessity of business practices and business models in the twenty-first century, must be optimally reflected in the processes, philosophy, and stakeholder relations of supply chain management (SCM) applications. It is the risk management-based supply chain management system that guides these reflection efforts and provides reasonable assurance regarding the achievement of such optimization.

The traditional business model in the aviation industry and all sub-sectors of the industry is being reshaped transformed with digital technologies. In this context, aviation activities can be carried out with the products and services of industry-related sub-sectors. Maintenance and repair, training, catering, and tourism agencies are examples of these sub-sector organizations connected to the industry. Hence, digitalization, with the activities of subsidiaries, is one of the sustainable sources of the industry in both economic and operational areas.

Digitalization, smart systems, and artificial intelligence are of primordial importance in the aviation industry, as using cutting-edge technology in air transportation is making the systems smart; thus, system errors are decreasing. Therefore, this is creating a considerable advantage to focus on human-sourced errors in both accidents and incidents in air transportation. Thus, this part presents digitalization and artificial intelligence (AI) with an innovation management-based approach. Most importantly, digitalization and artificial intelligence combined with innovation management both build and contribute in maintaining resilience in the aviation

M. Helmold et al., *Supply Chain Risk Management*,
Management for Professionals, https://doi.org/10.1007/978-3-030-90800-3_3

industry. With respect to the COVID-19 pandemic conditions, resilience is one of the leading aims to be achieved by civil aviation organizations.

Optimum risk management in the supply chain management requires good decision-making and good strategy development, due to both stakeholders and sectoral characteristics in the aviation industry. For effective supply chain risk management, the establishment of flexible organizational structures, suitable for digital transformation, in aviation organizations, adoption and adaptation of digital technologies, full integration with all administrative processes, and convergence and localization of the chain with local networks are considered effective strategies.

Forward-thinking companies are looking toward the adoption of digital technologies, vertical integration, and localization for an edge. Clearly, a supply chain is at the heart of any Aerospace and Defense (A&D) organization's success. Thus, effective and efficient supply chains enable A&D organizations to meet their strategic and financial goals. Moreover, they are incredibly complex ecosystems of different tiers of suppliers, original equipment manufacturers (OEMs); maintenance, repair, and overhaul (MRO) providers; and customers, including airliners and armed forces. And they are also very much global and diversified in nature (Miller, 2018).

Not only do companies need to deal with suppliers and customers across different geographies, but they also need to deal with an entire ecosystem of data, created by the digital disruption in the industry. In this respect, effective supply chain strategies not only help companies improve efficiency, control costs, and mitigate risks but also enable them to deliver value to the customers.

As in all industries, business models such as Industry 4.0 and digital transformation have increased, to maintain cost-effective business in the aviation sector. Both are changing and evolving. The change in the ways and methods of operation within the scope of the model also changes and transforms the necessary resources. While working with numerous and diverse sectors, such as the aircraft industry in their field of activity and tourism, catering, education, security, such as the air transportation industry, they also affect the sustainability of these sectors.

Recently, supply chain risk managers have started to focus their investments on innovation in line with the evolution and transformation areas of the supply chain, especially in robotics, automation, predictive analytics and artificial intelligence, and the Internet of Things (IoT).

AviSCRM is a fundamental part of the aviation industry and digitalization that significantly contributes to the optimization of the supply chain. Electronic service providers have a key role in the introduction of AI and digitalization. Providers such as SITA, Amadeus, and others offer advanced technologies to the aviation community. In this chapter, we present the implications of digitalization in the AVİSCRM-aviation industry, on supply chain risk management. Moreover, these technologies and services are useful in the post-COVID-19 era, as they enable touchless travel. In this part, digitalization and AI topics are presented with an innovation management approach in aviation.

The aviation industry is prioritizing investment in technology, smart systems operations, and infrastructure, to reduce its impact on operations fields, such as distance control, safety checking, and ticketing. However, a changing operational environment, especially due to pandemic restrictions, has also impacted flights and on-ground operations at airports in recent years and is likely to continue to do so.

3.2 Digital Transformation Environment in the Aviation Industry: Managing Transformation Risk in the Digital Aviation Industry Universe

The keywords on today's global aviation agenda have been updated as unmanned aerial vehicles, autonomous systems operating with artificial intelligence, humanoid robots, and Internet of Things. Moreover, technological developments and innovations in technology transform life. People are changing with technology, and models and elements in professional and social life are transforming accordingly. For this transformation to be healthy, organizations and individuals need to be flexible, up-to-date, and open to innovations that will complete and sustain the transformation.

Technology is rapidly changing every element of the industry and enabling the agile adaptation of supply chains for all potential challenges, from tsunamis to trade-wars and recently a global pandemic. Today, disruption is the new normal, and it is more frequently affecting supply chains. The magnitude and frequency of this disruption have been escalating, partly due to the globalization of supply chains, and partly due to new risks presented by geopolitical and climate change issues[1].

Digitization refers to the automation of processes and business models by connecting digital technology, information, and people. Airlines have different options for digitization, such as modernizing existing products and services with digital functionality or integrating additional digital solutions into the existing portfolio. Being one of the key players in the industry, airlines will digitalize if they ensure the assistance of competent, innovative partners to implement the innovations made possible through digitalization. Most airlines today have integrated digital processes, such as online check-in and real-time flight information for passengers (adapted from Mattig and Hausweiler, 2017). In this view, the efficiency level of digital applications in airlines can be improved by completing the shortage of employees experienced in managing supply chain risks, IT infrastructure, or digitalization.

The European Aviation High Level Group on AI has published a report evaluating the benefits of using AI in aviation and air traffic management. Accordingly, it has been determined that fields of activity, such as technology, especially smart maintenance, engineering, and prognostic tools, supply chains, and customer services in the aviation sector are of interest (Berti, 2020) (Fig. 3.1).

To comprehend the impact of digitalization in the aviation industry, it is useful to examine how different airline companies and governments integrate digitalization in practice. These digitalization processes will be examined under three headings, categorized as Industry 4.0 (Aviation 4.0), Internet of Things, and Human Resources. In this section, the innovations analyzed while examining the processes of digitalization in practice and its effect on the business structure are also briefly examined and presented below.

[1] https://supplychaindigital.com/digital-supply-chain/building-resilience-supply-chain-40-strategy

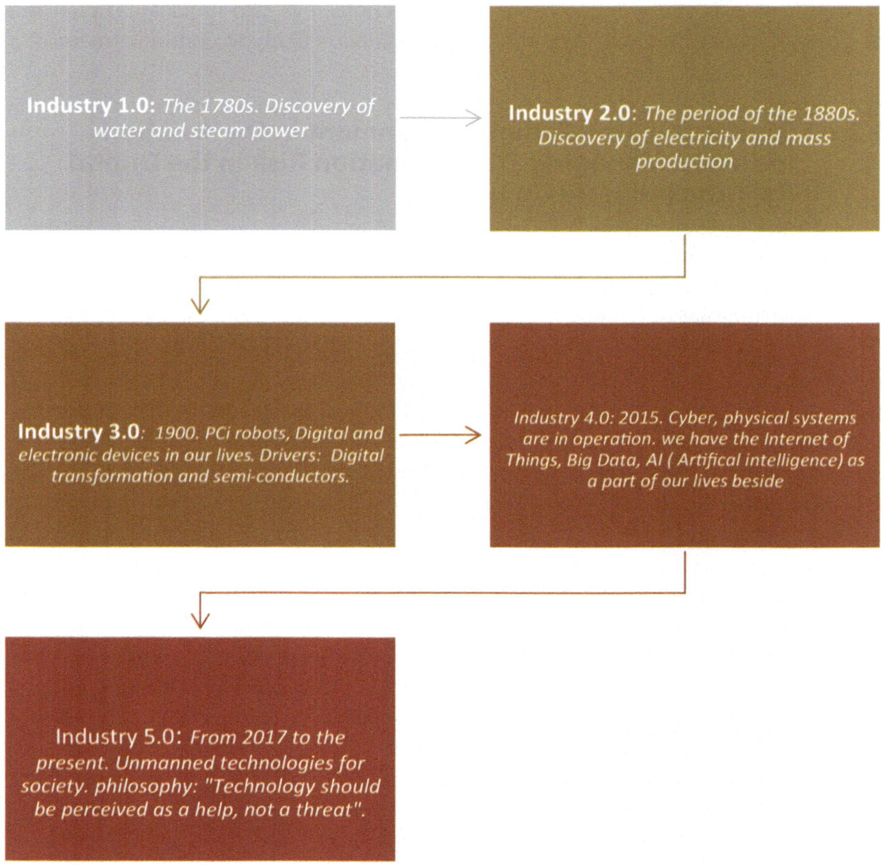

Fig. 3.1 Technological revolutions that transform all other sectors and the aviation industry. (Source: Authors)

3.3 Industry 4.0 and Aviation 4.0 (Digitalization)

Industry 4.0 is a collective whole of technologies and concepts of value chain organizations. Clearly, this fourth industrial revolution has taken its place in all areas of the aviation industry with its new activities. In this respect, technologies such as artificial intelligence, augmented reality, big data entries, new technologies, and the Internet of Things started to be used in production, and integration between these systems and the workforce was ensured. In this way, efficiency and productivity have been added to production. Overall, Industry 4.0 refers to the fourth industrial revolution, although it relates to areas that are not usually classified as industry applications per se, such as smart cities.

The new process, defined as Industry 4.0, includes a structure that will completely change the production and consumption relations. Therefore, Industry 4.0 defines both production systems that instantly adapt to the changing needs of the consumer, and automation systems that are in constant communication and coordination with each other (adapted from Alcin, 2016). Efficiency is paramount in the aviation industry, one of the fastest-growing global industries. Moreover, big data analytics, which is among the technologies of the fourth industrial revolution, has the potential to create a value shift in the aviation industry. Examples of important application areas of big data analytics in the commercial aviation industry are as follows: intelligent maintenance, risk management, air traffic optimization, customer satisfaction, cost reduction, revenue management, performance metrics, cost control and verification, fleet capacity increase, and freight control for fare adjustment, providing connected travel experience to passengers and airport performance management.

Industry 4.0, which also includes digital transformation, develops an orientation and transformation that will affect the world economy with all its elements and industries. Most importantly, this transformation is no longer optional. Industry 4.0 transformation, which is integrated with sustainable growth in the corporate strategy, risk management and policies, investments, all development plans, and related processes of aviation organizations, is the main framework.

The Industry 4.0 approach of the Germans is considered as an approach that focuses on production exploiting technology. The Japanese Society 5.0 is evaluated as an approach that focuses on people who produce and use the same technology. It covers production forms based on automation with high-efficiency levels. In this context, Supply Chain 4.0—as the next-generation digital supply chain, the application of the Internet of Things, the use of advanced robotics, and the application of advanced analytics of big data in supply chain management—requires to place sensors in everything, create networks everywhere, automate anything, and analyze everything to significantly improve performance and customer satisfaction. Moreover, the transformation into a digital supply chain requires two key enablers—capabilities and environment (McKinsey, 2021).

At this point, Industry 4.0 creates a milestone and organizations are in deep need of improving and updating of their supply chain risk management systems, according to the contingency approach, as in the business environment, which is transformed by being exposed to technological and environmental effects, management functions may change according to changing conditions.

Most supply chain systems, which have been reshaped and transformed with Industry 4.0, allow real-time and on-site monitoring of all processes in the supply chain, as well as products. Furthermore, the data pools obtained by monitoring constitute an infrastructure for artificial intelligence-supported automatic decision-making by managers. The biggest promise of the Internet of Things is interpreted as providing uninterrupted transparency from supplier to customer, processes that transmit signals to each other in a chain, and a distributed management initiative freed from centralized administration. Therefore, SCRM, a digital supply chain risk management infrastructure built with the right principles, offers significant advantages and opportunities (adapted from Digitalis, 2021):

- *Supporting decision-making with timely transparency across all elements of the chain*
- *Centralizing all supply chain-related data on the cloud and making it available for location-independent in-house use*

- *Optimizing based on big data*
- *Reducing the complexity of central management by decentralizing decision-making and automatic action*
- *Making the material flow leaner and more flexible*
- *Expanding the ability to develop solutions with easy interfaces instead of closed-box solutions in horizontal and vertical directions within the organization*
- *Increasing automation by facilitating human-machine interaction*
- *Minimizing the error rate in complex processes*

Digitalis (2021).

Accurate and timely decision-making, and, therefore, rapid information flow, is one of the determining factors in supply chain risk management. The most effective way to achieve rapid information flow today is the use of digital applications. With the inclusion of digital applications in the supply chain process, information can move in a much shorter time and in shorter ways than the flow of material. In today's supply chains, in-house integrations as well as inter-institutional integrations have become important. Therefore, it is necessary to establish value chains between institutions. Currently, these value chains may be achieved through digital applications and information flows over the internet. Thus, the integration of supply chain management will be ensured by the effective working of different functions together through digitalization and related application systems in the supply chain of the aviation industry.

As regards aviation, the main applications of the Industry 4.0 concept so far are related to aerospace production processes. Barbosa provided a contextual outline of how robotics, additive manufacturing, augmented reality, the Internet of Things, and simulation are currently applied in the aerospace manufacturing industry. In essence, it shows some of the innovations and daily benefits of Industry 4.0 in the aerospace industry (Barbosa, 2016).

Although there is still a long way to go before the first fully automatic aircraft is produced, the implementation of robots at Airbus and Boeing will enable monthly production rates of over 30 units for some aircraft types. InFactory Solutions, a new Airbus subsidiary, is advancing the corporate vision of the "Factory of the Future" with products and services for connected manufacturing in a fully connected and digital manufacturing environment. Airbus spin-off supplying Industry 4.0 systems for composites completes the first qualification and discusses future developments for defect position visualization. (*Informative short note:* InFactory Solutions (Taufkirchen, Germany) is an Airbus subsidiary created in 2016 to deliver automated, connected, and intelligent systems for manufacturing. It offers sensor systems, data analytics, and engineering consulting services mainly for composites production) (Gardiner, 2017).

Although there are some developments in technology, the reason for the emergence of Industry 4.0 is the economic competition between the East and the West. Clearly, Industry 4.0 has focused on manufacturing by adding machinery to the human workforce and even reducing the human workforce. With this revolution, it is aimed to implement self-managed smart production systems. In order to create a production system with Industry 4.0, some factors need to come together. These factors are as follows.

3.4 Big Data

Big data is larger, more complex data sets, especially from new data sources. These data sets are so voluminous that traditional data processing software just cannot manage them. But these massive volumes of data can be used to address business problems you would not have been able to tackle before (Oracle, 2021). Therefore, Big data helps companies shape their services and products according to the wishes and needs of their customers.

3.5 Internet of Things (IoT)

The idea of creating the Internet of Things belongs to British businessman Kevin Ashton, in 1999. He defined it as a communication system of sensory devices over a computer network. The Internet of Things (IoT) is a large-scale data flow environment powered by the deployment of global smart objects that constantly collect large amounts of data (Sun et al., 2017).

Airbus BizLab is currently working on a project to print aircraft parts with the help of a 3D printer. With the application of this technology, some burden will be taken off the shoulders of the very complex supply chain process, thus facilitating the aircraft manufacturing process. Production will not be tied to specific locations in central factories; instead, suppliers or even customers equipped with a 3D printer will be able to take over this process (Mattig and Hausweiler, 2017).

Using Virgin Atlantic, a fleet of Boeing 787 aircraft and cargo equipment connected by IoT devices, the total data generated on a flight using IoT exceeds half a terabyte and includes findings such as 20% reduction in delays, 15% reduction in deferred defects, and every airline engineer gaining daily hours (https://w3.accelya.com/blog/5-great-ways-airlines-are-using-the-internet-of-things).

EasyJet has designed and manufactured advanced uniforms integrating wearable technology for crew and ground personnel to increase safety in operation. Air New Zealand used wearable devices to monitor unaccompanied minors on short and long-haul flights (https://www.intechopen.com/books/aircraft-technology/aviation-4-0-more-safety-through-automation-anddigitization).

Being the first US carrier to use Radio Frequency Identification (RFID) baggage tracking technology, Delta Airlines has taken a step toward solving the problem of lost property or excessive waiting time. Passengers can see the location of their baggage on the way to the aircraft, on the aircraft, and on the way to baggage claim with push notifications on Delta's mobile application. Thus, the IoT enabled Delta Airlines to provide its customers with transparency and control over their luggage (https://www.supplychaindive.com/news/Delta-RFID-airline-logistics-use-case/529024/). Qantas Airlines has teamed up with Samsung Electronics Australia to launch an entertainment service that uses the Samsung Gear VR headset to provide passengers with a 3D experience in interactive 360° cinematic video format. In-flight VR headsets allow viewers to watch the latest in-flight movies, view the latest Qantas products, or see possible destinations (https://www.qantas.com/us/en/promotions/virtual-reality.html).

Rolls-Royce has recently partnered with Microsoft to use IoT technologies to make aircraft engines "intelligent." The engine manufacturer has adopted Microsoft's Azure IoT Suite and Cortana Intelligence Suite to diagnose potential failures in engines fitted to aircraft serving worldwide. Thus, information on engine health, air traffic control, route restrictions, and fuel usage will be collected from hundreds of sensors inside the engines and analyzed to detect any operational abnormalities or signs of developing malfunctions (Rolls Royce, 2019), (https://www.rolls-royce.com/country-sites/sea/discover/2019/delivering-better-engine-performance-withiot.aspx).

3.6 3D Printing

3D printings are fictionalized in a computer environment, and this fiction is transferred to reality utilizing devices and extracted as an object. These prints, which can reflect a kind of fiction or design from virtual to reality, are time and cost efficient to businesses.

3.7 Autonomous Robots

Autonomous robots are robots responsible to perform a task assigned to them. They try to perform a task with the macros assigned to them. Hence, they save both time and labor for businesses. This happens because while autonomous robots are involved in the production, they tend to perform a specific task both completely and at the desired level.

Cyber-physical systems will transform the Aviation 4.0 fuselage into a digital and intelligent aircraft. As a result, the amount and variety of operational data that can be collected onboard and through ground operations will increase exponentially. In Aviation 4.0, supervisory control and big data acquisition and processing networks in production processes enable automation and integration with IT systems. Moreover, aircraft operations broadcast on the employment of the CPS on a large scale. Thus, future air traffic management systems are designed as some cyber-physical systems system (CPSS) that requires tight coupling to provide the required capacity, efficiency, safety, and security system performance. Examples of cyber components including aircraft digital communication, weather/traffic forecasting, flight planning/optimization algorithms, situational awareness, and decision support software are in the form (Valdés et al., 2018).

Digital elements in the supply chain including predictive prediction with algorithms, definition of rule sets for decision-making in automated processes, machine learning algorithms to understand issues like quality or shipping bottlenecks, and automating operations with robots can be exemplified (Oliver Wyman, 2021). For example, DocuSign's electronic signature service offers the ability to electronically sign documents such as sales contracts, offer letters, account openings, and invoices to make remote work faster and easier.[2]

[2] https://www.docusign.com/products/electronic-signature. Access date: June 16, 2021.

As part of the DocuSign Agreement Cloud, eSignature integrates with a wide variety of procurement systems and software. Intelligent Insights uses artificial intelligence to help procurement teams quickly find and analyze the clauses in their contracts. Used with eSignature, Intelligent Insights can index and search contracts anywhere across multiple DocuSign eSignature accounts, internal systems, and external storage. Moreover, it can use analytics to create side-by-side contract comparisons that help procurement teams identify risks and opportunities in existing contracts.

Therefore, Blockchain is particularly interesting in creating more transparency and visibility across all supply chain activities. Organizations can create a decentralized record of all transactions to track assets from production to delivery or use by end-user. Clearly, this increased supply chain transparency provides more visibility to both buyers and suppliers to resolve disputes and build more trusting relationships. Another benefit is that the validation of data is more efficient to prioritize time on the delivery of goods and services to reduce cost and improve quality (Wilson, 2020a, b).

In aviation, for example, a digital supply chain can increase aircraft uptime through prediction of breakdowns, improved spare-part availability, and lightning-fast shipping. In retail, digital supply chains reduce the cost of logistics due to real-time, business case-based distribution network configurations which allows greater agility and responsiveness to variations in demand[3] (see following scenario)

Aviation Scenario: Predictive Forecasting for Replacement Parts

Imagine that an airline forecasting system predicts with a probability of 60 percent that a thrust reverser on a plane will fail within 18 to 22 days—likely in either Chicago or Atlanta. The airline orders the required thrust reverser from a distributor, and ships it to the central warehouse of the logistics company.

When the predicted breakdown occurs in Chicago, the on-board computer transmits the requirement for a new part to the Airline. Within 15 minutes, the part is labelled and sent via express air-cargo for same-day delivery.

The technician in Chicago receives the part along with a detailed repair plan on his tablet. Since the damaged thrust reverser cannot be repaired, it is sent back to the manufacturer to determine the cause of the breakdown. All relevant data is saved in a central database to further increase future prediction quality.

What's the impact? Automatic detection of the part failure by sensor saves time searching and ordering a replacement part. Advance prediction of the breakdown location enables early shipping and decreases delivery time. Overall AOG is decreased by 2.5 days, and logistics costs by 60 percent. (https://www.oliverwyman.com/our-expertise/insights/2017/nov/add-digital-to-your-supply-chain.html)

The digital supply chain also includes Cyber Technologies, Cloud Technologies, augmented reality, system integration, which are other reflections of digital transformation within the scope of Industry 4.0. These factors started to be used in production and enabled businesses to enter the competitive environment more tightly and compete. As such technologies include artificial intelligence, and after being

[3] https://www.oliverwyman.com/our-expertise/insights/2017/nov/add-digital-to-your-supply-chain.html

combined with human power, they have developed the ability to respond to most requests and needs. Thus, businesses have developed their ability to analyze together with the artificial intelligence as they receive help while producing their goods and services. Thus, it has tried to continue the production of the best goods and services that can meet the wishes and needs of people.

Undoubtedly, Industry 4.0 has created a transformation in many sector's business processes, production processes, business models, supply chains as well as in the aviation industry. Moreover, digital transformation-based new applications have gained speed to aviation operations. Thus, the aviation industry has increased its preference rate, with applications that will increase customer satisfaction during pre-flight, flight time, and post-flight time. Airline companies and airport operators that compete need to integrate Industry 4.0 and continue for the sustainability of their operations in the supply chain, as it should be prepared and in harmony with all kinds of changing technology and environment. Clearly, companies that cannot keep up with change will melt away in this competitive environment. Therefore, they need to adopt the Industry 4.0 system.

3.8 Industry 4.0 in Aviation

The aviation industry is among the sectors where advanced manufacturing and advanced assembly systems are used, and the quality and safety requirements are the highest. Being among them also requires being prepared for all kinds of areas that may change. Therefore, the use of new technologies is of great importance in the aviation industry. It operates within the aviation Industry 4.0, which includes all kinds of aviation activities from aircraft production to ground services. High-end technologies used in aircraft production not only make production effective and efficient but also save time for aircraft manufacturers. If we consider aviation in the world, the intensity of aircraft production and the flight was taken into consideration before the emergence of COVID-19. This intensity not only brought aviation further in the world but also global influences such as cultural and social influences became widespread. Furthermore, the rapid development of aviation shows that it is under the influence of Industry 4.0.

Another innovation brought by Industry 4.0 is business models. As new technologies affect existing business models, new business models are also emerging. Leasing could serve as an example of this model in aviation. Currently, the ownership of the aircraft remains fixed and it can be used through another business, rather than purchasing. Hence, businesses can use aircraft in their operations and reduce their costs by renting them, rather than paying the exorbitant aircraft prices. The leasing process is important for large airline companies. Airline companies with large and wide flight networks operate by increasing their frequency, and the frequency requires more aircrafts for the airline company. Thanks to leasing, it is possible to continue activities by renting aircrafts without purchasing them.

Flexible working is another business model brought by Industry 4.0. Standard work styles have gradually been replaced by non-standard work. Flexible working was a result of the economic crisis in the 1970s. Considering the new production order brought by Industry 4.0, more labor is required for excess service resulting from overproduction. In this case, the shift system can be considered, since in the shift system we can see the shift work of airline companies that operate both day and night, and accordingly, even the areas affected by aviation. With this system, the potential of the enterprise to respond to the wishes and needs of the customers is met. In addition, the aircraft maintenance organizations of the airline companies that continue their operations continue at full speed.

Airlines state that industry 4.0 has a lot of positive impact on their companies. It enables them to improve their existing projects and to be a partner in the competition. Furthermore, the questions posed in a survey were generally positive within Industry 4.0, and they talked about the need to integrate this new transition into them. In fact, in research conducted, the company employee was asked, "Do you use a roadmap for the planning of Industry 4.0 activities in your institution? Explain" and the answer they received was "Yes, Industry 4.0 is a very important period for all businesses. Planning for the use of these activities and determining a roadmap are very important. We have determined a roadmap for these activities. In the sectoral sense, we will implement the practices that will help us to survive against more advanced technologies and dynamic changes."

3.9 Industry 5.0

The term "Industry 5.0" relates to humans working with robots and smart machines. The concept is robots that help people work better and faster by leveraging advanced technologies such as the Internet of Things (IoT) and big data. In essence, it adds a personal human touch to the automation and efficiency pillars of Industry 4.0. It is stated that the high level of customization demand in the market also highlights the need for Industry 5.0 (Jardine, 2020).

For example, it is Toronto's Paradigm Electronics, which produces high-end speakers. While the company used Universal Robots' UR10 robotic arm to bring loudspeaker cabinets to high brightness, it was after a long time that it added a human to the production process, increasing production efficiency by 50%. This does not mean that robots will eventually be removed from the production cycle; on the contrary, Industry 5.0 is envisioned to enhance both machine and human roles in the manufacturing industry by leaving monotonous, repetitive tasks to the mechanical and opening the creative side to the biological one. This will allow staff to take more responsibility and more control of systems to improve the quality of production in all areas (Atwell, 2017). It has been less than a decade since Industry 4.0 first surfaced in manufacturing circles, but visionaries are already predicting the next revolution, Industry 5.0. If the current revolution highlights the transformation of factories into IoT-enabled smart facilities that use cognitive computing and interconnection via cloud servers, Industry 5.0 is set to focus on the return of human hands and minds to the industrial framework.

Industry 5.0 is interpreted as the revolution where man and machine reconcile and find ways to work together to increase production tools and efficiency. It may have already been applied among companies that have just adopted the principles of Industry 4.0. Even as manufacturers begin to use advanced technologies, they do not immediately make redundant a large part of their workforce and become fully computerized.

Industry 5.0 appears to have the potential to challenge and ultimately dismantle the assumption that connections, and therefore devices and people interacting in this environment, must be in it. This could eventually also result in the connection going beyond the physical limits of the production environment. In this view, people and devices can interact with the environment remotely. In fact, an engineer can interact with a production environment from a home office in a different country.

3.10 Human Resources

Human factor risk as human resources transforming in digital transformation

It is equally important to note that since the inception of Industry 4.0, the general view of what is considered an "industry" has changed (I_SCOOP, 2021).

It has traditionally meant "manufacturing"; thus, Industry 4.0 focused on environments where things would be built, such as factories and shipyards. At this point, it can be said that digital transformation also transforms concepts and perspectives. Moreover, the human factor is affected by these transformations. The human factor is the most critical risk in aviation. Therefore, human resources should be particularly focused on as a risk factor in digital supply chain management.

With the influence of digital business and organizational environments, the areas of expertise and skills needed in human resources are also transforming. Technology will also have an impact on the industry workforce, with employees empowered by real-time information and decision-making support from AI to focus on their core strengths. These trends look set to propel the industry into a period of accelerated digitalization (World Economic Forum, 2017).

In other words, "Digital transformation requires a different skillset from those working in today's economy and will create new types of jobs… Managing the impact of automation on employment, re-qualifying the industry workforce for the digital economy and creating a safety net for those working in a flexible workforce are the challenges of the industry, regulators. and will need to be addressed collaboratively by policymakers. Digitization and Artificial Intelligence will reduce the cognitive load on humans but will also have a significant impact on the need for human time and resources. Questions such as how aviation can best anticipate and manage this impact, and what changes it needs in recruitment, management, retention, and retraining practices to ensure adequate and appropriate human resources are successful in the aviation workplace will be important" (https://hermes.aero/?page_id=2186).

We can conclude that new technologies arising from digitalization have created numerous opportunities for optimizing air travel. However, digitization is not only beneficial for the customer, but it is also important for players in aviation to have a digitization strategy. Increasing profitability by optimizing flight performance is as important as improving the customer experience. It is very important to prepare for the future (https://www.intechopen.com/books/aircraft-technology/aviation-4-0-more-safety-through-automation-anddigitization).

Furthermore, we are experiencing COVID-19, which has become a pandemic by spreading all over the world, threatens and restricts both individual and social life, while constantly harming the economy and economic actors. The pandemic has also accelerated the rate of transformation of all sectors in terms of both the way they operate, and the components used while operating. In this view, the digital transformation, that has already begun, has accelerated with the pandemic. The aviation industry is one of the changing and transforming industries. In this already technology-intensive industry, the level of digitization of production and service components is increasing. The high level of digitalization both changes and transforms the changing business models, the changing structure human resources needs, and the content of products and services.

3.11 Managing Transformation Risk in the Digital Aviation Universe

Today's most critical risk is transformation risk

The aviation industry has both complex and integrated process in creating both services and products. For example, an airline needs air traffic services, passenger services, such as check-in and baggage control, catering, flight supervision, services by airports, and other aviation-related activities, in accordance with aviation law and requirements. The process is becoming more digitalized in this volatile business environment. For this reason, achievement of much needed integration is only possible through an optimized supply chain, supported with effective decision-making in a multi-criteria environment.

The use of digital technologies in their activities plays a pivotal role in the implementation of cost-effective strategies, as it allows them to simultaneously save significant resources and communicate.

Due to the changes and transformations created by digitalization in the production and service sectors, the supply chain system has begun to change, in terms of both operating systems and its stakeholders. Based on the principles of the contingency approach, suppliers also need to change both their production components and their logistics portfolios to be enabled for supplying digital products.

As of June 1, 2008, the International Air Transport Association (IATA) ordered the aviation industry to switch from paper tickets to electronic tickets. The basis of the transition to electronic tickets of all airlines worldwide is considered a form of digital transformation. Applications such as self-check-in kiosks, boarding passes, mobile boarding barcodes, mobile reservations, and Bitcoin have been accelerated in aviation, especially within the scope of airline companies and airport operators. These are valuable examples as concrete proof of how accelerated digital transformation has been.

Bitcoin has started to be used in many countries, such as Lithuania, Germany, Japan, Israel, Canada, Hong Kong, Malaysia, Turkey, the Philippines, the Netherlands, Singapore, Slovakia, Thailand, England, America, Vietnam, and South Korea. There are Bitcoin ATMs (America 1289, Canada 325, UK 105, Austria 93, Spain 38, Turkey 1, etc.) in approximately 260 countries and above (Kislakci, 2017).

The issues to be considered during the transportation, storage, and delivery of the digital product portfolio, contracts for the supply of digital products and delivery processes also have their characteristics. For supply chains to continue to produce and serve under these changing product portfolio conditions, they need to transform in their operational fields of activity, in data management systems, and risk management systems. Moreover, it is important that they update their organizational and operational structures to be open to change, flexible, and innovative.

Airline operators in the civil aviation sector, such as airport operators, ground handling operators, aircraft manufacturers, aircraft maintenance providers and repair organizations, training institutions, and spare parts suppliers, continued their activities by adhering to comprehensive measures, and occasionally, the supply chain was broken with the complete cessation of their activities. In terms of production planning, many industries have decided to halt or reduce production, under uncertain pandemic conditions. In some countries, such as in China, the containment of the pandemic was faster than in other countries. Countries that have contained the pandemic have started production again, and supply problems have started to emerge. Today, many newly industrialized countries are struggling to find containers. Therefore, in aviation, as in the automotive, computer, and telephone sectors, supply problems have started to be experienced in both production and service provision. As is known, the key elements in digital supply chain management are to make production, transportation, and warehouse operations manageable with data-based decisions, by providing end-to-end visibility.

Aviation is one of the most important industries affecting the supply chain, as it has a dual role in the supply system as both a supplier and an enabler. With the increasing acceleration of digitalization, digital production components, such as chips, have started to be used more in aircraft production (manned and unmanned aerial vehicles).

Air transport is a sector that increases human mobility both nationally and internationally. "The important role of air transport on human mobility has paved the way for the aviation industry to constantly come to the fore both in the spread of the epidemic and in prevention efforts" (Akca, 2020). Although people can reach different regions in a short time, thanks to air transportation, the spread of the epidemic increases globally, while airports are no longer merely areas used for flight activities and turn into trade centers, thus increasing human mobility at airports and increasing the risk of locally triggering the pandemic. For these reasons, one of the measures taken by the countries upon the recommendations was the restriction of transportation. "The World Health Organization recommends that measures should be implemented to limit the entry and exit of disease into countries" (World Health Organization, 2020). The World Health Organization has also published the measures to be taken at airports and flights during the pandemic and presented them to governments and airlines.

With advances in technology, information sharing has increased communication possibilities between businesses. As a result of advances in technology, it has eliminated time and place constraints and facilitated and accelerated the flow of products and information between businesses (Yıldızöz, 2006). With information technologies, product demands can be obtained directly from sales points. Thus, businesses can access market information more quickly. In the light of these developments, it becomes difficult for businesses to operate alone and thus the supply chain gains more importance (Tutkun, 2007). A typical digital supply chain could consist of several steps, although the only mandatory steps for digital assets are the following: creation, delivery, and consumption. Therefore, the digital supply chain is distinct from digital asset management as the focus is not on how to create or manage the digital assets but the end-to-end supply chain of these assets, particularly from the point of production to the point of consumption. Thus, different travel players, like aircraft manufacturers, travel agents, ground handlers, in-flight attendants, and IT partners, may be involved to support these functions for each of the assets at different levels (Singh, 2013).

New and changing risk sources are emerging due to the digitalization of supply chain management as a whole, and, with all its elements, the digitalization of stakeholder relations in the supply chain, the execution of collaborations in digital environments, and the digitalized business environment.

It is, therefore, important to improve the traditional supply chain risk management with a contingency approach and to restructure it in a way that will produce optimum results in the digital environment. Including the capacities and capabilities of human resources in the restructuring, it is predicted to be critical in terms of managing the human factor risk.

Aviation is a very resilient industry, accustomed to dealing with many operational challenges. However, pandemic-related causes are starting to be addressed as part of normal daily network planning and operations in airlines, airports, and ground handling operations; yet some may lead to more systematic permanent changes. Therefore, business models and management systems may be expected to reshape according to the pandemic environment. This means that mode of digitalization and AI artificial intelligence-based systems will replace current systems.

There have been great technological developments in the passenger aircraft production sector, led by Airbus. Although there are not many aircraft manufacturers, competition is high, with cost-effective production efforts. Aircraft manufacturers are aware that technology and digitalization is the most important factor that will make a difference in competition. Indeed, they are working hard on it. Soon, it will be possible to produce pilotless aircrafts. Furthermore, during the pandemic period, investments and projects based on sustainability have increased. In line with the sustainable growth targets, with the time opportunity created by the decreasing operations, the industry stakeholders are expected to reduce the negative environmental impacts, reduce the impacts on global warming, create green and smart airports, achieve low carbon emission, less noise pollution, etc. They have increased their digitalization investments and projects to manage the risk sources of losses.

To conclude, the aviation industry is undergoing a major transformation with the spread of digitalization and three-dimensional production techniques. Parts of aircraft engines can now be produced much lighter and more durable, thanks to additive manufacturing. Likewise, sensors placed on the aircraft engine with digitalization monitor all the dynamics of the jet engine and allow the development of special maintenance schedules, instead of standard maintenance intervals (General Electric Turkey, 2021).

3.12 Digital Applications and Implication Areas in the Aviation Industry and AviSRM

Safety & security come first in Aviation

Digital applications in the aviation industry as well as civil aviation activities and services are implemented within the context of the priority of safety and security. Innovations are adopted within the scope of these digital applications. It is included in products and services to make a difference, compared to the periods prior to its use to make a visible positive change in the operation carried out and to adapt to the developing technology. Digitization in aviation greatly contributes to the achievement of the goals of reducing costs, performing operations uninterruptedly and on time, accelerating, and keeping human error at acceptable levels, especially in terms of safety and security.

Clearly, digitization brings a host of opportunities to the airport industry. Mobile check-in apps, self-service bag drop, indoor geo-location, electronic bag tags, interactive digital displays—everything boils down to one thing: the digital revolution is transforming the airport industry. However, digitization also creates its own unique array of technical, cultural, and legal challenges which must not be overlooked (ACI World, 2018).

Industry 4.0 has brought about some changes in the aerospace and defense industry, as well as in other industries. Aviation companies that want to improve their operations and increase their revenues have gone through digital transformation. What is important is that it is not possible to become a "digital business" using only new technologies. In other words, broad-mindedness is required with the applications used, with the business models and with the way of organization. Digital technologies are shaping the aviation industry in the following concepts:

- *Advanced robots*
- *Additive manufacturing*
- *Augmented reality*
- *Simulation*
- *Cloud and cyber security*
- *Big data and analytics*

Currently, aviation companies and organizations are working to provide a better customer experience. While increasing the efficiency in their operations, they also use some innovations for their employees. Products and services are introduced under the name of innovation in aviation, to shorten the waiting time of passengers in check-in processes, to reduce maintenance costs, and to keep human error at acceptable levels, in maintenance equipment, and maintenance process, to ensure cockpit and cabin safety during flight, especially in large airports. Furthermore, algorithms are used to help personnel find directions, mobile technologies that enable pilots to quickly access the information they need to use in the cockpit to create a real operational perception in flight training, warning systems used to ensure safety in the air traffic tower, in-flight entertainment systems that will make a difference for airline operators. Algorithms are used in virtual reality and augmented reality applications and in all areas affected by flight operations.

According to Grasso (2020), suppliers facing complex global risk factors should re-evaluate and prepare themselves proactively by working to become more effective organizations.

Manufacturers are supported by suppliers to provide parts and systems during the assembly phase of the aircraft. For example, large companies, such as Boeing or Airbus, decide to retain or use subcontractors, after evaluating their capabilities, resources, and objectives, and deciding which one is more suitable for them. Thanks to the digital transformation involving digital applications, artificial intelligence, and smart systems, aircraft manufacturers are enabled to optimally implement their cost-effective decisions.

Blockchain is the technique that allows data to be exchanged directly between two parties without the need for any intermediary. Parties in a computer network perform transactions anonymously with encrypted identities. Each transaction is then added to a new transaction chain that cannot be changed and is automatically distributed to all other users in the same network. In this way, the security of the transactions carried out is ensured.

3.13 Digital Technical Applications

Blockchain

Lufthansa, which signed a content partnership agreement with Switzerland-based Winding Tree company in 2017, contributes to the development of the first Blockchain-based marketplace in the travel industry.

Thanks to the Marketplace developed by Winding Tree using the Ethereum network, it is aimed to increase the profit margin of service providers on the one hand and to make travel cheaper on the other hand.

Today, there are global reservation system providers and agency channels called GDS between airlines and passengers, the amount that the said intermediary layer collects from the airlines and passengers under the name of commission and service fee reaches billions of dollars every year.

With a digital wallet application to be developed for the loyalty program called KrisFlyer, Singapore Airlines aims to "digitize" the miles accumulated in the accounts of Program members, which will give their members the opportunity to meet this different technology, and to be traded instead of money in retail workplaces that are also members of the program. Singapore Airlines is working with KPMG Digital Village and Microsoft on this project (Nergiz, 2018).

Advanced Robots

Intelligent machines that can perform various tasks themselves without the need for human control are called autonomous robots. Robots, which are used in many areas from assembly lines to warehouse logistics, are preferred because they reduce work times and can perform complex works. Robots, which have a wide range of uses in the aerospace and automotive industries, create added value during the production phase and support efficiency, productivity, and profit.

Additive Manufacturing

For sectors where competition is intense, it is very important to present a product cheaply, quickly, and with high quality. While the products are in the testing phase, virtual prototypes may not always show the desired performance, and a physical prototype is needed for this. The work of creating a three-dimensional object by stacking various layers on top of each other is called additive manufacturing. Prototyping, which is a step in which the designed product has reached the desired level, helps to get feedback quickly. With the development of 3D printers, prototyping began to be used in many fields from architecture to aviation.

Augmented Reality

It is a technology that combines the real world with virtual graphics through a handheld or head-mounted display. This technology, which is also used in the aviation industry to simplify and speed things up, can reduce the workload on people. It also increases quality while reducing the need for training and support. For example, it supports training in aviation with its virtual cockpit. Apart from this, there are many documents that technicians need to look at during the process, such as maintenance processes, manuals, and technical procedures that must be followed in aircraft maintenance. With the augmented reality application, an augmented reality glasses to be worn by the technicians during the procedure can be easily detected and the problem can be fixed quickly.

Amadeus Electronic Ticketing Direct

Electronic Ticketing Direct enables authorized travel agents to issue electronic tickets and report these transactions directly to airlines' revenue accounting systems without having to report them first to the Billing & Settlement Plan (amadeus.com, https://amadeus.com/en/portfolio/retail-travel-agencies/electronic-ticketing, accessed on June 25, 2021).

Ticketing is the process of issuing and selling a travel document to a person. Clearly, the ticket sales process is a complex and specific activity. In this regard, it is necessary to know English terms, understand signs and abbreviations, and have a good grasp of the details of ticketing, in order to perform ticketing processes in the most accurate way. Amadeus is one of the global reservation systems used by airline companies and travel agencies worldwide, where cancellation, refund, and change operations can be carried out, as well as flight ticket reservation and sale. Apart from sales transactions, this system, which also includes information pages about the fee practices and rules of airlines, is very important for travel agencies (TÜRSAB Association of Turkish Travel Agencie, 2021).

As is known, information security management starts from the ticket purchase stage in airlines. Amadeus also stores all the necessary information of the passenger in its database. In addition, Amadeus is one of the largest sales platforms used for hotels, air tickets, transfers, and train tickets, which are extensively used worldwide. In essence, when one buys tickets online, Amadeus is probably the system running in the background. The information recorded in the database, as a result of ticketing, is called PNR (Passenger Name Record) and all transactions are tracked through this PNR code until the completion of the passenger's journey. Clearly, PNR information is the most important information in the aviation industry.

Pegasus Airlines

ICRON is one of the providers of Optimized Decision-Making and Supply Chain Optimization software solutions. They have entered into a partnership with Pegasus Airlines, Turkey's leading low-cost airline and one of the region's frontrunners, to digitalize and optimize the airline's end-to-end planning, decision-making, and operations. The first phase of this partnership—which aims to ultimately optimize all of Pegasus' ground operations, through ICRON's integrated, automated planning, and decision-making software platform—is the implementation of ICRON's Ground Handling Services Optimization Solution (ICRON, 2019).

Big Data and Analytics

Big data is complex data stacks that are collected in a wide variety, large volume, and quickly from many sources with different methods. Since it is process-oriented, it is very important to collect and analyze data within the aviation industry and to make use of these data as appropriate.

Thus, obtaining this data can bring strategic advantages to commercial airline companies, in this sector where intense competition is experienced. Furthermore, with the increasing use of social media in today's world, access to data has been facilitated. In this way, airlines started to collect tons of information about their customers and record their action trends. Therefore, businesses that reach and analyze customer requests and needs the fastest can offer services according to the desired ones. This, indeed, helps airlines to offer a personalized service, which accesses valuable data from passengers' personal information, travel habits, special requests, and needs to food and beverage preferences on board, hotel, and car rental habits, while increasing loyalty.

Cyber Security

While technology develops and makes daily work easier, yet, it entails some risks. Cyber security, according to its short and simple definition, is the access of information by unauthorized persons by infiltrating the system. In the above section, we stated the value of access to data and its accurate analysis and how it can give companies a strategic advantage.

Especially the technological developments that are related to Industry 4.0 increase the risk of cyber security. Clearly, threats are growing with virtual systems developing in manufacturing and supply chains. In the same way, such security problems are experienced in a sector where competition is intense.

Simulation

Simulation, which is a technology used in many fields from the health field to the construction sector, is a real-life event, situation, structure, etc. It is a technology that allows a product to be transferred to a virtual environment and tested. For aviation, simulation systems are a technology used for the training of users. They are used in many different fields of aviation, especially pilot candidates, to test and experience the difficult situations they may encounter in real life.

For example, in the "Hudson Miracle" in 2009, a US Airways A320 piloted by Chesley Burnet Sullenberger was launched into the river by flocks of birds and lost both engines. There were 150 passengers and 5 crew members aboard the aircraft. With the information obtained after the incident, it was revealed that the captain pilot had previously received training on this scenario. Thanks to this training, he saved the passengers' lives.

Drones

Audi and Airbus are jointly conducting pilot projects in the cities of Ingolstadt and Hamburg to develop the flying taxi concept. Drone air taxis, also called drone copters, are currently being tested outside the EU with some pilot studies in Dubai and China. According to the research of Roland Berger Consulting, it is aimed to provide transportation of approximately 100 thousand passengers by drone by 2050.

When the development process of drones is examined, it can be seen that cargo drone projects, which started as a pilot application for drone transportation and delivery in the past years, have started to being implemented at the point reached today. Especially the COVID-19 outbreak has significant potential in the widespread use of this technology in the logistics sector. In this context, cargo drones are being tested by many logistics companies, largely in Australia, Singapore, Iceland, and Switzerland, with the necessary permission and incentive initiatives of local authorities. It can be seen that the big retail sectors, such as Amazon, logistics service providers such as DHL, and many leading companies serving in other sectors, have started to use drone technology in shopping delivery or various distribution services, such as food or medicine. Thus, it is estimated that this technology will be used increasingly in the near future term, as an alternative mode of transportation in the field of logistics.

Clearly, drones have a very functional usage network in emergencies that may arise from the health field. Drone technology can be used in the fight against epidemics such as COVID-19, SARS, MERS; natural disasters, such as climate change, earthquake, flood, avalanche; disasters that cause resource shortages, such as food and water; crises such as human-induced conflict, terrorism, and mass migration; and every possible occurrence. It is extremely beneficial in delivering the necessary materials to urban and rural areas quickly and safely in all kinds of emergency situations.

It is believed that drones, which are especially used in disaster and humanitarian aid logistics and to meet the urgent needs in the field of health, can save the lives of many people, by ensuring that vital drugs or materials can be delivered to places that are difficult or impossible to access with other modes of transportation. Thus, drones find an important field of application. For example, food aid and medical supplies will be delivered to rural areas whose roads are closed due to heavy snowfall, and the lives of aid personnel will not be jeopardized against any avalanche that may occur. In addition, drones help search and rescue teams to determine risky buildings after an earthquake and decide whether it is safe to enter the buildings.

It is appropriate to underscore that drones serve not only in the air, but also underwater, with underwater drones. Underwater drones are primarily used for underwater data collection, mapping, and reconnaissance. Deep sea surveys, scanning of seismic fault lines in the sea, sampling from the seafloor, shipping logistics materials to a region in the sea, and inspection and maintenance of ships or boats are also done with these drones. In addition, drones can find widespread application in civil defense fields, such as precision agriculture and firefighting, for real-time data collection. Especially in the agricultural industry of the future, drones are an indispensable technology instrument for smart and sustainable agriculture, thus forcing conventional agricultural operations to change. Drones will enable monitoring the instant productivity of agricultural lands by making automatic measurements in the field at certain periods, independently.

It is stated that with the active use of drone technology in urban passenger and goods transportation as an innovative model of transportation, it is foreseen to make a significant contribution to the overall range of future transportation systems. "The European Innovation Partnership on Smart Cities and Communities" (EIP-SCC), supported by the European Union (EU), launched the "Urban Air Mobility" (UAM) initiative to deploy driverless drone air taxis for transportation within an area of approximately 100 km in cities. In this context, Drone Air Taxi projects are underway.

Online Applications

In digital transformation, economic developments, constraints and contractions due to the economy, and transformations in business and education life also have an impact. For example, the pandemic has also created an environment that accelerates digital transformation for social life, business life, and individuals alike. Undoubtedly, one of them is the increasing and permanent distance education and remote work models.

Looking at all these contexts, people have started to spend more time at home due to the COVID-19 pandemic. This is one of the most important measures to be taken, in order to be less affected by the epidemic. Therefore, the number of people spending time in the digital world has increased, as countries want to be protected as much as possible, by closing their border gates. To socialize, people now prefer digital platforms instead of meeting in person. Although these meetings, which are held with video and audio participation, do not replace in person meetings, they are the most important chat environments in current conditions. Thus, recently, applications such as WhatsApp, Zoom, and Microsoft Teams are the most widely used ones.

In addition, it is predicted that new business models that develop during the pandemic will be permanent. Therefore, digital transformation has also initiated a transformation in business models of the aviation industry as well as of other industries.

Digital Manufacturing in the Aviation Industry

New technologies used in production also create changes in the production process and process steps in the industry. All elements of the production process, from the production resources used to the control and monitoring processes, are also in transformation. This accordingly transforms the risks in the production process and during the procurement of products. It may be possible to fully understand the impact of transformation with striking examples in the aviation industry. For example, in the production of the A350, aircraft wings are not manual and are produced completely automatically. Clearly, this is not the only example of automatic production in aviation, as it is possible to see similar production techniques not only in the aviation sector, but also in various other sectors, such as automotive and construction. Automation can be applied to increase security, efficiency, and human value. Clearly, it can reduce hazards while maintaining the goals set in production.

Automated Production and the Role of Human Workers

In aviation, it is much more convenient to transfer some jobs to robots in the production processes. For example, drilling locating can be a time-consuming and tedious task. While performing this task by robots speeds up the process, the very valuable human resource can be exploited in more critical processes.

In addition, automatic systems are not merely a technology used in the production process. It is not possible for this technology, which is found in every field of aviation, to always be sufficient. For example, although the plane has autopilot, two more human pilots participate in each flight. This is due to safety concerns. As can be seen from the example of Hudson's Miracle given in the sections above, in some experienced situations, human cognition and decision ability are required. Until the robots' thinking and decision-making ability reach human dimensions, they will not be sufficient on their own, except for automatic production processes.

At the same time, a negative effect of automated systems is the reduction in the need for labor. Automated systems with industrial developments have already replaced human workers in many areas. It can be argued that some occupational groups will be compromised due to the further development of automation in the future. For example, an aircraft system that can think and make decisions like a human could be detrimental to pilots. Furthermore, the need for labor may also be reduced by transferring manual work to robots on the production line.

Mini Robots

Airbus, one of the aircraft manufacturers, develops automation in production by using robots, produced by a company called Kuka, which are autonomous navigation solutions that can move in all directions and have a payload of 90 tons, work with high precision, and work for 48 hours without the need for charging. Due to the different workstations and the huge fuselage sections, space in the Airbus hangar is limited. The ability to turn from a standing start is the greatest advantage of the Kuka Omni Move platform. The Mecanum wheels move in every direction and operate with the utmost precision even with a maximum payload of up to 90 tons (Edwards, 2016).

In addition, Rolls-Royce engineers are developing miniature robots that could be used in future jet engine maintenance applications. The Intelligent Engine initiative is studying a wide variety of advanced robotic technology, ranging from snake robots that work their way through the engine like an endoscope, to miniature, collaborative swarm robots that crawl through the insides of an engine (https://www.assemblymag.com/articles/94496-rolls-royce-develops-robots-to-crawl-into-jet-engines). The robotic technologies have the potential to offer significant benefits for customers by reducing the cost of engine maintenance, increasing the availability of an engine, and ensuring any maintenance required is completed as quickly as possible (https://www.rolls-royce.com/media/our-stories/insights/2018/swarm-robots.aspx; Rolls-Royce Develops Robots to Crawl Into Jet Engines, 2018, https://www.assemblymag.com/articles/94496-rolls-royce-develops-robots-to-crawl-into-jet-engines). Clearly, these robots are designed to facilitate aircraft engine repair processes with their different capabilities and to reduce the great costs in this field. Thanks to these robots, the engine does not need to be removed from the aircraft every time to perform maintenance. Because of this technology, it will be possible to reduce aircraft engine maintenance costs, extend the operating time of the engine, and ensure that the required maintenance is completed quickly. For aviation companies, this could be very profitable in repair processes.

Blockchain

Digital transformation in aviation began when the International Air Transport Association (IATA) ordered the aviation industry to switch from paper tickets to electronic tickets on 1 June 2008. Thereafter, digital transformation applications started to be implemented in various areas, such as self-check-in kiosks, boarding pass, mobile boarding barcodes, and mobile reservations. With the emergence of these innovations, entrepreneurs who went into different pursuits developed the Bitcoin and Blockchain platform.

Although the concepts of Blockchain and Bitcoin emerged much earlier than they both became known, the low trust of people in the security of transactions, via the internet at that time, delayed the implementation of this platforms. However, the

Blockchain platform, which came to the fore again with the development of technology and the Internet, made a big leap. As a result, Blockchain came to life with Bitcoin. Bitcoin, with the symbol ₿, is a crypto currency or virtual currency used via the Internet and not affiliated with any central authority or intermediary institution.

Samples to Bitcoin Applications in Aviation

- *The first Bitcoin ATM in Turkey was opened at Istanbul Airport. This ATM converts deposited money into Bitcoin regardless of currency.*
- *Avione Jet is the first private jet charter company to use Bitcoin in Turkey.*
- *Pegasus is Turkey's first low-cost airline company that will serve with Bitcoin's Blockchain Technology.*
- *ABITSKY is the first online system to sell flight tickets with crypto money.*
- *In Latvia, airBaltic became the first low-cost airline to accept payments in Bitcoin three years ago.*
- *Low-cost airlines (low-cost carriers) have integrated into the Bitcoin system very quickly.*
- *Air transport and tourism-travel companies are trying to keep their customers by trying to adapt themselves to this new change by offering Bitcoin payment option as an alternative to traditional credit card and bank transfers.*

Blockchain is the name given to the technology that allows data to be exchanged directly between two parties without the need for any intermediary. In other words, it is an ever-growing distributed database in which records are linked to each other by cryptographic elements.

Resilience, traceability, integrity, and disintermediation are the four most basic features of Blockchain.

Dubai Airport: Cell Phone Instead of Passport

Passengers using Terminal 3 and departing from the United Arab Emirates (UAE) can use smart gates (e-gate) at the terminal because of a project implemented as a result of the cooperation of Emirates Airlines and Dubai Airport-related government agencies in 2017. After the mobile application UAE Wallet is installed on the mobile phone, the passenger's UAE identity card, passport information, and e-gate card are brought together in a digital environment. Thus, passengers benefiting from this innovation are expected to complete their passport control process in a very short time, such as 9–12 seconds. The process in question is completed by scanning the fingerprint of the passenger on the e-gate and scanning the screen of the mobile phone.

BAE is working with a company called Object Tech on this important project that uses Blockchain infrastructure.

Using Lufthansa Blockchain

Blockchain technology is used by airlines to sell tickets to passengers using global reservation system providers and agency channels called GDSs (Global Distribution Systems) as an intermediary. However, these intermediaries demand a large amount of money from the airline companies in return for the services they provide. Lufthansa, who wants to eliminate this cost factor, has started to develop the first

Blockchain-based marketplace in the travel industry by making a content partnership agreement with the Swiss-based Winding Tree company in 2017, aiming to sell tickets to its passengers without an intermediary. Thus, by using the Blockchain platform, it starts selling tickets to its passengers without intermediaries, thus reducing its cost expenses.

Smart Airports

Guiding signal-finding technologies will provide indoor routing, walking times to boarding gates, or boarding alerts. It includes augmented reality, smart kiosk machines, social media-enabled services, airport games, loyalty services, queue management, airport mobile application, and a continuous IoT (Internet of Things) framework (İGA Airport, 2021).

In addition, a technology-driven baggage delivery system will enable passengers to register their baggage quickly and easily. In this context, passengers who register online or at airport kiosk machines can weigh their baggage at the baggage tag generation corner at the airport terminal and use their boarding passes to produce tags for their baggage. Furthermore, technologies aid travel shopping, creating an experience worth remembering.

SABRE Airline Solutions

Sabre Airline Solutions is a platform that provides operations related to an airline's operation, which include planning and marketing, corporate operations, and customer sales and services. Sabre Airline Solutions uses software as a service technology, to provide flexible solutions that adapt as a business grows. Sabre Airline Solutions enable businesses to create products that appeal to their targeted customers, reach customers who shop for air travel, care about their customers at every touchpoint, and work efficiently to deliver the products expected to customers. The following are the main features offered by Saber Airline Solutions (Sabre, 2017):

- Cargo management
- On-board catering and supply
- Income analysis
- Pricing and revenue management
- Launch control
- Online direct
- Flight operations
- Maintenance planning
- Crew management
- Recovery
- Airport management

Artificial Intelligence

Artificial intelligence (AI) technology is highly optimizing flight operations and impacting the commercial aviation industry. World's leading airline companies are implementing AI and other emerging technologies to offer personalized services and enhance customer experience. For example, self-service kiosks are automating operations and security checks at the airport. Going forward, AI will play a critical role in the aviation industry.[4] There are various successful AI applications in Aviation as follows (Aithority, 2021):

- *Passenger identification*
- *Baggage screening*
- *Fraud detection*
- *Customer support*
- *Cost optimization*
- *Predictive maintenance*
- *Recommendation engine*
- *Chatbots*
- *Journey management system*

The aviation industry leverages AI with machine learning, computer vision, robotics, and natural language processing. Key benefits include predictive maintenance, pattern recognition, auto-scheduling, targeted advertising, and customer feedback analysis to improve overall customer experience (Aithority, 2021).

İGA Istanbul Airport

Being the "smartest" airport in Turkey, Istanbul Airport distinguishes with the mobility-oriented, innovative technological services it offers to its passengers, in addition to the standard airport services. With the important digital services currently offered at Istanbul Airport such as e-passport, smart translation service, mobile application, smart parking, 5G, smart security and robots, İGA is trying to produce "technological value" for Turkey (İGAirport, 2020).

A mobile application is the software designed and coded specifically for devices, such as tablets and smart phones. Some services that cause loss of time are received more quickly through the mobile application at the airports. A mobile application is a system in which transportation vehicles such as trains, shuttles, and taxis can be reserved according to the airport density or traffic and weather conditions according to the time remaining for the departure of the plane or the duration of the flight during the journey starting from home, and automatically planning according to all accessible information (İGAirport, 2019).

For example, at Istanbul airport, in the parking lot, mobile payment, maintenance, washing, repair and refueling services, space reservation, and blocking can be carried out through the mobile application. In the terminal, 2D and 3D maps, live location information, store locations, personalized flight planning, in-terminal navigation, calculation of baggage waiting process and turning it into an advantage, in-terminal product ordering are provided via mobile applications (İGAirport, 2019).

---

[4] https://aithority.com/predictive/ai-applications-in-aviation-and-travel-industry/. June 25, 2021.

Supply Chain Applications

Lufthansa

Outsourcing and Supplier Management Outsourcing for the implementation of big data is Lufthansa's main strategy. In November 2014, Lufthansa signed a $1.25 billion outsourcing agreement with IBM to take over its IT infrastructure services division and personnel. Lufthansa has a long history of outsourcing. It always outsources infrastructure and applications. There are no in-house developers at Lufthansa.

The Code of Conduct, which has been binding for all bodies, managers, and employees of the Lufthansa Group since 2017, was supplemented by a Supplier Code of Conduct in 2019. In this Supplier Code of Conduct, the Lufthansa Group lays out its position that it also expects business partners and suppliers to adhere to the principles as a fundamental aspect of the business relationship. The standards at its core are not only the basis for responsible conduct and fair competition, but also seek to identify legal and reputational risks at an early stage and avoid them. The Lufthansa Group has published the Code of Conduct on its website https://investor--relations.lufthansagroup.com/fileadmin/downloads/en/financial-reports/annual-reports/LH-AR-2020-e.pdf.

"A smart supply chain is one element of a successful digital transformation. This is because digitalization and changing customer expectations, with regard to information and mobility are driving Logistics 4.0. Automated processes, telematics, big data, sensor technology, and cloud solutions are helping companies to digitalize their supply chains and have led to improvements in many areas of the transport and logistics industry." (https://www.lufthansa-industry-solutions.com/de-en/solutions-products/supply-chain-logistics-40/) (Fig. 3.2).

Lufthansa Industry Solutions was recognized as a relevant player in the digital factory in the three use case clusters "Predictive Analytics & Maintenance", "Traceability," and "Asset & Plant Performance Monitoring" by teknowlogy. According to teknowlogy, the leading independent European market analysis and consulting company for the IT industry, LHIND has proven to be able to address all related use cases in these categories in airlines, MRO operations or cargo handlers https://www.lufthansa-industry-solutions.com/de-en/solutions-products/supply-chain-logistics-40/.

Lufthansa Industry Solutions is a service provider for IT consulting and system integration. A subsidiary of Lufthansa Cargo AG, the firm empowers its clients through their digital transformation journeys. Its customer base includes organizations from within and outside the Lufthansa Group, as well as over 200 companies, in a number of business lines. The organization helps companies to digitize and automate their business processes. As a result, the organization does not only focus on the IT required but also on the customer's business as a whole, as well as its internal and external challenges. This is because digital transformation impacts a company's entire structure and culture and goes beyond company borders to collaborate with partners, customers, and suppliers (Galea-Pace, 2020).

Fig. 3.2 Lufthansa Industry Solutions. (Source: https://www.lufthansa-industry-solutions.com/de-en/solutions-products/supply-chain-logistics-40/)

Airbus

Digitization is at the heart of Airbus' strategy. Airbus works with over 12,000 direct suppliers, thus necessitating a solution provider that can swiftly and smoothly integrate its software into existing procurement systems. Optimizing business relationships is critical, as Airbus seeks to increase its strategic agility through digitalization for iconic global companies. By deciding to apply digital transformation solutions in the global supply chain of the aerospace manufacturer, Airbus collaborated with Bellevue-based Icertis. As one of the cloud-based enterprise contract management providers, Airbus will leverage the Icertis Contract Management (ICM) platform and ICM Sourcing application to develop its source-to-contract solution across various divisions of Airbus (Lawrence, 2020).

By combining Airbus' rich sales and purchasing contracts on a single platform, digital optimization of Airbus' vendor relations will be possible. Thus, it will be possible to accelerate trade negotiations and benefit from improved compatibility. Airbus executives believe that "with the ICM platform and ICM Sourcing application, they will digitally transform their business foundations in the supply chain, enabling them to provide best-in-class supplier evaluation, selection, contracting and collaboration, all while reducing supply chain risk." With the product portfolio, it will be possible for businesses to combine market opportunities with their supply chains more effectively (Lawrence, 2020).

As regards the manufacturing of aircraft, Airbus has applied more and more composites to its products, increasing it from approximately 4.5% in the A300 (1974) to approximately 40% in the A350 airframe. Composites were first applied in secondary structures, expanded into primary building sections, and then into large-scale components. Airbus has a unique, extensive experience in this technological area. A fundamental and imperative criterion for the rise of composite materials is the technological maturity required to meet acceptable maintenance costs along with performance and cost advantages for the customer. The main strengths of composites are high strength/low density ratio, corrosion resistance, and advantageous fatigue behavior (no fatigue in service conditions). The choice of a technology is the result of a trade-off that systematically includes all the driving factors (Rösner & Jockel-Miranda, 2006), in this context in production materials which would mean for Airbus to change suppliers as well. This change brings along new risks within the scope of the change in the supplier structure, new agreements, and communication.

Airbus is a manufacturer of aerospace and defense products and related services. It has 180 international locations and 12,000 direct suppliers. It has launched Skywise, a new aviation data platform that provides big data integration and advanced analytics. The Skywise data platform developed and used by Airbus has achieved great success in analyzing and predicting faults. As such, an increase in security and operational efficiency has been achieved (Think tech, 2020).

Fraport A.G.

Unlike manufacturing companies, Fraport's management does not focus on the supply chain. Instead, the focus is placed on the quality of the services offered and the functionality of the infrastructure required for this. It is crucial, however, that business partners and suppliers are selected carefully. The Group companies each have their own procurement management (Fraport A.G., 2020).

Digitization at Frankfurt International Airport

In every business, customer satisfaction and services are of prime importance. Some new technologies are likely to have a major impact on airports over the next decade, including Frankfurt International Airport (FRA). Fraport, the operator of Frankfurt Airport, thinks that with the implementation of new technologies ever-improved operations based on a more efficient infrastructure will be achieved. According to Fraport, Digital transformation requires acceptance and participation. Therefore, the successful implementation of any digital strategy depends on finding a common orientation with all people involved. Fraport appears to have a sufficient and suitable infrastructure; thus, they may integrate many already existing digitization initiatives (ACI World, 2018).

Lockheed Martin

Lockheed Martin describes its supply chain management philosophy as the "SCM+: Supply Chain Management Plus Program." A similar situation exists in Europe. While the share of SMEs among Airbus' suppliers is 65% in France, this ratio reaches 90% in Germany. The average ratio has currently reached 80%.

Qantas: In-Flight Virtual Reality Systems and Augmented Reality Applications

Qantas has launched a virtual reality (VR) app, which allows travelers to explore immersive destination content before booking their flights.[5] Australian flag carrier

[5] https://www.futuretravelexperience.com/2016/11/qantas-virtual-reality-app-offers-immersive-pre-travel-experience/. Accessed June 26, 2021.

airline Qantas has reportedly discussed plans to entirely outsource its ground handling operations. The outsourcing initiative revealed that the company's long-term strategy to reshape the company involved jeopardizing approximately 2500 job positions (Supply Chain, 2020). Furthermore, it shows that Qantas is changing their supply chain strategy. At this point, we may think that their risk portfolio will change. Therefore, their risk management strategy and concept will be revised by their managers.

GE Aviation

A new application that leverages Blockchain to monitor progress in the food supply chain, developed by GE Aviation in collaboration with TE-FOOD: This application uses Blockchain to help monitor the necessary cleanliness checks of aircraft, crew, and passengers prior to take-off. Developed by Microsoft Azure, this solution is currently available, and airlines, airports and industry groups are experimenting with the application. "GE Aviation's business model encompasses airlines flying with GE engines," according to David Havera, GE Aviation general manager of Blockchain solutions. He underscores that they are doing their best to ensure that passengers fly again without further ado. As already stated, Blockchain technology is known as the underlying structure of cryptocurrencies such as Bitcoin with its high-security record keeping technology; however, it also has diverse uses. For example, companies using Blockchain can store and track an almost infinite number of digital records, similar to combining unique building blocks. The Blockchain in the new app uses encryption and private keys to help protect the personal information and medical records of passengers and airline employees. In addition, it allows airlines to share this information worldwide (GE Turkey Blog, 2021).

Heathrow Airport

Heathrow Airport is one of the busiest airports in the world and generally operates at 100 percent capacity. It leverages artificial intelligence and big data in specific tasks of air traffic control and runway management. More data insights have allowed Heathrow Airport to increase its capacity and ultimately its revenues (Think Tech, 2020).

Intelligent Data Sharing

As in many industry sectors, there is a tendency toward reducing paper and printed materials in air transportation. IATA's goal is a paperless process and "intelligent data sharing." The emergence of apps and software for freight forwarders that facilitate all stages from invoicing to freight tracking to occur digitally implies a paperless future is at hand.

This system is quite beneficial to aviation logistics. Clearly, it is a greener system and less cumbersome than physical paperwork. Thus, user-friendly apps and software save senders' time and energy, providing operators with quick responses and intuitive processes to follow. At the same time, all the information they need is readily available regardless of one's location.

Furthermore, these innovations create advantages for suppliers in the field of customer relations. In addition to providing a cost-effective, efficient, and environmentally friendly method of shipping, it builds customers' confidence by leaving much less room for human error.

The digital transformation of procurement processes, which offers a variety of short-term development perspectives, has been progressing steadily over the years. Therefore, making optimal use of digital solutions provides significant performance gains in purchasing organizations.

Aviation businesses use many innovative systems to easily take decisions that minimize delivery times. Computerized decision support systems, data analysis to identify needs and reduce costs, and various collaboration portals to monitor suppliers' performance comprise the innovations used in the field of purchasing.

RED Entertainment System

Virgin America's inflight entertainment system, RED, has a Linux-based operating system. Created by Panasonic, this system is powered by AMD. RED has a system that will track where passengers are going during the flight using Google Maps. Moreover, passengers can buy food and drink without waiting for cabin crew, talk to other passengers on the plane online, and donate to charities. In addition, thanks to RED, passengers can watch TV and movies, by paying a fee. Furthermore, passengers can listen to music of all styles with its rich music library. This system has been developed and introduced in a much more advanced form by many airline companies, and being the founder of the functional display on the back of the seat (Paul, 2007).

Threats in Supply Chains

Raw Material Constraints in Part Productions

Demand for the automotive industry started to increase as the need for cars increased slightly with the lifting of the bans; however, there was a pause in car production due to the shift of canceled reservation and chip production for other industries. Moreover, this has affected cargo transportation, as some of the cars are transported by airplane. Due to the use of chips in electronic devices used in aviation (Electronic Flight Bag-EFB, etc.), the demand for these devices cannot be met. Due to the negativity in microfluidic chip production, stagnations in health will both cause disruptions in technological developments and make it difficult to prevent epidemics such as COVID-19, prone to affect aviation.

Container Supply Risk

In the 1950s, US ship operator Malcolm McLean realized that a lot of time was spent transferring cargo from ship to land and from land to ship, and he developed giant steel boxes. A breakthrough in transportation, containers were first used in transatlantic trade in 1966. Currently, "container transportation" takes the biggest share in maritime transportation. With the outbreak of the COVID-19 pandemic worldwide, most countries became unable to export. This, in turn, reduced the use of containers in terms of logistics. However, China, which recovered more quickly compared to other countries, followed the global monopoly approach by reserving almost all the containers. The French Newspaper Le Monde summarized this situation with the headline "Dependence on China inflamed maritime transport prices." Thus, the market has evolved into a China-USA country pair, as China, which has a monopoly on container supply, exports to the USA. Although there are many products in their warehouses and ready for shipment, in places other than this country pair market, containers are very difficult to find; even if they are found, fewer containers can be booked at prices much higher than the normal price, both due to the high freight price and the failure of the supply to meet the demand.

3.14 Importance of Digital Supply Chain Management

As shown in Fig. 3.3, Boeing supplies the parts of the aircraft it produces by establishing many partnerships globally. In order for the orders received by airlines to be delivered on time, it is vital that these parts arrive at the assembly site on time. Therefore, the Industry 4.0 revolution has had a significant impact on the digitalization of the supply chain.

Clearly, digital supply chain management is an emerging internet-based information architecture that can be used to facilitate information flow in global supply chain networks. With the assumption that objects have digital functionality and can be identified and tracked automatically, IoT can dramatically simplify how to manage the supply chain and quality factors (Xu, 2011). Thus, information flow between the manufacturer and the supplier can be easily provided.

Currently, due to the intense competitive environment, businesses have begun to face difficulty in self-sufficiency and have started to establish loyalty relationships with other businesses. In this context, businesses operating in the aviation industry try to keep all processes undergoing transformation in the supply chain under control and manage risks, from the beginning of production to the presentation to the customer, in order to be sustainable, to compete, and to achieve their goals in cooperation with their stakeholders. In the light of technological developments, it is a dynamic concept that increases as information is shared among businesses, and cultural and geographical barriers come to the fore as a global production source, thanks to information sharing and technologies. The sustainability of all activities in the supply chain process largely depends on transparent information sharing and trust-based collaborations with stakeholders. Thus, digitalization and technological information sharing tools play a critical role in obtaining cost-effective results in order to maintain transparency among the stakeholders in the supply chain and to ensure effective information sharing. According to Gunasekaran and Ngai (2004), the supply chain aims for improved customer satisfaction and hence for overall

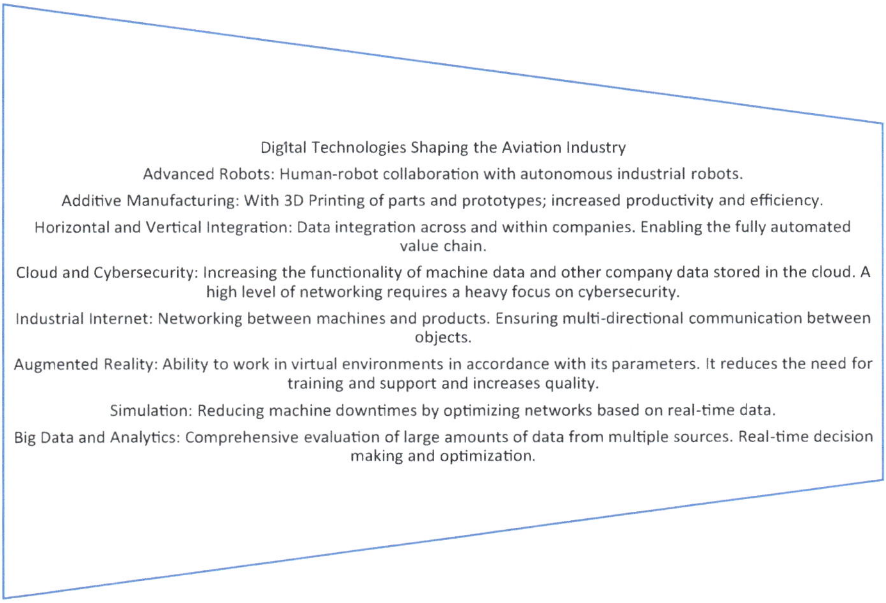

Fig. 3.3 Digital technologies in the aviation industry. (Source: Authors)

competitiveness in a global market. In global business competition, companies believe that greater transparency in supply-chain operations and collaboration is very important for success. Supply-chain transparency in ordering, inventory, and transportation is a prerequisite for optimization and is critical for making business decisions. Desired transparency in the supply chain requires both the development and effective using digital tools, which provide all players with open communication and shared information in every stage of the order-to-delivery process (Gunasekaran & Ngai, 2004).

In order to deliver the right product to the right customer at the right time, at the right price, all risks related to the processes in the supply chain must be well managed. Furthermore, it is important that stakeholder relations are based on trust and transparency while managing these risks.

Relationships should also be well managed. In traditional supply chain management systems, the focus is on cost-effectiveness and speed. Since this does not include the management of stakeholder relations and the optimization of comprehensive communication channels, it may prevent risks from being managed at the desired level. With the digital transformation, supplier and customer relations have started establishing through digital communication rather than face-to-face communication. In addition, the activities of the procurement process, the emergence of new technologies, such as information sharing, service software, and social media have made the communication between the enterprises and their supply chain stakeholders simultaneous and effective.

The goal of increasing quality while reducing the production costs of the traditional supply chain has become more achievable with the digitalization of products and business models. With Electronic Data Interchange Software, businesses can share documents regarding commercial relations between them completely electronically and at any time. Thus, businesses are enabled to save time-consuming paper processes, time, and human resources. In addition, recording information and documents in digital environments, monitoring simultaneous activities, simultaneous control, and supervision of the process, which is one of the most critical problems for businesses, they also reduce the risk of information and documents being lost. But the risk of information leaks from digital platforms has also been transformed. It is particularly important for businesses to manage the risks that change and transform along with digital applications.

Aviation is one of the industries where the digital transformation is applied at the highest level. Digital applications and smart systems are used in the production processes of products and services, aiming to safety. Thus, with digital transformation, innovations are included in the product and service production process, in order to ensure the highest level of safety and security, to reduce interruptions in products and services, to achieve corporate strategies, to adapt flexibly to the transforming business and business environment, and to respond to the needs of the day.

Currently, aviation companies work toward providing a better customer experience. While increasing the efficiency in their operations, they also use digital applications and smart systems for their employees. Therefore, in aviation, products and services are introduced under the name of innovation in order to shorten the waiting time of passengers in check-in processes, to reduce maintenance costs, and to keep human error at acceptable levels, as well as in maintenance equipment, equipment and maintenance process, in order to ensure cockpit and cabin safety during flight, especially in large airports. Furthermore, algorithms are used to help personnel find location and direction, mobile technologies enable pilots to quickly access the information they need to use in the cockpit in order to create a real operational perception in flight training, warning systems are used to ensure safety in the air traffic tower, and in-flight entertainment systems to have an effect on for airline operators. Digital transformation is used in virtual reality and augmented reality applications, and in all areas related to flight operation.

Digital applications are shaped by the change and transformation of the needs of both product and service manufacturers and customers in the aviation industry, due to digital transformation. Another area where digital transformation is strongly felt in the aviation industry is airports.

Today, passengers can follow their own travel processes, get or change flight information before arriving at the airport, get their boarding pass from the kiosk devices of the airline companies or ground handling company when they arrive at the airport, and deliver their luggage from specially reserved counters if they have done online check-in (Artar & Turkay, 2021).

Conclusively, for the aviation industry and the aviation supply chain, digital transformation is changing technologies and trends, stakeholder relationships, chain processes, traceability, control, and auditing of processes. At this point, it is recommended that the supply chain be implemented by developing a value chain-oriented risk management system, since digital transformation enables more transparent applications, access to information, and simultaneous monitoring. Therefore, digital transformation in the supply chain is a dynamic process in which technologies are integrated into chain activities for specific purposes. These aims are basically to improve operations, prevent interruptions, increase speed, make relations transparent, reduce costs, increase revenues, and thus provide optimization in risk management.

There are numerous and diverse supplier structures in the aviation industry. Hence, when cooperation in the aviation supply chain is achieved at a desired level, it may be possible to benefit from the advantages of digital applications, such as Blockchain.

3.15 Conclusion and Final Remarks

The aviation industry is driven by countries that possess advanced technologies and have managed to integrate digital applications and processes. By way of example, Boeing is one of the world's largest aircraft manufacturers. It is stated that Boeing has 28,000 suppliers. Moreover, Boeing purchases approximately 800 million parts per year, and the total number of employees in the supply chain reaches 500,000. Boeing's 787 aircraft consists of more than 2 million parts. Main subsystems such as engine, landing gear, avionics are also outsourced from about 40 large suppliers. Therefore, supply stands out as one of the vital risk sources for the sustainability of the aviation industry.

In order to increase the integration with the stakeholders and turn the suppliers into risk partners, it is foreseen that the information flow in the network and cooperation in the design and/or development processes should be achieved in digital applications and related investments.

In the current dynamic, variable, competitive production and business environment of the current aviation industry, safety and security are key priorities in industry, while industry stakeholders and suppliers have to manage their operations and activities cost-effectively and increase performance, and, thus manage sustainability risks. For example, it can be seen that new and modern airports are constantly being designed with new digital systems, smart systems, and technological application approaches.

Risks are driven by trade wars, the coronavirus outbreak, and supply chain organizations, and/in capabilities. Today, suppliers in aviation, the automobile industry, pharmaceuticals, etc., which have not adequately incorporated risk management and mitigation strategies, are facing serious shortages and/or delays from their Chinese partners. The combined effects of these risks have made it even more evident that supply chains, no matter how mature, are far more inelastic. Therefore, operational strategies currently focused on "digital" should also include a strong risk preparedness component, greater transparency, and sustainability (Grasso, 2020). Schlüter et al. (2017) stated that due to the digitalization of supply chain networks, a large number of real-time data will be available and allows quicker recognition and responses to potential risks.

Digital Transformation and Transforming Risks

Aircraft manufacturers have many suppliers. Examples of such suppliers in the hardware space include companies such as DevCom, Las Aerospace, GE Aviation, and Goodrich Corp. Artificial intelligence and artificial intelligence technologies are the ones used on the supply chain, provided to aircraft manufacturers by these companies. Moreover, General Electric and Rolls-Royce are engine suppliers. These companies use numerous technologies in engine production. They also aim to minimize emissions with their advanced analytical methods. Clearly, in the production of engines they use AI technology in their production premises, like almost all companies in the sector. In addition to all these, although it has not been identified in the aviation industry yet, there is no doubt that Blockchain technology will be given prominence in the next 10 years. In this view, digital platforms may be used most especially in the purchase of parts, engines, and hardware, which aircraft manufacturers buy from their suppliers.

Clearly, this situation arises from the dynamics of improving operations and capacity and providing a better customer experience. Rapidly developing air transportation with the effect of advancing technology and globalization has diversified the risks and increased the number of them together with the increasing number of passengers and traffic and the rate of use of technological advancements.

As in other sectors, the technologies that trigger Industry 4.0 are reshaping and transforming the aviation industry with all its stakeholders and components. Aviation industry organizational participants, such as both manufacturers and suppliers, use digital technologies to carry out cost-effective activities, manage their risks, adapt to the digital age, increase their revenues, and thus achieve their sustainability goals in economic, social, and operational areas. However, it is important for an organization to manage its risks, create risk scenarios, develop business models, develop its organizational structure to be flexible and open to innovations, and strengthen stakeholder relations on the basis of cooperation, partnership, and transparency, so that an organization can use digital applications effectively by taking advantage of digitalization. In addition, organizations must ensure that their digital investments meet internal and external customer needs and important business objectives, toward achieving their economic, social, and operational goals.

AviSCRM is a fundamental aspect of management in the aviation industry. Supply chain risk management (SCRM) may improve both the cooperation and collaboration level among stakeholders in supply chain, and improve both the managerial and operational performance of the chain. A supply chain, designed to increase the awareness level about risks entailed in digital operation and to optimize risk management, enables supporting sustainability for all value chains.

Companies are actively striving toward risk mitigation. The current focus is investment to mitigate risk and increase resilience for rapid recovery, and profit restoration. Clearly, COVID-19 has been the catalyst that led more companies to understand the magnitude and importance of investing in a supply chain. Costs may increase, but so too can the chance of business survival.[6] In order for businesses to manage their supply chain risks, it is important that they perceive this digitalized supply chain, which is connected end-to-end, together with both the process and its stakeholders, and gain the potential to use Industry 4.0 technologies and develop it. To build on these trends and cope with the changed requirements, supply chains need to become much faster, more granular, and much more precise (McKinsey, 2021).

The number of devastating cyber-attacks since the 1980s has progressively increased. As devices and machines become interconnected in the world, great threats are also encountered in the face of increasing opportunities. As high-end machines process complex interconnected data on a daily basis, it is critical that this information is both secure and accessible in real time (Kahraman, 2021). The smart Aerospace & Defense (A&D) businesses would be supported by the suppliers of the future, who would be equipped with real-time information sharing platforms, so as to ensure an uninterrupted supply for critical parts in real time and with minimal waste. The relationship between original equipment manufacturers (OEMs) and their suppliers would go beyond buyer-supplier relationship to "being a part of the business," giving rise to a new range of risk-and-revenue-sharing business models (Miller, 2020).

In this respect, innovative technologies on sustainability and efficiency shape the sustainability strategies of organizations in the aviation industry. Digitalization and artificial intelligence are considered to be the source of this strategy. In a way that supports cost-effective management purposes, digital applications increase efficiency by increasing usage performance. In addition, digitalization will also improve the level of organizational awareness and success in achieving goals related to sustainable growth, together with supplier stakeholders of organizations in the aviation industry.

In addition, companies operating in this industry have become large-scale, multinational structures as a result of mergers, and sometimes under the direction of government structures. These giant companies focus on the development of original and technology-intensive products to sustain their existence and drive this process through innovation. Thus, forecasting exactly what kind of permanent changes could take place is difficult, since pandemic conditions may be under control thanks to worldwide vaccination, but current restrictions may create both current and future new operational challenges.

A concentrated data-driven SIOP (sales, inventory & operations planning) optimization approach and a comprehensive review of product mix, demand signals, and supply constraints is the first step in mobilizing corrective actions (Grasso, 2020) in AviSCRM (Aviation Supply Chain Risk Management).

Important applications of big data analytics in the commercial aviation industry facilitating smart maintenance, risk management, air traffic optimization, customer satisfaction, cost reduction, revenue management, performance measurements, cost control and verification, load control for fleet capacity increase, and ticket price adjustment provide connected travel experience and airport performance management.[7]

---

[6] https://supplychaindigital.com/digital-supply-chain/building-resilience-supply-chain-40-strategy

[7] https://thinktech.stm.com.tr/uploads/raporlar/pdf/21202091831971_stm_sivil_havacilikta_buyuk_veri.pdf

The aviation industry is one of the major cornerstones of the economy in the recent past, present, and future. The size of the investments made, their effects on the environment and economy, social contributions as well as the number of employees, and the number of people benefiting from the service clearly show that this is a determinant and transformative industry which adds value for either human and economics. For the post-pandemic take-off in the aviation industry, the use of applications that will affect the perception on the basis of trust is foreseen as a supportive strategy for the re-take-off.

3.16 Case Study: Boeing

"Through our robust and growing supply chain capability, Boeing offers industry-leading distribution and repair solutions to customers across the commercial, government, business and general aviation markets," commented William Ampofo, vice president of Global Services Supply Chain. "Streamlining our operations under a single brand will further strengthen the services and support our customers know and trust from Boeing, Aviall and legacy KLX Aerospace. We will work closely with customers and suppliers to help them realize the benefits of the industry's most integrated, optimized and responsive global supply chain" (https://supplychaindigital.com/supply-chain-2/boeing-advancing-its-supply-chain-better-serve-customers).

3.17 Case Study: TAV Airports Holding

The sudden and rapid digitalization that we all had to face during the pandemic accelerated the growth of e-commerce, by roughly 5 years, according to McKinsey. The acceleration of e-commerce is anticipated to support increased cargo traffic worldwide. Although only 1% by weight of all commodities is carried by air freight, the items carried make up 35% of global trade by value. Acceleration of e-commerce is thus expected to drive above trend growth for cargo in the future. In this context, the acquisition of Almaty Airport in Kazakhstan, once complete, will capitalize well on these trends. Almaty has the potential to become one of the most important cargo hubs in Central Asia. On the supply side, reduced regulations, efficiency gains, low-cost carriers, and digitalization have pushed ticket prices down making air travel more accessible to all. Furthermore, increased awareness for environmental and social governance and cost pressures will push airlines to increase fuel efficiency which would further move prices down in the longer term. Thus, with increasing demand, especially in emerging economies and cheaper supply, the industry is still poised for growth once pre-pandemic passenger levels are reached. While Embraer projects a global growth rate of 2.6% per year in the next decade, Boeing expects average world passenger growth to reach 4% in the next 20 years. Therefore, with its strong balance sheet, world-class intellectual capital, and a long-term outlook that stands intact despite the pandemic, we are confident that TAV Airports can manage the challenges of this period well and again establish a position of superior growth once normalization occurs. We would like to thank our supportive shareholders and our employees for navigating this great brand successfully into the future, through historically turbulent times (TAV Airport Holding, 2020).

TAV Technologies, a subsidiary of TAV Airports, was awarded at the 11th IDC CIO Summit, organized by the International Data Corporation (IDC) Turkey office. The DAP platform, developed by TAV Technologies with its own resources, received an award in the category of "Informatics Solution Creating the Best Customer Experience." With nine airports in its portfolio, TAV signed the protocol established by the European Union's agency responsible for aviation security, EASA, to protect the health of passengers and employees against COVID-19. Operated by TAV Airports, Izmir Adnan Menderes, Ankara Esenboğa, Zagreb, and Skopje Airports were selected as the best airports in Europe in their categories at the Airport Service Quality ASQ awards given by the World Airports Council (ACI World). TAV Airports was among the best in social media in the "Airports" category at the Social Media Awards Turkey 2020, Turkey's most comprehensive social media awards (TAV, 2020: https://webcmstavairports.tav.aero/files/1615449193_Faaliyet%20Raporu%202020%20TR.pdf).

Aviation is a major service industry, generally based on transporting passengers and cargo to faster and longer distances than other alternatives. Since aviation is a very comprehensive and broad industry, it proceeds with the organizational harmony of many industries. This organization covers the process from the production of an aircraft to the market, and the quality completion of this process is enabled through the effective, full, and timely management of the supply chain.

There are many types of organizations in aviation that affect each other. Some of these can be listed as aircraft manufacturers, aircraft spare parts manufacturers, support service providers, accessory and component manufacturers, airlines, airport operators, ATC units, aircraft maintenance organizations, ground handling/ground handling operators, academies, and schools providing flight training. Although all these stakeholders provide services differently from each other, they all affect and are affected by each other and by the aviation industry as a whole. Thus, the aviation supply chain plays a pivotal role in starting the process and reaching the consumer, and any disruption or delay has the potential to change the entire chain.

References

Alcin, S. (2016). A new theme for production: Industry 4.0. *Journal of Life Economics, 3*(2), 19–30. https://doi.org/10.15637/jlecon.129

Akca, M. (2020). The impact of Covid 19 on the aviation sector. *Journal of Eurasian Social and Economic Research, 7*(4), 45–64.

Artar, O., & Turkay, U. I. (2021). Digital transformation of airports in the aviation industry. *Working Paper Series, 2*(1), 86–97. http://workingpaperseries.ticaret.edu.tr/index.php/wps/article/view/45

ACI World. (2018). Fraport's digital strategy: Focusing on projects that make a difference. *ACI Insights*. Article: https://blog.aci.aero/fraport-digital-strategy-focusing-on-projects-that-make-a-difference/. Assessed on 25 June 2021.

Aithority. (2021). https://aithority.com/predictive/ai-applications-in-aviation-and-travel-industry/. June 25, 2021.

Assemblymag.com, https://www.assemblymag.com/articles/94496-rolls-royce-develops-robots-to-crawl-into-jet-engines, 2018.

Atwell, C. (2017). Yes, industry 5.0 is already on the horizon, AUTOMATION & IIOT, Machine Design. https://www.machinedesign.com/automation-iiot/article/21835933/yes-industry-50-is-already-on-the-horizon

Berti, A. (2020). FLY AI: The role of artificial intelligence in aviation. Analysis, Airport Technology (FLY AI: the role of artificial intelligence in aviation airport-technology.com)

Barbosa, G. F. (2016). Aviation manufacturing towards to industry 4.0: A review. In *4th international conference and exhibition on mechanical & aerospace engineering*, October 03–04, 2016 Orlando, USA, New Exploration in Mechanical & Aerospace Engineering, Retrieved at June 2021 from https://mechanical-aerospace.conferenceseries.com/abstract/2016/aviation-manufacturing-towards-to-industry-4-0-a-review

Da Xu, L. (2014). *Enterprise integration and information architecture: A systems perspective on industrial information integration* (Advances in systems science and engineering (ASSE)). CRC Press. ISBN 1439850240, 978143985024.

Digitalis. (2021). Digital supply chains. https://dijitalis.com/dijital-tedarik-zinciri

Edwards, D. (2016). Kuka's monstrous robotic vehicle manoeuvres gigantic Airbus components with 'millimetre precision'. *Robotics & Automotion News*. https://roboticsandautomationnews.com/2016/06/30/kukas-monstrous-robotic-vehicle-manoeuvres-gigantic-airbus-components-with-millimetre-precision/6005./

Fraport. (2019). GRI report 2019. https://www.fraport.com/content/dam/fraport-company/documents/konzern/verantwortung/publikationen/eng/sustainability/2019/fraport-gri-report-2019_final.pdf/_jcr_content/renditions/original./fraport-gri-report-2019_final.pdf. June 22, 2021.

Fraport. (2020). Combined non-financial Statement 2019, Fraport AG, www.fraport.com, Combined non-financial Statement 2019 - Fraport AG.

Galea-Pace, S. (2020). Lufthansa industry solutions: Accelerating digitalization. *Supply Chain Digital, Magazine*. https://supplychaindigital.com/supply-chain-2/lufthansa-industry-solutions-accelerating-digitalisation. June 22, 2021.

Gardiner, G. (2017). InFactory Solutions with Airbus, Composites World, Gardner Business Media. https://www.compositesworld.com/articles/infactory-solutions-qualifies-afp-sensor-on-mtorres-equipment. Accessed at 20 June 2021.

GE Turkey Blog. (2021). Retrieved at March 24, 2021 from https://geturkiyeblog.com/havacilik-endustrisinin-daha-hizli-toparlanmasina-yardimci-olabilecek-uygulama/

General Electric Turkey. (2021). Aviation. https://geturkiyeblog.com/ge-teknolojileri/havacilik/. Access date 21 June 2021.

Grasso, D. (2020). The complex risk factors facing aerospace and defense, think tank, supply chain brain. Accessed at 21 June 2021 from https://www.supplychainbrain.com/blogs/1-think-tank/post/31121-the-complex-risk-factors-facing-aerospace-defense

Gunasekaran, A., & Ngai, E. W. T. (2004). Virtual supply-chain management. *Production Planning and Control, 15*(6), 584–595. https://doi.org/10.1080/09537280412331283955. [Taylor & Francis Online], [Web of Science®], [Google Scholar].

https://blog.satair.com/cyber-threats-in-aviation-industry

https://blog.satair.com/blockchain-in-aviation

https://investor-relations.lufthansagroup.com/fileadmin/downloads/en/financial-reports/annual-reports/LH-AR-2020-e.pdf

https://supplychaindigital.com/digital-supply-chain/building-resilience-supply-chain-40-strategy

https://w3.accelya.com/blog/5-great-ways-airlines-are-using-the-internet-of-things

https://www.intechopen.com/books/aviation-and-its-management-global-challenges-andopportunities/aviation-of-the-future-what-needs-to-change-to-get-aviation-fit-for-the-twenty-first-century

https://www.lufthansa-industry-solutions.com/de-en/solutions-products/supply-chain-logistics-40/

https://www.oliverwyman.com/our-expertise/insights/2017/nov/add-digital-to-your-supply-chain.html

https://www.qantas.com/us/en/promotions/virtual-reality.html

https://www.rolls-royce.com/media/our-stories/insights/2018/swarm-robots.aspx; Rolls-Royce Develops Robots to Crawl Into Jet Engines, 2018, https://www.assemblymag.com/articles/94496-rolls-royce-develops-robots-to-crawl-into-jet-engines

i_SCOOP. (2021). Industry 4.0: The fourth industrial revolution – Guide to Industrie 4.0. Retrieved April 2021 from https://www.i-scoop.eu/industry-4-0/

ICRON. (2019). Pegasus Airlines partners with ICRON to digitalize and optimize end-to-end operations. News, Icron Technologies. Accessed on 26 June 2021 from https://icrontech.com/news/pegasus-airlines-partners-with-icron-to-digitalize-and-optimize-end-to-end-operations/

IGAirport. (2019). Sustainability report 2019. https://www.igairport.aero/sites/sustainability/en/news/2019-sustainability-report-published.

IGAirport. (2020). Istanbul Airport was granted the "Best Digital Transformation in Europe" Award. Accessed by https://www.igairport.aero/en/press-releases/best-european-airport-for-digital-transformationistanbul-airport/news/294755/istanbul-airport-was-granted-the-best-digital-transformation-in-europe-award/.

Jardine, J. (2020). Industry 5.0: Top 3 things you need to know, Learning Center GxP Lifeline, Master Control. https://www.mastercontrol.com/gxp-lifeline/3-things-you-need-to-know-about-industry-5.0/. Accessed at 16 June 2021.

Kahraman, H. (2021). Digital transformation for aerospace and defense industry, Industry 4.0. https://www.endustri40.com/havacilik-ve-savunma-sanayi-icin-dijital-donusum/

Kislakci. (2017). *Air News Times*. https://www.airnewstimes.com/talip-kislakci-havacilikta-dijital-donusum-ve-bitcoin-727-yazisi.html

Lawrence, M. (2020). Airbus selects Icertis for digital transformation of its supply chain. *Technology, Magazine, Supply Chain*. Accessed by https://supplychaindigital.com/technology-4/airbus-selects-icertis-digital-transformation-its-supply-chain at June 22, 2021.

McKinsey. (2021). Supply Chain 4.0 – the next-generation digital supply chain. https://www.mckinsey.com/business-functions/operations/our-insights/supply-chain-40%2D%2Dthe-next-generation-digital-supply-chain

Miller, R. (2018). Why supply chain management is important in aerospace and defense? Ernst & Young Global Limited (EY), UK. Accessed by https://www.ey.com/en_gl/aerospace-defense/why-supply-chain-management-is-important-in-aerospace-and-defense at 04.21.2021

Miller. (2020). *Why supply chain management is important in aerospace and defense*, Ernst & Young Global Limited, https://www.ey.com/en_cn/aerospace-defense/why-supply-chain-management-is-important-in-aerospace-and-defense

Nergiz, A. (2018). "Blockchain" applications in the airline industry, havayolu101. https://www.havayolu101.com/2018/07/17/havayolu-sektorunde-blockchain-uygulamalari/ adresinden alındı.

Oliver Wyman. (2021). Add digital to your supply chain - and add value, insights. Accessed at 16 June 2021 from https://www.oliverwyman.com/our-expertise/insights/2017/nov/add-digital-to-your-supply-chain.html

Oracle. (2021). What is big data. Retrieved at April, 2021 from https://www.oracle.com/big-data/what-is-big-data/

Paul, M. (2007, 08 10). Hands-on with Virgin America's RED in-flight entertainment system. *Engadget*. https://www.engadget.com/2007-08-10-hands-on-with-virgin-americas-red-in-flight-entertainment-syste.html

Rolls Royce. (2022). *Powering better performance and customer experience with the Internet of Engines*. Accessed by https://www.rolls-royce.com/country-sites/sea/discover/2019/delivering-better-engine-performance-with-iot.aspx Rolls Royce, https://internetofbusiness.com/10-real-life-examples-iot-aviation/

Rösner, H., & Jockel-Miranda, K. (2006). Airbus airframe – New technologies and management aspects. *Materialwissenschaft und Werkstofftechnik: Entwicklung, Fertigung, Prüfung,*

Eigenschaften und Anwendungen technischer Werkstoffe, 37, 768–772. https://doi.org/10.1002/mawe.200600062

Sabre Airline Solutions. (2017). *Airline customer sales & service set your business free with our solutions portfolio.* Accessed by, https://www.sabreairlinesolutions.com/images/uploads/Sabre_Airline_Solutions_Overview.pdf

Schlüter, F., Diedrich, K., & Güller, M. (2017). Analyzing the impact of digitalization on supply chain risk management. In *26th IPSERA conference*, Budapest/Balatonfured, 2017.

Singh, A. (2013). Importance of digital supply chain in airline industry. *Phocuswright.* https://www.phocuswire.com/Importance-of-digital-supply-chain-in-airline-industry. Accessed at 9 June 2021.

Sun, L., Liu, J., Higgs, R., & Zhou, L. (2017). *IEEE international conference on computational science and engineering (CSE) and IEEE international conference on embedded and ubiquitous computing (EUC)* (pp. 437–442).

Supply Chain. (2020). Qantas outsourcing documents leaked. *Magazine, Supply Chain Digital.* Accessed 26 June 2021 at https://supplychaindigital.com/supply-chain-2/qantas-outsourcing-documents-leaked

TAV Airports Holding. (2020). 2020 annual report. https://ir.tav.aero/uploads/documents/Documents03032021144252_.pdf. Accessed on 11 June 2021.

Think Tech. (2020). Big data technology and applications in civil aviation. https://thinktech.stm.com.tr/uploads/raporlar/pdf/21202091831971_stm_sivil_havacilikta_buyuk_veri.pdf. Accessed on 25 June 2021.

TÜRSAB Association of Turkish Travel Agencie. (2021). Announcement about ticketing and Amadeus system training. https://www.tursab.org.tr/duyurular/ticketing-ve-amadeus-sistem-egitimi-hakkinda-duyuru. June 25, 2021.

Tutkun, H. İ. (2007). *Analysis of its applicability in business before designing and organizing the supply chain management structure.* Unpublished Master Thesis, Dokuz Eylul University Social Sciences Institute, Izmir.

Valdés, R., Comendador, V. F. G., Sanz, Á. R., & Castán, J. A. P. (2018). Aviation 4.0: More safety through automation and digitization. *Aircraft Technology.* https://doi.org/10.5772/intechopen.73688

Wilson, G. (2020a). Boeing: Advancing its supply chain to better serve customers. *Technology, Supply Chain, Supply Chain Digital Magazine.* https://supplychaindigital.com/supply-chain-2/boeing-advancing-its-supply-chain-better-serve-customers. April 02, 2021.

Wilson, G. (2020b). Boeing: Improving supply chain operations in Asia-Pacific, Supply Chain. https://supplychaindigital.com/supply-chain-2/boeing-advancing-its-supply-chain-better-serve-customers. May 17, 2020. Accessed 16 June 2021.

World Economic Forum. (2017). Digital transformation initiative aviation, travel and tourism industry in collaboration with Accenture, January 2017, White paper. https://reports.weforum.org/digital-transformation/wp-content/blogs.dir/94/mp/files/pages/files/wef-dti-aviation-travel-and-tourism-white-paper.pdf

World Health Organization. (2020). *Updated WHO recommendations for international traffic in relation to COVID-19 outbreak.* Accessed by https://www.who.int/news-room/articles-detail/updated-who-recommendations-for-international-traffic-in-relation-to-covid-19-outbreak

Yıldızoz. (2006). *Supply chain management and its application,* Unpublished master thesis, Social Science Institute, Yıldız Technical University, http://dspace.yildiz.edu.tr/xmlui/bitstream/handle/1/6998/0024622.pdf?sequence=1&isAllowed=y

Global Supply Chains 4

When it is obvious that the goals cannot be reached, don't adjust the goals; adjust the action steps.

– Confucius

4.1 Structure of Supply Chain

In times of globalization, the companies rely largely on an optimal structure of supply chain to achieve competitive advantages.

4.1.1 Dimensions of Supply Chain

The administration of the flow of goods and services in the business entities is commonly described as supply chain management. The issues in supply chain management are often discussed in several dimensions, for example:

(a) *Material*. This involves the different stages of the transformation of raw materials into work-in-process and finally, the finished products.
(b) *Activities*. A plethora of activities are important to supply chain management throughout the processes of procurement, production, and distribution.
(c) *Organization*. The supply chain management requires a good coordination of many business entities and in each business entity, the coordination of many different divisions.
(d) *People*. A large number of people with different interests are involved along the supply chain, for example, the employees of the manufacturer, the customers, the suppliers, and the distributors. In addition to the issues of

M. Helmold et al., *Supply Chain Risk Management*,
Management for Professionals, https://doi.org/10.1007/978-3-030-90800-3_4

industrial-organizational psychology, there are also social and ethical issues. These are especially complex in an international environment.

(e) *Information*. In many industry sectors (e.g., automotive industry), the efficient exchange of information along the supply chain beyond the boundaries of the business organizations has long become an essential factor for the business success.

4.1.2 Process Modelling with SCOR Framework

Due to the increasing complexity of the global supply chain, the implementation of professional diagnostic tools has become indispensable for the configuration and reengineering of the supply chain. Such tools are rather helpful in scrutinizing alternative processes, with the aim of business performance optimization in a sustainable manner.

Supply Chain Operations Reference (SCOR) model is among the most popular process-driven tools for capturing internal and cross-company business processes, introduced by the Supply Chain Council. The implementation of SCOR model normally follows a "top-down" order. In the first step, the corporate strategy is to be divided into subtasks for the middle management. Those subtasks are defined as business processes for the responsible stakeholders. In turn, the processes then break down into specific activities for stakeholders within and beyond the boundaries of the business organization (Wang et al., 2010) (Fig. 4.1).

SCOR classifies supply chain processes in six categories: Plan, Source, Make, Deliver, Return, and Enable.

- Plan: Processes that balance aggregate demand and supply to develop a course of action which best meets sourcing, production, and delivery requirements.
- Source: Processes focusing on procurement of goods and services in accordance with the planned or actual demand.
- Make: Processes dealing with the transformation of raw materials into finished products in accordance with the planned or actual demand.

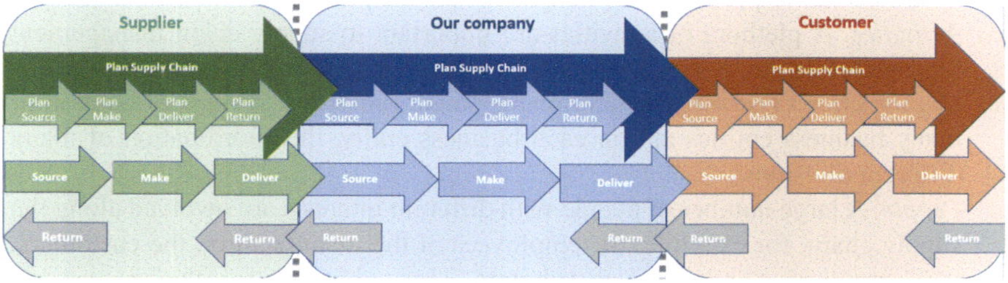

Fig. 4.1 Modelling supply chain processes with SCOR model. (Source: Author according to SCOR Framework)

- Deliver: Processes dealing with the distribution of finished goods and services in accordance with the planned or actual demand.
- Return: Processes designed to handle returning or receiving returned products for any reason.
- Enable: Processes which facilitate the above processes, including the management of business rules, performance, and supply chain network.

4.2 Demand-Driven Global Supply Chains

4.2.1 Globalization, Deglobalization, and Glocalization

The term "globalization" is often used to describe the growing interdependence of different nations worldwide due to process of interaction and integration. The pertinent academic research primarily in the past has focused on the economic aspect of the process and dedicated to the increasing interdependence of different economies through cross-border movements of products, services, technologies, and capital (Joshi, 2009).

In the previous literature, there was a consensus among the leading economists that globalization with diminishing trade barriers would lead to an overall economic growth and raise the living standards of the world population. Through access to global markets, the corporates could benefit from the economies of scale. The improved access to global technology and innovation, as well as to global talents, accelerate the business progress in the future. With the free choice of production locations worldwide, manufacturers are able to achieve higher cost-efficiency. In addition, the access to global capital market enables a fast expansion.

However, the regional benefit from globalization has been unequal. The statistics implies, compared with the noticeable economic growth in the emerging countries (e.g., China and India), the growth in the industrial countries turned out insignificant. In other words, the gap in economic power of the individual countries seems to be closing (see Fig. 4.2).

After intensified globalization processes in the recent decades, this development is being increasingly criticized for the uneven distribution of gains. As the "elephant graph" based on the income development of the worldwide private households from 1988 to 2008 (developed by the researcher Branko Milanovic) shows, a minority of households with the highest income in most countries have shown the fastest income increase in the above period of time. On the contrary, the households with the lowest income level have been locked out of the global economic growth. While the living standards of the middle class in the industrial countries as a whole are still superior to that of their counterparts in the developing countries, the stagnation of their income is causing insecurity and anxiety (see Fig. 4.3).

The term "deglobalization" is used to describe the reverse development of globalization—the diminishing interdependence of different nations, especially in the economic context. The movements of deglobalization in the recent years are marked

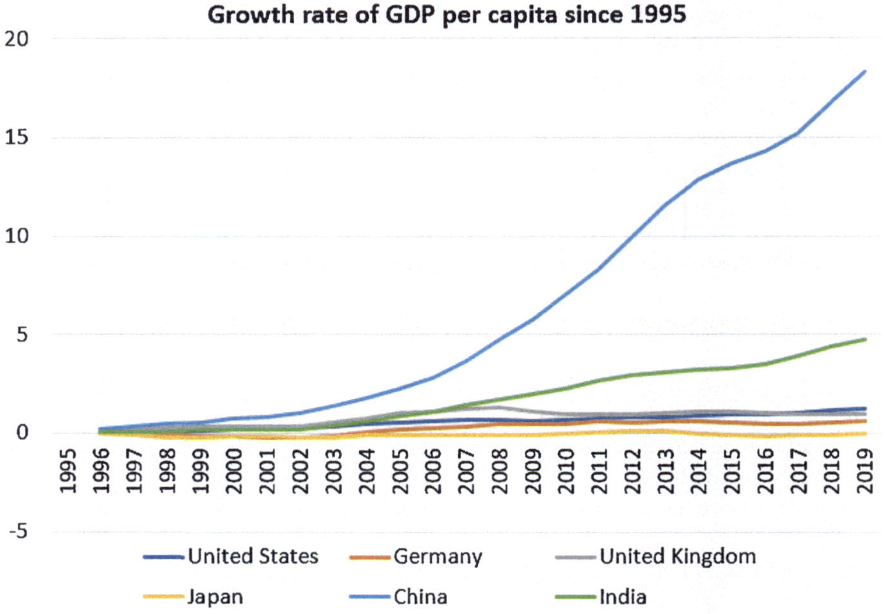

Fig. 4.2 Growth rate of GDP per capita from 1995 to 2019. (Data source: World Bank https://data.worldbank.org/indicator/NY.GDP.MKTP.KD.ZG)

by the rising of conservative political forces and a series of prominent events, for example, the BREXIT and the trade war with China launched by the previous President of the United States Donald Trump. In spite of the decline of global trade, it is yet no evident that the backlash will trigger a turning point of the trend of globalization (Martin, 2018).

Nowadays, not only multinational large companies, but also SMEs are entering international markets and operating with overseas production locations and suppliers. The challenges of a global supply chain are not confined to the greater geographic distances and time differences. More importantly, the business organizations have to adhere to different laws and regulations, technical standards, as well as special features of the local markets across the globe. The concept of harmonization of the global and local requirements is addressed with the term "glocolization."

The organization of global supply chain is often customer centered to achieve optimal customer satisfaction, alternatively being sequential (push-based or pull-based), or otherwise as a simultaneous network with the support of modern internet technology (Laudon & Laudon, 2014, p. 379).

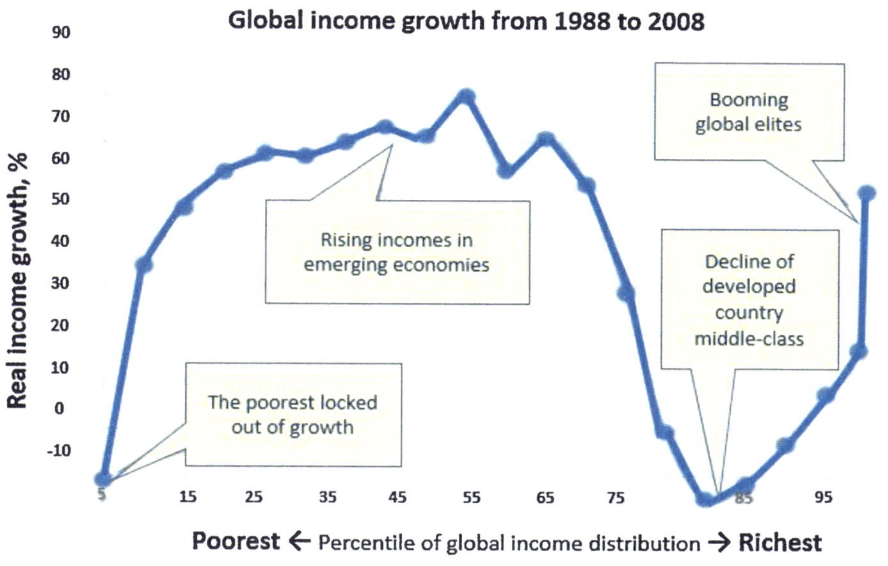

Fig. 4.3 The "elephant graph": global income growth from 1988 to 2008. (Source: author adapted from Milanovic, 2016)

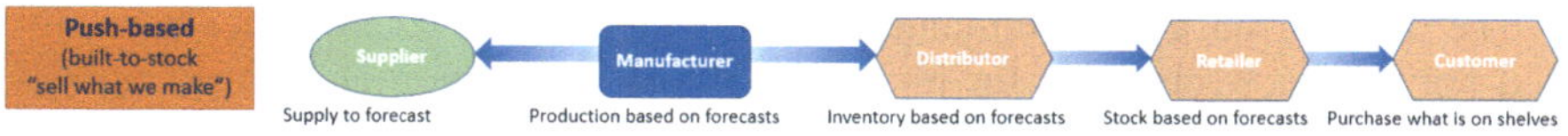

Fig. 4.4 Push-based supply chain model. (Source: author adapted from Laudon & Laudon, 2014, p. 380)

4.2.2 Push-Based Supply Chain

The focus of production plan in a push-based model lies in the demand forecast of the manufacturer. The finished products are delivered to the finished-products warehouse and subsequently, "pushed" through the distribution channel to customers (see Fig. 4.4). In other words, the customers can only choose from what has been produced by the manufacturer. This supply chain model is also referred to as "built-to-stock" (Laudon & Laudon, 2014, p. 379).

4.2.3 Pull-Based Supply Chain

The pull-based model is also known as "built-to-order." In this model, production activities are triggered by the information through distribution channel about customer demand (orders or purchases). In this way, only products with market demand

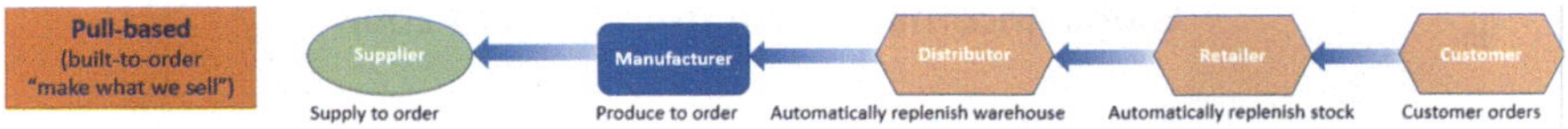

Fig. 4.5 Pull-based supply chain model. (Source: author adapted from Laudon & Laudon, 2014, p. 380)

are produced, avoiding waste of resources caused by suboptimal production plans (see Fig. 4.5). However, the coordination of information on actual demand with production schedules, procurement, and distribution activities poses an additional challenge on supply chain management in comparison to the push-based model (Laudon & Laudon, 2014, p. 179).

4.2.4 Internet-Driven Global Supply Chain Network

The modern internet technology enables a constant, high-speed exchange of supply chain information within and beyond the boundaries of the business entities, leading to an integrated supply chain network with both upstream and downstream supply chain partners. This could drastically improve the service level of supply chain, in terms of reducing costs through efficient use of resources and lower inventory level, matching demand and supply to achieve optimal customer satisfaction, and shortening lead time (Laudon & Laudon, 2014, p. 379) (Fig. 4.6).

The rapid advances of communications and information technologies have created not only new channels for procurement and distribution at internet marketplaces, but also new business models like virtual manufacturing. In addition, logistic services are being further specialized with the participation of logistic exchanges. Altogether, the internet-driven global supply chain has many advantages, especially the increase of sales through accurate market information, efficient use of resources, and reduced supply chain costs.

4.3 Risk Management for Global Supply Chain

4.3.1 Challenges of Global Supply Chains

Depending on the degree of destructive outcomes, the impacts of supply chain risks may be described as deviations, disruptions, and disasters. Due to high complexity of business environment and logistic networks, global supply chains are challenged with increased risk exposures through natural disasters, pandemics, terrorist attacks, and other environmental and economic changes, leading to severe disruptions and disasters (Chen et al., 2013).

The task of supply chain risk management is to deal with risks and uncertainties in collaboration with other participants in a supply chain (Norrman & Jansson, 2004). The risk factors in supply chain management are dealt with at three levels:

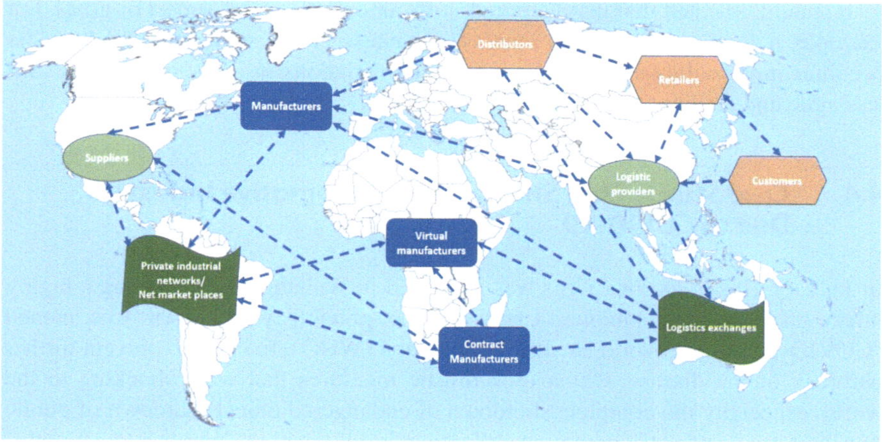

Fig. 4.6 Internet-driven global supply chain network. (Source: author adapted from Laudon & Laudon, 2014, p. 380)

strategic, operational, and tactical. The instrument applied for supply chain risk management can be either preventive or responsive. The following are some of the most popular methods (Kilubi & Haasis, 2015):

- Multiple sourcing (maintaining alternative suppliers).
- Implementation of functional IT systems to support inventory management and supplier management.
- Capacity redundance (increasing safety stock and production capacity).

4.3.2 Sustainability and LARG Supply Chain Management

The sustainability movement in the recent decades plays a particularly important role in risk management of global supply chains. To maintain a positive corporate image in the public, the business model and business processes need to be communicated as sustainable: beneficial both to the current and to the future generations. The sustainability has three dimensions: economic, environmental, and social (Helmold et al., 2020).

The sustainability of supply chain is often discussed under the LARG paradigm:

- *L*ean: maintaining minimum inventory
- *A*gile: able to respond smoothly to market changes
- *R*esilient: able to recover quickly from disruptions
- *G*reen: providing environment-friendly products

It should be noted that there are trade-offs among the above subset of goals. For example, reduction of inventory increases leanness. At the same time, the business becomes more vulnerable toward unexpected variations in the supply chain, thus less agile and resilient.

4.4 Case Study: Chip Shortage for Automotive Industry Due to COVID-19

In January 2020, a corona virus was identified in Wuhan, China, causing a highly infectious severe pneumonia. Later on, the previously unknown was named "COVID-19" by the World Health Organization (WHO). In order to prevent further outbreak of the disease, China took drastic measures that were shocking to the world, especially the complete shutdown of endangered cities, shutdown of public transportation, and self-quarantine obligation for all travelers. Within a few months, the disease turned into a pandemic and posed a great challenge on the global supply chain as force majeure (see Fig. 4.7).

While several business fields like internet marketplaces (e.g., Amazon, Alibaba), video communication services (e.g., WebEx, Zoom or MS Teams), and online streaming (e.g., Netflix) achieved unexpected drastic increase of sales in the course

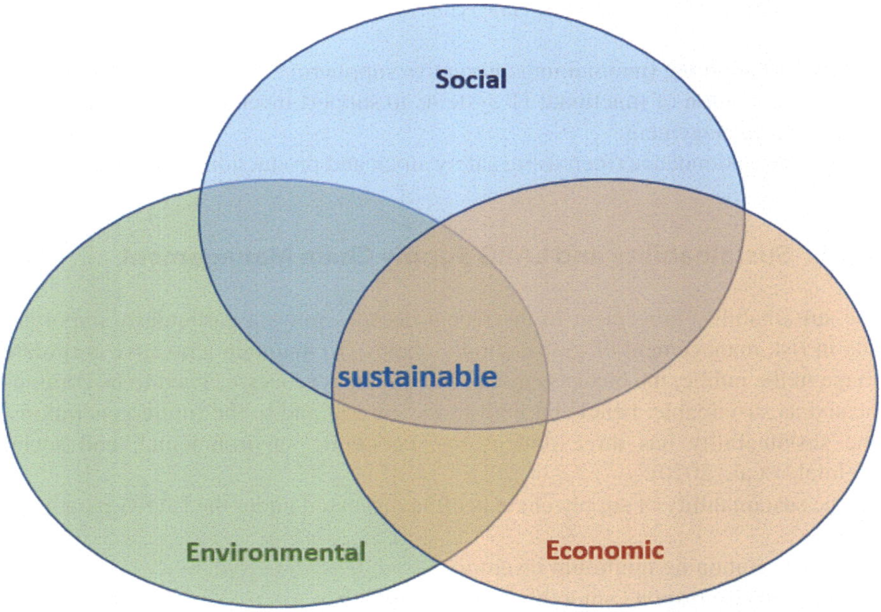

Fig. 4.7 Dimensions of sustainability. (Source: author)

of COVID-19 outbreak, most industry sectors suffered major disruptions in the global supply chain (e.g., the automobile industry).

Similar as during the previous financial crisis in 2008, following an overall income decline of the world population, the market demand collapsed across the globe. Countermeasures like large discount actions in different car segments to mitigate the crisis showed little effect. In the European Union, the entire market demand dropped by more than 75% in mid-2020 (FAZ, 2020).

In response to the negative economic development, the leading carmakers like Mercedes, BMW, Audi, Volkswagen, and Peugeot cancelled largely their global purchasing ordering for raw materials and components, including airbags, chips, and multimedia touch screens from Asia. As a result, the Asian manufacturers of the low-margin chips and built-in microelectronics transformed some major production capacities to focus on more profitable products with market demands like smartphones and gaming machines (Busvine and Steitz, 2021).

With effective pandemic control measures in place like the compulsory use of FFP2 masks and social distancing, as well as the positive development of COVID-19 vaccinations, the world market of automotive industry was re-boosted at the beginning of 2021 and carmakers offered new facelifted models. However, they lost much of the sourcing capacities for the chips that are essential for the in-car electronics, since the Asian suppliers have turned to more profitable products for non-automotive customers like producers of gaming and home entertainment devices. Due to the lack of chips, the company Renault was not able to serve the customer orders for more than 100.000 cars in 2021 (Busvine and Steitz, 2021).

Altogether, high opportunity costs were incurred for the carmakers, due to the complexity of global supply chain and the lack of control possibilities (see Figs. 4.7 and 4.8).

Murat Aksel, member of Volkswagen Executive Team for Purchasing, described the current global chip shortage as "urban warfare" (Deutsche Wirtschaftsnachrichten, 2021; Heise, 2021). The supply chain disruptions are currently causing production stoppage from time to time and force the car manufacturers to reduce their own production capacity. For instance, Mercedes has introduced reduced worktime for the manufacturing sites in Germany.

To work around the problem of chip shortage, Peugeot chose to implement mechanical speedometers, instead of modern digital speedometer in the new car model 308. By doing so, Peugeot gave up much of the profit for the 308-model; however, it was able to keep up the pace of production operations with a positive contribution margin (Sueddeutsche Zeitung, 2021).

This case study illustrates how fragile the just-in-time delivery of automotive industry with a global supply chain could be. It shows that the competitors in the upstream supply chain may come from a completely different industry sector like the gaming industry, as the suppliers' capacities could be diverted to products like Sony PlayStation and Microsoft Xbox, instead of chips for car production. In general, increase of inventory and redundance can make the supply chain more robust to overcome temporary disruptions.

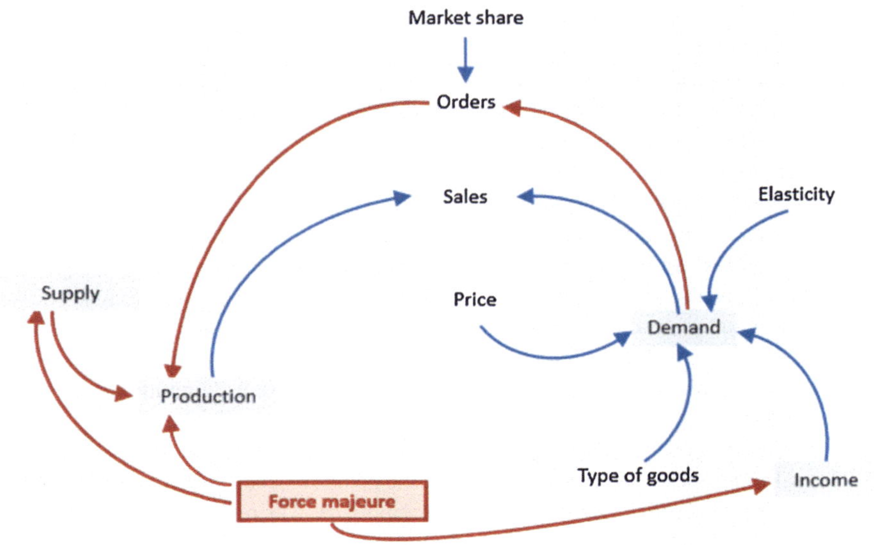

Fig. 4.8 Challenge of COVID-19 as force majeure for global supply chain. (Source: author according to Sinha et al., 2020)

COVID-19 pandemic helped the business organizations to identify the weaknesses in their business operations. Volkswagen plans to develop its own chips to become more independent from the global supply chain (NTV, 2021; Menzel and Murphy, 2021).

References

Busvine and Steitz. (2021). https://www.n-tv.de/wirtschaft/Chiphersteller-lassen-Autobauer-auflaufen-article22376720.html

Chen, J., Sohal, A. S., & Prajogo, D. I. (2013). Supply chain operational risk mitigation: A collaborative approach. *International Journal of Production Research, 51*(7), 2186–2199.

Deutsche Wirtschaftsnachrichten. (2021). https://deutsche-wirtschafts-nachrichten.de/510641/Wir-sind-im-Haeuserkampf-Chip-Lieferketten-fuer-Europas-Autobauer-an-mehreren-Stellen-gebrochen

FAZ. (2020). https://www.faz.net/aktuell/wirtschaft/corona-folgen-autoabsatz-in-der-eu-sinkt-um-76-prozent-16776719.html

Heise. (2021). https://www.heise.de/hintergrund/Sind-im-Haeuserkampf-VW-sieht-keine-rasche-Loesung-fuer-schwere-Chip-Lieferkrise-5990333.html

Helmold, M., Dathe, R., Dathe, T., Gross, D.-P., & Hummel, F. (2020). *Corporate Social Responsibility (CSR) im internationalen Kontext* (p. 24). Springer.

Joshi, R. M. (2009). *International business*. Oxford University Press.

Kilubi, I., & Haasis, H.-D. (2015). Supply chain risk management enablers: A framework development through systematic review of the literature from 2000 to 2015. *International Journal of Business Science & Applied Management (IJBSAM), 10*(1), 35–54.

Laudon, K., & Laudon, J. P. (2014). *Management information systems. Managing the digital firm* (pp. 379–380). Pearson.

Martin, M. (2018). Keeping it real: Debunking the deglobalization Myth, Brexit, and Trump: "Lessons" on integration. *Journal of International Trade Law and Policy, 17*, 62–68.

Menzel and Murphy. (2021). https://www.handelsblatt.com/unternehmen/industrie/software-chips-solarenergie-die-autonome-bewegung-diess-verordnet-vw-nach-der-e-mobilitaet-schon-die-naechste-revolution/27144790.html

Milanovic, B. (2016). *Global inequality: A new approach for the age of globalization*. Harvard University Press.

Norrman, A., & Jansson, U. (2004). Ericsson's proactive supply chain risk management approach after a serious sub-supplier accident. *International Journal of Physical Distribution & Logistics Management, 34*(5), 434–456.

NTV. (2021). https://www.n-tv.de/wirtschaft/VW-entwickelt-Computerchips-kuenftig-selbst-article22525786.html

Sinha, D., Bagodi, V., & Dey, D. (2020). The supply chain disruption framework post COVID-19: A system dynamics model. Foreign trade review, November 4, 2020.

Sueddeutsche Zeitung. (2021). https://www.sueddeutsche.de/wirtschaft/chipmangel-autoindustrie-1.5272966

Wang, W. Y. C., Chan, H. K., & Pauleen, D. J. (2010). Aligning business process reengineering in implementing global supply chain systems by the SCOR model. *International Journal of Production Research, 48*(19), 5647–5669.

Cultural Elements in SCRM

5

Human natures are much the same; however, the conventions are widely different.

—*Confucius (551 B.C.–479 B.C.)*

5.1 Introduction to Operations Management

Business operations are the processes that transform inputs (e.g., raw materials and labor) into output (goods or services), therefore a core component of the supply chain. Operation management aims at the efficient use of resources, in order to best meet the market demand. For a successful supply chain risk management, it is essential to address the cultural elements of operation management in a multicultural environment.

The EPRG Model is an effective instrument for the planning and assessment of international business strategies. The framework helps the corporates to define the relationship of the different cultures involved in the multinational business organizations (Sect. 5.2).

The definition of culture by Hofstede is a well-accepted description of the culture concept. According to Hofstede, culture is "the collective programming of the mind" manifested in the shared values and behaviors, which divides people into distinctive cultural groups (Hofstede, 2007).

According to Hofstede, the ultimate task of management is the coordination of all participants' efforts toward common goals. Since interpersonal relationships are influenced by cultural values, obviously, management processes should be designed in a way that is culturally appropriate (Hofstede, 2007).

The contradicting characteristics of cultures often lead to conflicts or frustration in international communications. Thus, cultural understanding and patience for

M. Helmold et al., *Supply Chain Risk Management*,
Management for Professionals, https://doi.org/10.1007/978-3-030-90800-3_5

dealing with the cultural differences are indispensable elements for the effective management of a global supply chain.

Researchers in the past have developed various theoretical culture frameworks which have proven effective both in cultural researches and in management practice.

In the following sections, two prominent culture dimension models, the Value Survey Model (VSM) by Hofstede (Sect. 5.3) and the concepts of Edward Hall (Sect. 5.4), will be discussed with some details.

5.2 EPRG Model for International Business Strategy

5.2.1 Background of EPRG Model

The first version of the international strategy development model by Howard V. Perlmutter, a well-known expert of international management, was published in 1969 (Perlmutter, 1969). Today, this model remains a widespread instrument for management practice and an important concept for the teaching of business administration. The framework of EPRG Model helps companies to analyze the advantages and disadvantages of alternative relationship models between the Headquarter and the overseas subsidiaries, so as to identify the optimal organization structure (Sect. 5.2).

5.2.2 Ethnocentrism

Ethnocentrism means that there is a dominant culture in the organization, which is usually the culture of the headquarters. The strategic management decisions, as well as the operational processes including control functions are largely centralized. To ensure the performance standards, the subsidiaries are constantly guided by the coaches at the headquarters. New recruits for key positions at the subsidiaries in host countries are often sent to the headquarters for training before they officially take office. Sometimes, such key positions are reserved for expatriate staff sent by the headquarters.

The management processes in an ethnocentric structure are efficient in communicating the consistent standards of the organization to the subsidiaries, saving costs both in terms of time and money. However, under circumstances, the centralized employee pool for key personnel and the travel expenses could become a financial burden. In addition, the organization fails to benefit from the potentials of local innovations and market opportunities, due to the fact that the local cultures and market requirements of the subsidiaries are not sufficiently taken into account. This could be a major drawback when entering the emerging market.

5.2.3 Polycentrism

Polycentrism means that the strategic management is largely decentralized, so that local requirements can be best attended to. Compared to ethnocentrism, however, with this approach the headquarters lose some control over the subsidiaries and the coordination of business activities at different locations becomes much more complex. A major drawback of the polycentric approach is therefore the loss of opportunities for economies of scale.

5.2.4 Geocentrism

Geocentrism is a compromise between ethnocentrism and polycentrism, which takes into account the objectives of both the home country and the host countries of the company. Key personnel are selected based on their experience and skills, without preference of their cultural background. This approach is intended to benefit the company with a collaborative network between headquarters and subsidiaries. Theoretically, this is the ideal form of an international business organization. In the practice, however, the planning decision should be made based on a thorough analysis on all alternative solutions including implementation details.

5.2.5 Regiocentrism

Similar to geocentrism, regiocentrism is another form of compromise between ethnocentrism and polycentrism. The subsidiaries' strategies, rules of conduct, and employee pool for the key personnel are standardized for the predefined regions (e.g., continents).

5.3 Hofstede and Value Survey Model (VSM) Framework

5.3.1 Background of Value Survey Model (VSM)

This model remains to this day among the most cited theories in academic research on intercultural communications, and it is also frequently used in management practice. The model was developed by the Dutch culture researcher Geerte Hofstede based on the empirical data he collected during his field research in the Company IBM in 74 countries between 1967 and 1976.

As results of the initial statistical analysis and further research in the following decades, Hofstede defined culture in the following dimensions (Hofstede, 2007):

- Power distance.
- Individualism vs. collectivism.
- Masculinity vs. femininity.

- Uncertainty avoidance.
- Long-term orientation.
- Indulgence vs. restraint.

5.3.2 Power Distance

The influence of each individual is distributed unequally in a society. The term "power distance" describes the readiness of the less powerful members in the group to accept the inequality of power.

The countries with high power distance often have a long history of a political system of absolute power, for example, the imperial power in the Chinese history (see Fig. 5.1).

In a corporate culture with high power distance, the management decisions are made according to the hierarchical order. According to the tacit rules of conduct, the junior members in the group are not expected to challenge the authority of their seniors. Therefore, the executives are rarely criticized by their subordinates, especially not in public, and their decisions stay largely unquestioned.

When dealing with business partners with high power distance, it is important to identify the true decision-makers at the very beginning and treat them with due

Fig. 5.1 The throne of the last emperor in China, a symbol of absolute power. (Source: the author)

respect according to their status. The decision-making process in such organizations could be relatively fast; however, it is prone to errors and irrationality. Managers tend to micro manage and overrule their subordinates. Revision of a decision may be associated with complications in the power structure.

Managers of a low-power distance business organization usually see themselves as the coach of their teams. Important business decisions are often made after prior consultation with the stakeholders. Thus, resistance in change management is reduced by the efforts of consensus building in advance. However, the internal communication could be time-consuming.

5.3.3 Individualism Versus Collectivism

Individualism and collectivism are two extremes of the culture dimension that describes the degree of integration of individuals in a society.

A strong individualism indicates that members of the business organization focus on their individual performance and self-determination. The employees in an individualistic culture tend to express their opinions openly. Their roles in the organization are means to personal aspirations. Employees of organizations shaped by strong individualism can be capable of teamwork, if it brings the group members forward.

In a collectivist setting, individuals tend to identify with their social groups. In the interest of the group, the members are often willing to give up part of their personal interests and to disregard some common rules of conduct when deemed necessary. In addition, social distance is less in a collectivistic culture and members of society share more intimate information with each other.

For effective intercultural communication, it is important to understand each other and treat the differences tactfully.

5.3.4 Masculinity Versus Femininity

The dimension masculinity vs. femininity stands for the dominant values of a society. The masculine values are those that are traditionally considered as male virtues, for example, heroism, the professional success, assertiveness, and wealth. The feminine values are centered by caring for each other, maintaining the harmony and modesty (see Fig. 5.2).

In a business organization with high masculinity, there is an intense competition among the employees in terms of their individual performance. However, this does not mean that they are incapable of teamwork.

In a society of high femininity, group harmony and consensus are among the most important considerations in management decisions such as job promotions or salary raises. In order to solve problems at work, employees sometimes prefer not to contact the responsible person directly, but to approach someone who maintains a closer personal relationship with the person seeking help (Dathe & Helmold, 2018).

Fig. 5.2 A symbol of heroism: Tree of Remembrance, St Patrick's Cathedral, Dublin, Ireland. (Source: the author)

5.3.5 Uncertainty Avoidance

The culture dimension uncertainty avoidance indicates how the society deals with situations when the consequence of the action is unclear.

With a high degree of uncertainty avoidance, conscientious work attitude is one of the major criteria for performance evaluation. Employees need explicitly formulated rules, guidelines, and codes of conduct. Ambiguity of information causes mental pressure and anxiety.

Organizations with low uncertainty avoidance, on the other hand, are more open to different opinions, new technologies, and organizational changes.

Some Asian cultures are typically characterized by a low level of uncertainty avoidance. The local markets widely embrace cutting-edge technologies such as digitalized payments and electric vehicles, despite of the uncertainty of possible negative consequences at the time of the introduction of the technical novelty (see Figs. 5.3 and 5.4).

Fig. 5.3 Supertrees in Singapore, a symbol for openness to innovation. (Source: the author)

Fig. 5.4 Curious Chinese tourists in Munich, Germany: Yearly, over 100 million Chinese tourists travel overseas to explore foreign cultures. (Source: the author)

5.3.6 Long-Term Orientation

There are often conflicts between short-term desires and long-term interests. The long-term orientation represents the willingness to invest in the long-term future at the expense of sacrificing short-term pleasure. Cultures with strong long-term orientation are open to progressive changes (see Fig. 5.5).

In cultures with a long-term orientation, business executives go to great lengths to maintain long-term business relationships. Problems are solved with a pragmatic approach, often based on trust-relationships between stakeholders. Companies with weak long-term orientation tend to stick to existing rules and traditions, and exhibit less agility in dealing with a changing environment.

5.3.7 Indulgence Versus Restraint

In an indulgent society, human desires for pleasures and idleness are widely accepted, while morality and social norms are dealt more leniently (see Figs. 5.6 and 5.7). Individuals tend to express their emotional impulses in an extroverted manner.

Fig. 5.5 A young couple posing in western customs at the Bund, Shanghai, China. (Source: the author)

In organizations shaped by restraint, there is a strong sense of professional duty and a low tolerance for emotional impulses.

5.4 Culture Concepts by Edward Hall

The following concepts of the American anthropologist and ethnologist Edward Twitchell Hall Jr.'s are introduced in this section:

- Context orientation.
- Monochronic vs. polychronic understanding of time.
- Private sphere and territory.

5.4.1 Context Orientation

The term "context orientation" describes the style of communication in terms of how information is conveyed and the role of social network in the communication process.

Fig. 5.6 An acrobat showing his art at a market in Dublin, Ireland. (Source: the author)

In low-context organizations, the information is communicated explicitly, that is, the communication partners try to provide the information as precise as possible in the spoken message. Additional background knowledge based on personal relationships is not important.

Fig. 5.7 A street artist in Barcelona, Spain. (Source: the author)

The communication in a high-context culture is associated with many unspoken rules commonly known in the community, so that messages are difficult for strangers to understand. Contextual factors such as personal relationships, non-verbal communication, and the circumstances of the meeting often play an essential role in the communication. Occasionally, corporate strategies are coordinated at an informal lunch among selected participants, instead of at formal meetings with the officially responsible persons.

5.4.2 Monochronic or Polychronic Understanding of Time

In a typical monochronic culture, business operations are conducted steps by step in a given order. It is an important task to keep up the predetermined schedules. Personal relationships are not important for the coordination of team operations.

In polychronic cultures, however, people are more used to carrying out several activities at the same time, and the schedule is only a relevant reference. The priority of the tasks can be constantly modified by the changing circumstances and the personal relationships. Members of a polychronic cultures normally react quickly to changes; however, they are also prone to distractions.

5.4.3 Private Sphere and Territory

According to Hall, each person considers an invisible, circular space around himself as his private sphere. The various perceptions of the extent of the private sphere largely define the appropriate physical distance in communication. One feels uneasy if others enter the private sphere without permission. On the other hand, clearly exceeding the appropriate distance can also be perceived as a negative sign of lack of trust or even hostility.

Territory is an extended private sphere, which includes the places or objects that a person perceives as his personal property. Entering the territory without permission is considered as an intrusion which provokes hostility. The understanding of territory varies from culture to culture.

5.5 Case Study: What the Chinese Market Needs from Carmakers

The premium car manufactures have been steadily increasing their market share in the recent years in China, where there is a growing middle-class community. Nowadays China is the main market for premium car dealers like Volkswagen Group: Audi, Porsche, as well as Daimler and BMW (Manager Magazin, 2020).

In order to accommodate the special demand of the Chinese customers, Audi and BMW have developed a long version of its A6 and 5er premium line. It took the competitor Mercedes longer to bring on a special long version of the E-class model to the Chinese market (Grünweg, 2009) (Fig. 5.8).

A long version of car means that the body of the standard model is stretched by up to 15 cm (6 inch). This modification provides additional space to the backseat of the car. The need of the customers has its cultural background.

As a collectivistic society, the Chinese people often travel in larger groups, for example, with their business partners or family members. To facilitate the communication with contextual references, important conversations are usually conducted on the backseat (Grünweg, 2009). Therefore, the extra length that provides additional space and comfort at the back of the car becomes a valued feature.

Due to the large power distance, premium cars are bought to demonstrate the status of the owners. This explains the high demand for import cars despite of high expenses for luxury tax and the customs. Compared to the purchase of premium cars in the rest of the world, the Chinese customers are at an average 15 years younger and there are 30% more female buyers (Pander, 2020).

Due to the low uncertainty avoidance, the modern E-mobility as a symbol for new technology is most welcome in the Chinese market. Tesla has been importing most of the electric cars from the USA to China, in order to satisfy the high demand.

The government fuels the demand further with subsidies and traffic rules in favor of carbon-neutral cars. To improve the air quality in the urban areas, currently cars with combustion engines are only allowed on the road on certain weekdays. Some households therefore keep more than one vehicle to stay permanently mobile.

Fig. 5.8 Traffic in Beijing, China. Many Chinese drivers prefer cars with extended body. (Source: the author)

However, such restriction does not apply to the electric cars. This means additional cost advantages for the e-cars. In the first half year of 2020, 392.000 electric cars were sold in China, while 400.000 in total were sold in the EU. The demand at the Chinese market is fast growing.

Tesla's good understanding of the cultural elements of the global supply chain has been rewarded with a large market share. Late 2020, Tesla opened a new "Giga factory" in Shanghai for the production of its local brands like Nio. The researchers believe, with the "Musk Factor," China will remain the leading electric car market in the world in the next 50 years (Pander, 2020).

References

Dathe, T., & Helmold, M. (2018). *Erfolgreich im Chinageschäft: Strategien und Handlungsempfehlungen für KMU*. Springer.

Grünweg, T. (31, July 07 2009). Spiegel Mobilität. Von Limousinen in der Langversion für China: Im Reich der zweiten Reihe: https://www.spiegel.de/auto/aktuell/limousinen-in-der-langversion-fuer-china-im-reich-der-zweiten-reihe-a-635299.html. Retrieved 04.05.2021.

Hofstede, G. (2007). Asian management in the 21st century. *Asia Pacific Journal of Management, 24*(4), 411–420.

Manager Magazin. (13, October 2020). Starke Wachstumsraten: Chinas Konjunktur und Automarkt erholen sich. Von https://www.manager-magazin.de/politik/weltwirtschaft/china-autoabsatz-sowie-im-und-exporte-steigen-im-september-kraeftig-a-081dfe19-5cd6-45b3-bf7c-2af737901 1ea. Retrieved 04.05.2021.

Pander, J. (06, October 2020). Spiegel Mobilität. Von "Auto China"-Messe in Peking: Vorteil Deutschland: https://www.spiegel.de/auto/auto-china-messe-in-peking-vorteil-deutschland-a-fc6a94fe-d0ad-49dc-b66f-560ddc815071. Retrieved 04.05.2021.

Perlmutter, H. V. (1969). The tortuous evolution of multinational enterprises. In: *Columbia Journal of World Business*. 4. Jg., Heft 1, 1969, p. 9–18.

Lean Supply Chains and Lean Production

6

Perfection is not attainable. But if we chase perfection, we can catch excellence.

—Vince Lombardi (1913–1970)

6.1 Valued-Added and Waste

Added value can be defined as products, services, processes, and activities, which generate a certain value to the organization and enterprise. Value-added must be regarded from the customer viewpoint and is everything for which the customer is willing to pay for. It is important that value-added is recognized and perceived as value by the client. Many studies have shown that we only add value to a product for less than five to fifteen percent of the time, the rest of the time is wasted (Helmold & Terry, 2016a, 2016b). The opposite is non-adding value or waste as shown in Fig. 6.1. Waste (Japanese: Muda, 無駄) is anything that adds cost or time without adding any value or any activity which does not satisfy any of the above conditions of value-added is a waste or a non-value-adding activity in a process. The focus in operations management must therefore be in eliminating activities such as waiting time or rework (Ohno 1990; Liker, 2004). Enterprise must target value-added process and eliminate or reduce waste, whereby waste can be visible (obvious) or invisible (hidden) as shown in Fig. 6.2.

6.2 Fishbone Diagrams to Identify Waste

Fishbone or Ishikawa diagrams (also called herringbone diagrams, cause-and-effect diagrams, or Fishikawa) are causal diagrams created by Kaoru Ishikawa (Japanese: 石川 馨 Ishikawa Kaoru, 1915–1989) that show the cause-effect situation of a

M. Helmold et al., *Supply Chain Risk Management*,
Management for Professionals, https://doi.org/10.1007/978-3-030-90800-3_6

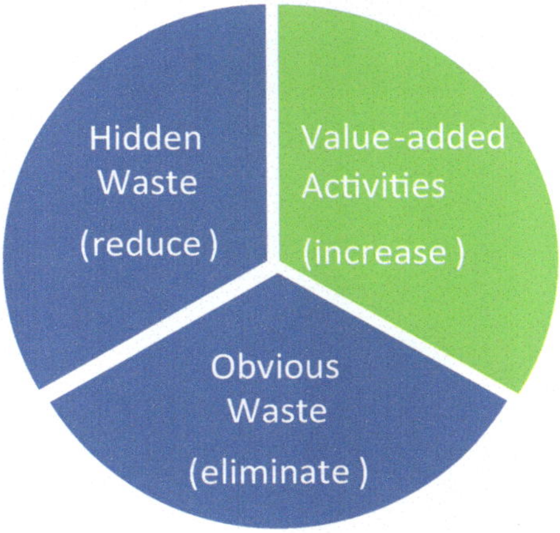

Fig. 6.1 Value-added and waste. (Source: Marc Helmold)

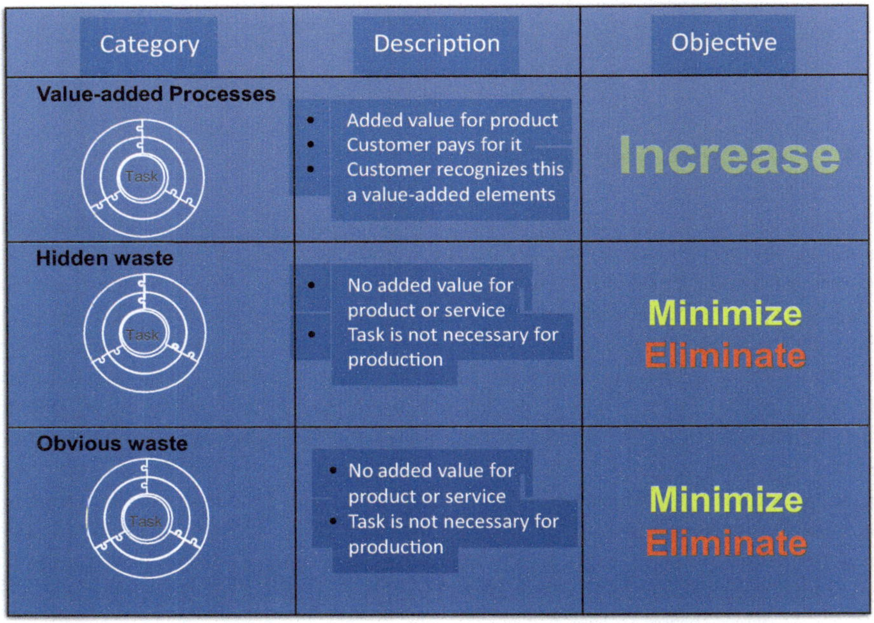

Fig. 6.2 Actions for value-added and waste. (Source: Marc Helmold)

specific event. Common uses of the Ishikawa diagram are areas of design, supply, production, and quality defect prevention to identify potential factors causing an overall effect. Each cause or reason for imperfection is a source of variation. Causes are usually grouped into major categories to identify and classify these sources of variation. The target of value-add and quality is shown as the fish's head, facing to the right, with the causes extending to the left as fishbones; the ribs branch off the

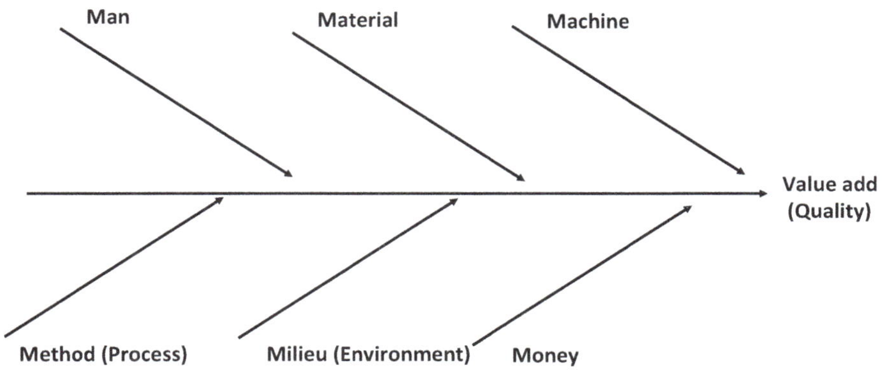

Fig. 6.3 Ishikawa diagram. (Source: Author's source)

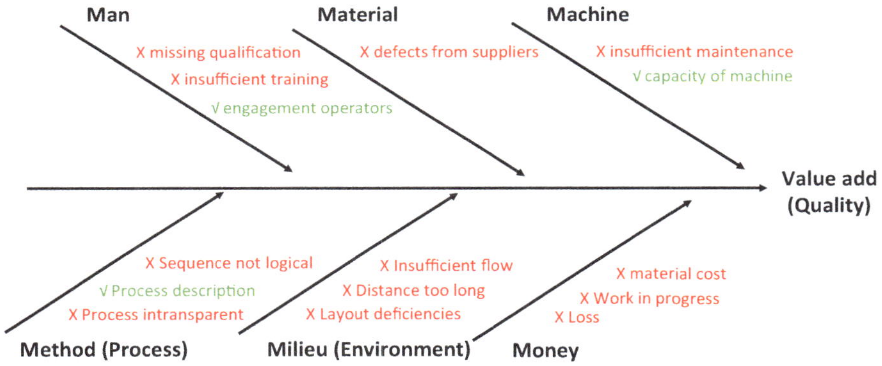

Fig. 6.4 Ishikawa diagram with waste and value-added. (Source: Author's source)

backbone for major causes, with sub-branches for root-causes, to as many levels as required. Figures 6.3 and 6.4 show two examples of the Ishikawa diagram.

6.3 Advantages and Disadvantages of Fishbone Diagrams

The advantages and disadvantages are shown in the following text..

Advantages

- Highly visual brainstorming tool which can spark further examples of root causes.
- Quickly identify if the root cause is found multiple times in the same or different causal tree.
- Allows one to see all causes simultaneously.
- Good visualization for presenting issues to stakeholders.

Disadvantages

- Complex defects might yield a lot of causes which might become visually cluttering.
- Interrelationships between causes are not easily identifiable.

6.4 5S Analysis in Supply Chains

5S is the name of a workplace organization method that uses a list of five Japanese words: seiri, seiton, seiso, seiketsu, and shitsuke. Transliterated into Roman Script, they all start with the letter "S." 5S is used to stabilize, maintain, and improve the safest, best working environment thus supporting sustainable QCDplus alpha. 5S is a systematic and structured work place optimization, originally be developed and used by Toyota. The objective is the identification and elimination of waste. In simple terms, the five S methodology helps a workplace remove items that are no longer needed (sort), organize the items to optimize efficiency and flow (straighten), clean the area in order to more easily identify problems (shine), implement color coding and labels to stay consistent with other areas (standardize), and develop behaviors that keep the workplace organized over the long term (sustain). 5S is a workplace organization method that uses a list of five Japanese words:

1. Seiri (整理).
2. Seiton (整頓).
3. Seisō (清掃).
4. Seiketsu (清潔).
5. Shitsuke (躾).

These five words can be translated as "Sort," "Set In order," "Shine," "Standardize," and "Sustain." The 5S methodology describes how to organize a work space for efficiency and effectiveness by identifying and storing the items used, maintaining the area and items, and sustaining the new order. The decision-making process usually comes from a dialogue about standardization, which builds understanding among employees of how they should do the work.

In some quarters, 5S has become 6S, the sixth element being safety or self-discipline (Fig. 6.5).

The advantages of the 5S system are the following:

- Creation of transparent layout and processes.
- Makes waste transparent.
- Eliminates unnecessary activities.
- Improves efficiency.
- Increases safety.
- Increases employee motivation simplification of the work environment.

Fig. 6.5 5S system. (Source: Author's source)

- Ensuring that all materials are instantly available.
- Ensuring that tools (screw driver, devices).
- Ensuring that required (work procedures, work sequence, etc.) information is instantly available by visualization.
- Reduction of waste.

The first element in the 5S concept is the sorting (seiri). In this step, it is important to distinguish between necessary and unnecessary things. Things in this context are materials, components, tools, gauges, information, things, and people. Unnecessary things must disappear. Removing these items which are not used in the working area may take a reasonable amount of time. Classification of all equipment and materials by frequency will help to decide if these items can be removed or not. The second step is the setting in order (seiton). The practice of orderly storage and warehousing is important so the right item can be picked efficiently at the right time, easy to access for the operators. Identification and allocation of materials, information, tools, and necessary things at fixed and visualized locations are important in this step. In the next and third step (seiso), it is mandatory to create a clean worksite without garbage, dirt, and dust, so problems can be more easily identified (leaks, spills, excess, damage, etc.). In the fourth step (seiketsu), standards for a neat, clean, workplace and operations will be set up through visual management. In the fifth and last stage (shitsuke), it is important to create the environment, patterns, management style, and behaviors that established standards are executed over the long term, and making the workplace organization the key to managing the process for success (Helmold & Terry, 2016a, 2016b).

6.5 Seven Types of Waste in Supply Chains

6.5.1 Transportation in Supply Chains

Excess transportation is a significant waste because the time, manpower, energy, efforts, and resources required to move items are something the customer does not care and does not want to pay (Ohno, 1990). Examples of wastes of transport are the transport of product from one functional area such as pressing, to another area such as welding, or the use of material handling devices to move batches of material from one machine to another within a work cell. It wastes time because operators are dedicating the available time of the work day to moving items from one place to another. It wastes energy and resources in that employee time could be better utilized and because some tools used for transportation (forklifts, trucks, pallet jacks) consume energy like electricity or propane. Also, by dedicating machines and operators´ time to waste activities they are no longer free and available to take on value-added activities. Figure 6.6 shows transportation waste. Reasons can be insufficient layouts and long distances between individual operations. The consequences of this waste are the increased time requirements and the decreased productivity. Decreased productivity will result in higher operating cost and can harm the profitability of the enterprise (Liker, 2004).

6.5.2 Inventory in the Supply Chain

Inventory consists of excessive material of finished goods, semi-finished goods, or raw material. Finished goods inventory is generally the most expensive inventory as

1. Transportation

Definition	Possible reasons
• Unnecessary transport of material • Transport is a necessary type of waste however it should be reduced to a minimum	• Insufficient arrangement of needed material and devices • Physical distance between material delivery and usage • Interim storage of material (buffer)
Consequences	**Examples**

• Additional space for transport
• Blocking of capacity due to additional logistic effort
• Possible damage of products
	• Long or additional transport of:
	  • Raw material
	  • Finished goods
	  • Tools and devices

Fig. 6.6 Transportation

it has labor and other overhead attached to it along with the cost of material consumed during production. In order to reduce this inventory, process improvements as well as a higher accuracy in forecasting customer requirements are required. Inventory waste refers to the waste produced by unprocessed inventory. This includes the waste of storage, the waste of capital tied up in unprocessed inventory, the waste of transporting the inventory, the containers used to hold inventory, and the lighting of the storage space. Moreover, having excess inventory can hide the original wastes of producing said inventory. The environmental impacts of inventory waste are packaging, deterioration or damage to work-in-process, additional materials to replace damaged or obsolete inventory, and the energy to light, as well as either heat or cool, inventory space. Figure 6.7 displays the definition, reasons, consequences, and examples for inventory. Inventory will have a negative impact on working capital and on cash flow, so that sophisticated production planning must focus on the optimum levels of inventory throughout the value chain and operations (Helmold & Terry, 2016a, 2016b).

6.5.3 Motion in Supply Chains

Motion waste is the excessive movement of man, material, or machines within the work space. Motion waste will lead to higher cost as the productivity decreases. Another problem of motion is the necessity for more time and capacity in operations than actually required. A proper workflow analysis and value stream mapping help to minimize this waste. Figure 6.8 outlines the definition, possible reasons, consequences, and examples of this waste.

2. Inventory

Definition	Possible reasons

• More material than needed according to planning in terms of:
  • Raw material
  • Semi-finished parts
  • Work in progress (WIP)
  • Finished goods
	• Problems regarding planning and logistic processes
	• Bad supplier delivery performance and quality
	• High product variety

Consequences	**Examples**
• Capital costs • Double handling, possible damages based on double handling, rework • Genuine problems won't be discovered and therefore not solved • Search effort • Scrap	• Overfilled warehouses • Overfilled place in production areas • Buffer stocks in producton • Crammed corridors • Crammed desks

Fig. 6.7 Inventory

3. Motion

Definition	Possible reasons
• Every type of movement that doesn't directly serve value creation	• Inaccurate analysis of all workflows Inappropriate layout • Insufficient delivery of material and arrangement of tools
Consequences	**Examples**
• Decrease of productivity • Increase of lead time and capacity • Insufficient ergonomics	• Long ways between tools, material and product or machine • Missing material or tools

Fig. 6.8 Motion

6.5.4 Waiting in Supply Chains

Idle time of operators or other employees in operations and waiting for work to arrive or to be told what-to-do is a significant waste. Waiting or standstill times must be avoided as waiting results into reduced efficiency and productivity. Other outcomes are longer lead times and decreasing engagement and motivation of employees as illustrated in Fig. 6.9.

6.5.5 Overproduction in Supply Chains

Overproduction waste is defined as producing too many products too early and in advance. That means that parts in a big quantity are existing inside operations management, even though these parts are not needed. Figure 6.10 displays possible reasons such as demand non-transparency or inadequate batch sizes. A consequence of this waste is that inventory increases drastically and that work-in-progress cost rise significantly.

6.5.6 Overprocessing in Supply Chains

Overprocessing is related to all activities and processes in operations, which are more than the customer really needs. Figure 6.11 highlights possible reasons such as insufficient technology, bad design, inefficiencies, or unawareness of customer-specific requirements. Overprocessing refers to any component of the process of manufacture that is unnecessary. Painting an area that will never be seen or adding

4. Waiting

Definition

- A period in which no activities take place.
- The employee is forced to wait and can't fulfil any value added activities. During the holding period the product is waiting for processing

Possible reasons

- Insufficiently synchronised material and information flows
- Insufficient line balancing of all processes
- Missing material or tools
- Lack of documentation
- Waiting for quality approval

Consequences

- Reduced productivity
- Decreasing efficiency
- Increased lead time
- Increase of capacity
- Decreased of employee motivation

Examples

- Waiting for material or tools e.g. crane
- Quality employees are not available
- Stopped processes due to missing resources (employees, defective machines, IT,...)

Fig. 6.9 Waiting

5. Overproduction

Definition

- If more is produced than the internal or external customer needs

Possible reasons

- Insufficient transparency of real demand
- Production according to supposed optimal batch sizes
- Instable processes
- Early use of available capacity

Consequences

- Generation of inventory (warehouse, WIP)
- Additional use of space
- Blocking of capacities (machines, employees)
- Double handling, decrease of product quality

Examples

- A lot of material in front of machines or assembly lines
- Crowded warehouses

Fig. 6.10 Overproduction

features that will not be used are examples of overprocessing. Essentially, it refers to adding more value than the customer requires. The environmental impact involves the excess of parts, labor, and raw materials consumed in production. Time, energy, and emissions are wasted when they are used to produce something that is unnecessary in a product; simplification and efficiency reduce these wastes and benefit the company and the environment.

6. Overprocessing

Definition

- Process weakness in terms of sequence, content, technologies and resources

Possible reasons

- Insufficient technology
- Not the most efficient procedure for the process
- Insufficient analysis and design of processes
- Due to process problems the product requirements in the specification are higher than required by the customer

Consequences

- High production costs
- Waste of material
- Low efficiency
- High need for resources (employee, machine, material)

Examples

- High tolerances
- Wrong, faulty and not needed process steps
- Not optimal utilisation of resources
- Duplication of efforts

Fig. 6.11 Overprocessing

7. Defects

Definition

- If right first time is not achieved

Possible reasons

- Lack of machine and tool maintenance
- Insufficiently trained employees
- Product not according to customer requirements
- Unstable or not standardized processes
- No problem solving process established

Consequences

- Additional need for material, tools and capacity
- Additional space for rework
- Increase of quality employees and checks
- Increase of lead time

Examples

- Increase of non-conformities
- Retrofitting and repairing defect parts
- Increased quantity of scrap
- Supply issues due to bad quality

Fig. 6.12 Defects

6.5.7 Defects of and in Supply Chains

Defects as shown in Fig. 6.12 refer to a product deviating from the standards of its design or from the customer's expectation. Defective products must be replaced; they require paperwork and human labor to process it; they might potentially lose customers; the resources put into the defective product are wasted because the product is not used. Moreover, a defective product implies waste at other levels that may

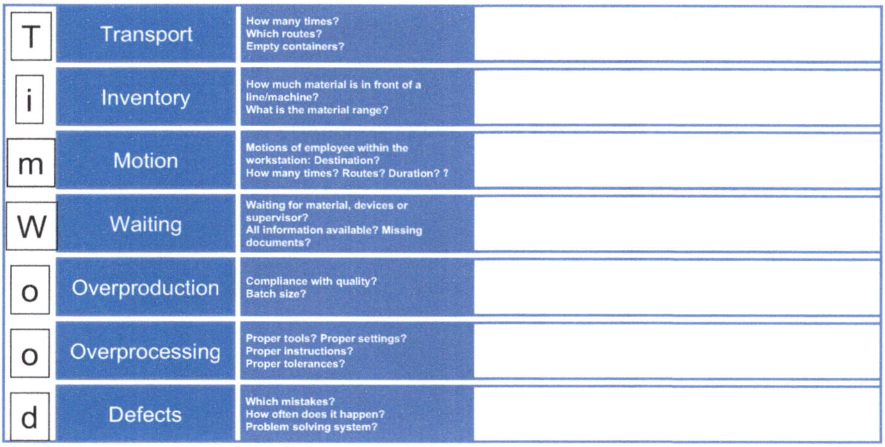

Fig. 6.13 TIMWOOD checklist

have led to the defect to begin with; making a more efficient production system reduces defects and increases the resources needed to address them in the first place. Environmental costs of defects are the raw materials consumed, the defective parts of the product requiring disposal or recycling (which wastes other resources involved in repurposing it), and the extra space required and increased energy use involved in dealing with the defects.

The checklist in Fig. 6.13 is the ideal tool to assess operations in terms of the seven wastes. It is a proven method for identifying waste in process and activities (Helmold & Terry, 2016a, 2016b).

6.6 Just-in-Time Production System

6.6.1 Introduction

The just-in-time production system or lean production system can be described as the ideal combination of four principles (Imai, 1986). These principles are the zero-defect principle, the pull principle, the tact, and the flow principle as displayed in Fig. 6.14.

6.6.2 Zero-Defect Principle

The starting point in Toyota's success story, zero defects is all about identifying errors or defects as closely as possible to where they occur. By so doing, and by neither accepting nor passing on defects, issues are resolved quickly and efficiently, avoiding subsequent re-work and quality issues. The zero-defect principle is a concept of the Toyota Production System and is aimed at the reduction of defects

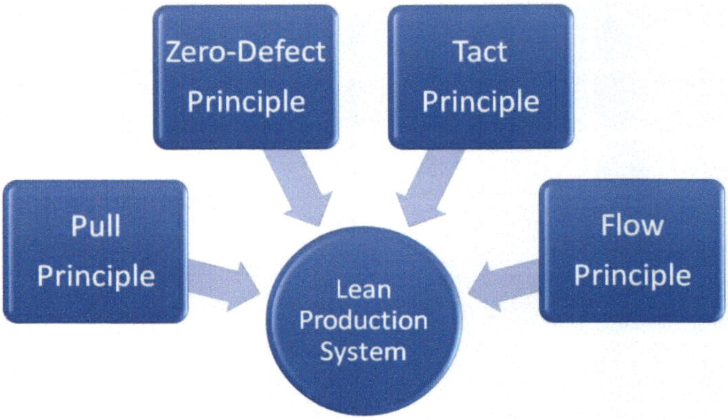

Fig. 6.14 Four lean production principles

through error prevention (Ohno, 1990). It is directed at motivating people to prevent mistakes by developing a constant, conscious desire to do their job right the first time. In reality, zero defects are not possible; however, the concept ensures that there is no waste existing in a project (Helmold & Terry, 2016a, 2016b). Waste refers to all unproductive processes, tools, employees, and so on. Anything that is unproductive and does not add value to a project should be eliminated is called the process of elimination of waste. Eliminating waste creates a process of improvement and correspondingly lowers costs. Common with the zero defects theory is the concept of "doing it right the first time" to avoid costly and time-consuming fixes later in the project management process. The concept of zero defects is grounded on four major elements for implementation in real projects:

- Quality is a state of assurance to requirements. Therefore, zero defects in a project means fulfilling requirements at that point in time.
- Right the first time. Quality should be integrated into the process from the beginning, rather than solving problems at a later stage.
- Quality is measured in financial terms. One needs to judge waste, production, and revenue in terms of budgetary impact.
- Performance should be judged by the accepted standards, as close to perfection as possible.

6.6.3 Pull Principle

The pull system is one of the lean manufacturing principles and is used to reduce waste in the production process. In this type of system, components used in the manufacturing process are only replaced once they have been consumed so companies only make enough products to meet customer demand. The opposite principle is the push system, in which as many products as possible are generated to be sold via marketing activities. The principles aim to avoid overproduction and stockpiling, thereby saving working capital, by letting demand dictates the rate at which goods or services are delivered. In this way the customer, or the next step in the chain, "pulls" value through the process.

6.6.4 Flow Principle

Value should be added in a smooth, uninterrupted flow, from the start to the end of the production process. The ultimate effect of this principle is that all process steps are focused and aligned to adding value, one piece at a time, removing all wasteful and unnecessary activities from the process. The advantage of a continuous flow in operations is that it features stability, continuity, balance, and does not waste time (the non-renewable resource). No time wasted on waiting between steps means time is being maximized for its capabilities. Operations are not able to introduce a waste-less process without the continuous flow, as it is the truly ideal process state. However, the troubles with continuous flow are that it is very hard to achieve, process steps are not generally balanced, and all process contains inherent waste activities. When one starts out to achieve continuous flow, many process problems will appear and come to the surface. Most individuals think this is bad—it is actually a good thing. The optimal process features continuous flow, and any problems that stand in your way from achieving continuous flow are problems that are now visible and can be rectified. The ideal flow is the one-piece flow as shown in Fig. 6.15.

6.6.5 Tact Principle

The German word for timing, tact refers to the rhythm at which goods or services are produced to meet customer demand. With a consistent, continuous rhythm providing a heartbeat for your production processes, it is far easier to regulate, responding flexibly and effortlessly as demand rises or falls. Tact time is defined as the

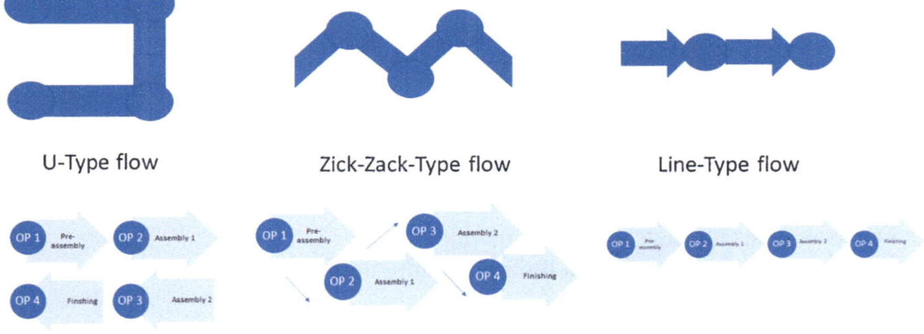

Fig. 6.15 Types of flows in operations. (Source: Marc Helmold)

Fig. 6.16 Tact time and other ratios

Tact time: (Customer tact)
$$\frac{\text{Available production time}}{\text{Customer demand}}$$

Optimum Manning level:
$$\frac{\text{Sum of cycle times}}{\text{Customer tact (Takt)}}$$

LBR: (Line balance ratio)
$$\frac{\text{Sum of cycle times}}{\text{Longest OP x No. OP}} \text{ x 100 \%}$$

LER: (Line efficiency ratio)
$$\frac{\text{Sum of cycle times}}{\text{Customer tact (Takt) x No. OP}} \text{ x 100 \%}$$

average time available (time available minus breaks, maintenance, or set-up) divided by the customer requested quantity as shown in Fig. 6.16.

The average time between the start of production of one unit and the start of production of the next unit, when these production starts are set to match the rate of customer demand. For example, if a customer wants 15 units with the available time of 9 minutes and the steady flow through the production line, the average time between production starts should be 36 seconds for one part or unit (9 minutes multiplied by 60 seconds = 540 seconds; 540 seconds divided by 15 units requested by the customer = 36 seconds per part). In fact, the tact time simply reflects the rate of production needed to match the demand. In the previous example, whether it takes 4 minutes or 4 years to produce the product, the tact time is based on customer demand. If a process or a production line is unable to produce at tact time, either demand levelling, additional resources, or process re-engineering is needed to correct the issue (Helmold & Terry, 2016a, 2016b).

- Directly tie production efficiencies to fiscal reporting.
- Reduce investigation time for root cause analysis.
- Shorten equipment ROI through increased utilization.
- Decrease costs through waste elimination.
- Increase customer satisfaction through quality improvement.

6.7 Andon

Andon (Japanese: アンドン or あんどん or 行灯) is a lean manufacturing tool referring to a system to notify management, maintenance, and other workers of a quality or process problem. The centerpiece is a device incorporating signal lights to indicate which workstation has the problem. The alert can be activated manually by a worker using a pull cord or button, or may be activated automatically by the production equipment itself. The system may include a means to stop production so the issue can be corrected. Some modern alert systems incorporate audio alarms, text, or other displays. An Andon system is one of the principal elements of the Jidoka method pioneered by Toyota as part of the TPS and therefore now part of the lean concept. It gives the worker the ability, and moreover the empowerment, to stop production when a defect is found, and immediately calls for assistance. Common reasons for manual activation of the Andon are part shortage, defect created or found, tool malfunction, or the existence of a safety problem. Work is stopped until a solution has been found. The alerts may be logged to a database so that they can be studied as part of a continuous-improvement program. The system typically indicates where the alert was generated, and may also provide a description of the trouble. Modern Andon systems can include text, graphics, or audio elements. Audio alerts may be done with coded tones, music with different tunes corresponding to the various alerts, or pre-recorded verbal messages. Usage of the word originated within Japanese manufacturing companies, and in English is a loanword from a Japanese word for a paper lantern (Imai, 1986) (Fig. 6.17).

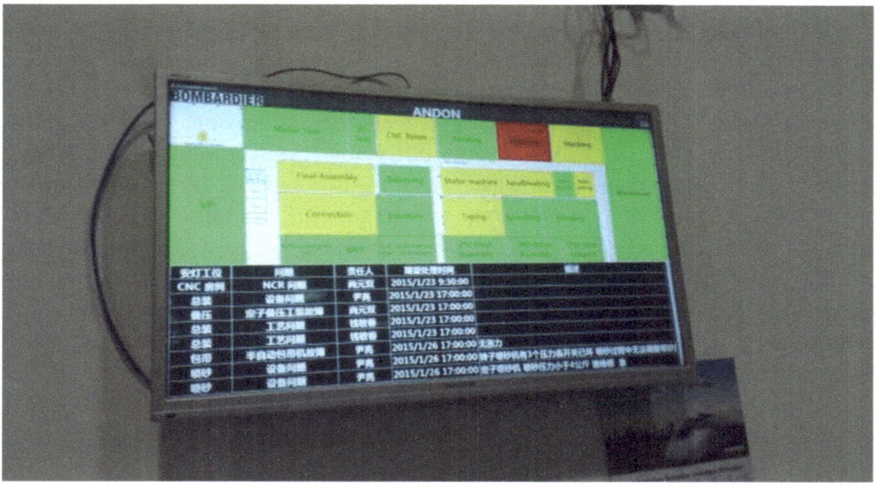

Fig. 6.17 Andon

6.8 Poka-Yoke

Poka-yoke (ポカヨケ) is a Japanese term that means "mistake-proofing." A poka-yoke is any mechanism in a lean concept, a process that helps an equipment operator avoids (*yokeru*) mistakes (*poka*). Its purpose is to eliminate product defects by preventing, correcting, or drawing attention to human or other errors as they occur. The concept was formalized, and the term adopted, by Shigeo Shingo as part of the TPS. It was originally described as baka-*yoke*, but as this means "fool-proofing" (or "idiot proofing") the name was changed to the milder *poka-yoke*.

6.9 Gemba and Shopfloor

Gemba (現場also described as *gemba*) is also a Japanese term meaning the real or right place. A production environment considers the shop floor as the most important place and the employees in the operation and support functions as most important human capital for adding value.

6.10 Shadow Boards

Shadow boards are specific boards for parts, tools, equipment in operations, manufacturing, or service areas to reduce waste and waiting time.

The aim of the shadow board is to achieve an organized workplace where tools, supplies, and equipment are stored in appropriate locations close to the work area or work stations. It provides the basis for standardization in the work place. They are a simple and inexpensive tool which provide tangible efficiencies and cost savings as well as intangible benefits. Figure 6.18 shows a shadow board for screws in Mitsubishi Japan. The appropriate storage, allocation, and preparation of screws avoid waiting time and the possibility of errors. The advantages of using shadow boards include avoiding waste, such as time looking for the appropriate tool or even having to buy a new one, wasted time in looking for supplies, and interchanging tools between tasks. Shadow boards also provide the ability to quickly gauge the location of tools and equipment or if they are missing. Shadow boards are used in the sort and set in order stages of the implementation and operation of a 5 s system in a workplace and kaizen initiatives. Shadow boards can be of different sizes and located in many different areas of a process or plant. The key is that they are appropriately located and hold all the necessary tools for the area or work station.

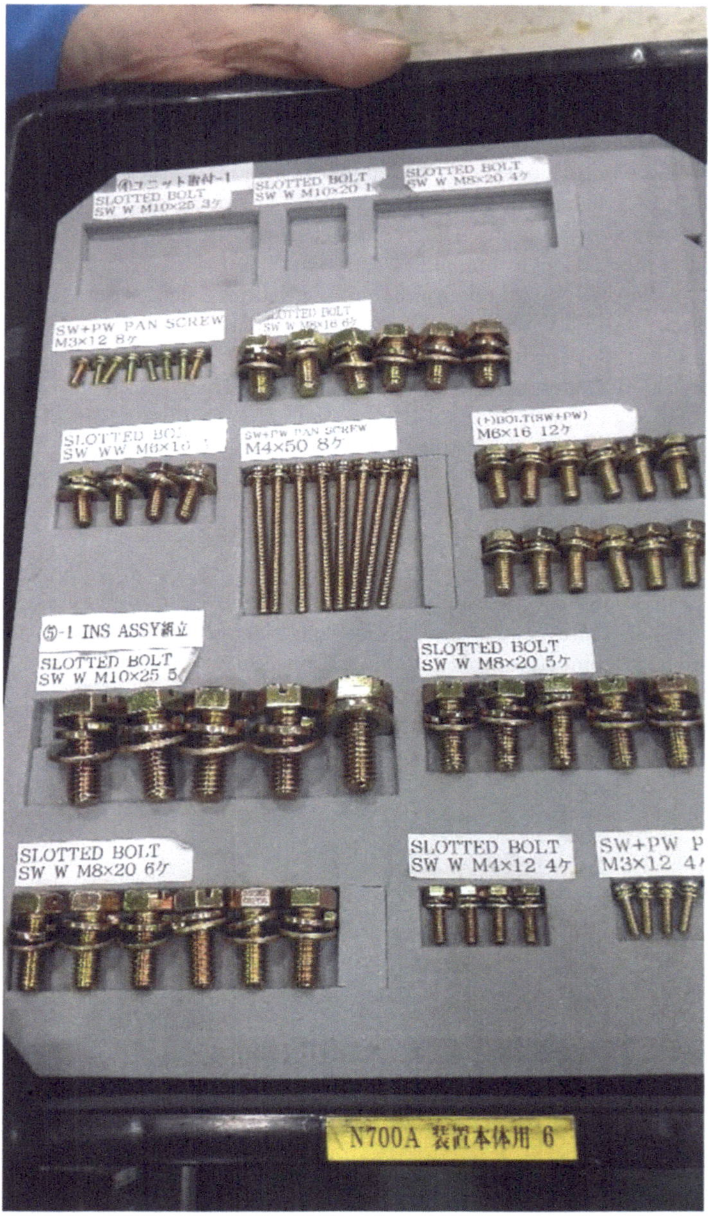

Fig. 6.18 Shadow board. (Source: Helmold. Shadow board. Mitsubishi Shinkanzen production in Osaka)

6.11 Health and Safety

Health, safety, and environment (HSE) is the concept and paradigm that implements and secures practical aspects of environmental protection and safety at work. From a health and safety standpoint, it involves creating organized efforts and procedures for identifying workplace hazards and reducing accidents and exposure to harmful situations and substances. It also includes training of personnel in accident prevention, accident response, emergency preparedness, and use of protective clothing and equipment. From an environmental standpoint, it involves creating a systematic approach to complying with environmental regulations, such as managing waste or air emissions all the way to helping operations´ departments reduce the company's carbon footprint. Successful HSE programs also include measures to address ergonomics, air quality, and other aspects of workplace safety that could affect the health and well-being of employees and the overall community. Figure 6.19 displays HSE requirements in a Chinese operations environment.

6.12 Overall Equipment Effectiveness (OEE)

Manufacturing a product is a complex process, without metrics and guidelines. It is very easy to lose control and have your business managed by your production. OEE is a tool that combines multiple manufacturing issues and data points to provide information about the process. By analyzing and calculating data, it also functions as a framework for root cause analysis. Through a documented process of

Fig. 6.19 Health, safety, and environment. (Source: Author's source)

combining the underlying data, OEE provides specific process information. All members of the manufacturing team, from assembly technicians to financial personnel can use the data to understand the current state of the manufacturing process. By having a predetermined framework of the impact of machine availability, performance, and quality, OEE provides a framework to track underlying issues and root causes. OEE also provides a framework for improvements in the manufacturing process. By using key OEE concepts such as The Six Big Losses waste exposed by tracking, OEE can be understood and efficiencies can be improved. The components of this framework are as follows:

- Availability.
- Performance.
- Quality.

OEE is a very simple metric to immediately indicate the current status of a manufacturing process and also a complex tool allowing you to understand the effect of the various issues in the manufacturing process and how they affect the entire process (OEE = Availability x Performance x Quality). Availability refers to the machine or cell being available for production when scheduled. At the most basic level, when a process is running it is creating value for the end user. When a process is stopped, it is creating a cost with no associated value. Whether it is due to mechanical failure, raw materials, or operator issues, the cell or machine is either producing or not producing. By comparing scheduled run time to actual run time, the availability component of OEE allows for a determination of lost production due to down time. Performance is determined by how much waste is created through running at less than optimal speed. By comparing the actual cycle times against ideal cycle times, OEE allows for a determination of how much production was lost by cycles that did not meet the ideal cycle time. Quality focuses on identifying time that was wasted by producing a product that does not meet quality standards. By comparing the quantity of good to reject parts, the percent of time actually adding value by producing good product is exposed. By itself, OEE only provides data about your manufacturing process. Companies that use OEE as a metric have found success when combining it with general lean manufacturing programs and also as part of TPM systems. When using OEE with these systems, the benefits become significant: Fig. 6.20 shows an example of the OEE. High performing companies can achieve an OEE higher than 85 percent. In the calculation, the OEE has the elements availability (83.3%), performance (90.0%), and quality (98%). Based on the actual figures, it is now possible to optimize each at the inefficient categories. The availability ratio is below 90% and needs special actions for improvements.

Fig. 6.20 OEE calculation. (Source: Author's source)

6.13 Kanban

Kanban (看板) is a visual system for managing work as it moves through a process. It is a concept related to lean and just-in-time (JIT) production, where it is used as a scheduling system that tells you what to produce, when to produce it, and how much to produce. Initially it arose as a scheduling system for lean manufacturing, originating from the Toyota Production System (TPS).

6.14 Supermarkets

Supermarkets ordinarily are located near the supplying process to help that process see customer usage and requirements. Each item in a supermarket has a specific location from which a material handler withdraws products in the precise amounts needed by a downstream process. As an item is removed, a signal to make more (such as a kanban card or an empty bin) is taken by the material handler to the supplying process. Toyota installed its first supermarket in 1953 in the machine shop of its main plant in Toyota City (Ohno, 1990). Toyota executive Taiichi Ohno took the idea for the supermarket from photos of American supermarkets showing goods arrayed on shelves by specific location for withdrawal by customers.

6.15 Case Study: Bombardier in China

Bombardier is recognized as a successful foreign enterprise in the Chinese rail industry. Bombardier is also a specially qualified Western enterprise which supplies railway passenger trains (high-speed trains and intercity passenger trains), metro vehicles, monorail trains, APM systems, and metro vehicle maintenance/services. Bombardier Transportation in China has six joint ventures, seven wholly foreign-owned enterprises, and around 7000 employees (Bombardier, 2020).

A wide range of our rail transportation and aerospace products are currently in service in the Chinese market. In total, more than 30,000 rail vehicles, locomotives, bogies, and propulsion systems are in operation or on order in China, including more than 3500 high-speed train and intercity passenger train cars, 580 electric locomotives, over 2000 metro cars, and maintenance for 1600 metro cars as part of China's growing urban mass transit market. Bombardier is also supplying, or has already supplied, APM systems to China's five largest cities: Beijing, Guangzhou, Shanghai, Shenzhen, and Hong Kong. In addition, Bombardier has supplied 104 tram cars for two other Chinese megacities (Nanjing/Suzhou), and in 2017 won its first monorail contract in China, for 240 cars. A total of over 14,000 Bombardier bogies are currently in use in China's mainline and urban mass transit vehicles, while Bombardier's propulsion and signaling equipment, largely supplied to third-party metro car builders, are in operation in more than 30 Chinese cities.

Figure 4.14 displays the assembly and testing line of high-speed trains in Bombardier Sifang Transportation. Figure 4.14 shows the visualization room of the International Procurement Office (IPO) in Shanghai. International purchasing offices or supplier management centers are part of the internationalization and change of corporate model in supplier management (Helmold, 2020). Multinational corporations such as Volkswagen, Daimler, Siemens, Bosch, or Bombardier have purchasing offices in regions such as China, India, or Eastern Europe, which offer savings potential or are geographically far removed from the parent company. Medium-sized partners expand through smaller offices or through collaboration with partners, purchasing offices, or institutions such as the German centers in the metropolitan areas of China (Helmold & Terry, 2016a, 2016b). In addition to offices, the German centers also offer contacts to government representatives or Chinese suppliers in order to make purchases from China (Helmold & Terry, 2016a, 2016b). In 2015, Deutsche Bahn opened an international purchasing office. Previously, the logistics division, DB Schenker, had successfully established itself in many locations over the years. In 2005, companies such as Bombardier Transportation or IBM opened an international purchasing office in Shanghai, China. In 2015, Deutsche Bahn decided to open a point-of-sale office in the same location. Developments

Fig. 6.21 8S example in China. (Source: Author)

show that it is advisable to establish an international purchasing office in China. Advantages can be outlined as follows:

- Proximity to markets with a high degree of product and know-how maturity, for example, automotive industry or railway industry.
- Establish relationships with Chinese manufacturers and ensure compliance with quality requirements.
- Transfer of customer and production requirements to the suppliers.
- Early involvement of suppliers in the product development process as well as joint development.
- Exploitation of savings through direct purchasing as well as through the use of local pre- and semi-finished products in the production process of the suppliers.
- Acquisition of own end products in domestic markets.
- Proximity to other high maturity Asian markets, for example, Japan or South Korea.

Figure 6.21 depicts an example of the 5S concept in China at ZhongWang in Shenyang. The company changed in a very creative way the 5S philosophy into eight categories (8S).

References

Bombardier. (2020). Retrieved 1.2.2020. https://rail.bombardier.com/en/about-us/worldwide-presence/china/en.html.

Helmold, M. (2020). Lean Management and Kaizen. Fundamentals from Cases and Examples in Operations and Supply Chain Management. Springer Cham.

Helmold, M., & Terry, B. (2016a). *Lieferantenmanagement 2030. Sicherung der Wettbewerbsfähigkeit durch wertfokussierte Lieferantenbeziehungen*. Springer.

Helmold, M., & Terry, B. (2016b). *Global sourcing and supply management excellence in China*. Springer.

Imai, M. (1986). Kaizen. Der Schlüssel zum Erfolg der Japaner im Wettbewerb. Frankfurt: Ullstein.

Liker, J. K. (2004). *The Toyota way*. McGraw-Hill.

Ohno, T. (1990). Toyota production system. Beyond large Scale Production. New York: Productivity Press.

Upstream SCRM

7

What gets measured gets improved.

—*Peter Drucker (1909–2005)*

7.1 Supplier Side

The supply side is the function, which secures that inputs are available for the transformation process as shown in Fig. 7.1. Transformation is any activity or group of activities that takes one or more inputs, transforms and adds value to them, and provides outputs for customers or clients. Inputs, for which the supply management is responsible, are mostly products and services coming from suppliers in the upstream side of the value chain. These products or services are directly involved in the transformation into end-products to customers. However, inputs can be also indirect categories or services, which are not directly included in the transformation process (desks, machines, training services, etc.).

The term "supply management" as key value-adding function replaces old definitions of procurement or purchasing (Helmold & Terry, 2016). This definition is in line with Porter's description of value chains. A value chain is a set of activities that a firm operating in a specific industry performs in order to deliver a valuable product, service for the market. The concept comes from business management and was first described and popularized by Michael E. Porter in his 1985 best-seller, *Competitive Advantage: Creating and Sustaining Superior Performance* in the upstream supply management or the supply side. Figure 7.1 displays the operations, the upstream supply side (supply management), and the downstream supply side (customer or demand side side). In Porter's value chain framework (see Fig. 7.2), Inbound Logistics, Operations, Outbound Logistics, Marketing and Sales, and Service are categorized as primary activities. Secondary activities include Procurement, Human Resource Management, Technological Development, and

M. Helmold et al., *Supply Chain Risk Management*,
Management for Professionals, https://doi.org/10.1007/978-3-030-90800-3_7

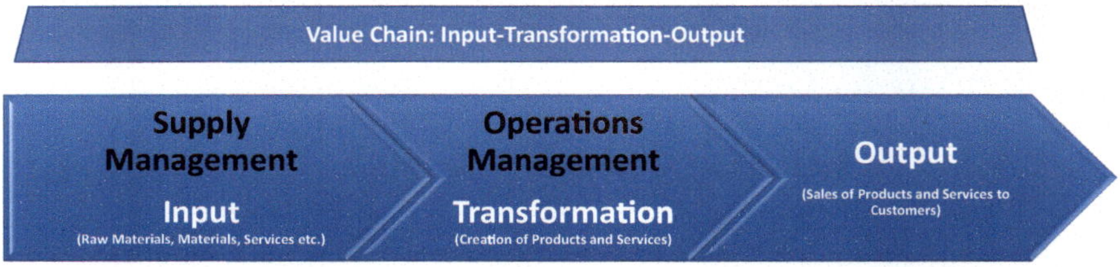

Fig. 7.1 Supply management managing the input and supplies. (Source: Author's source)

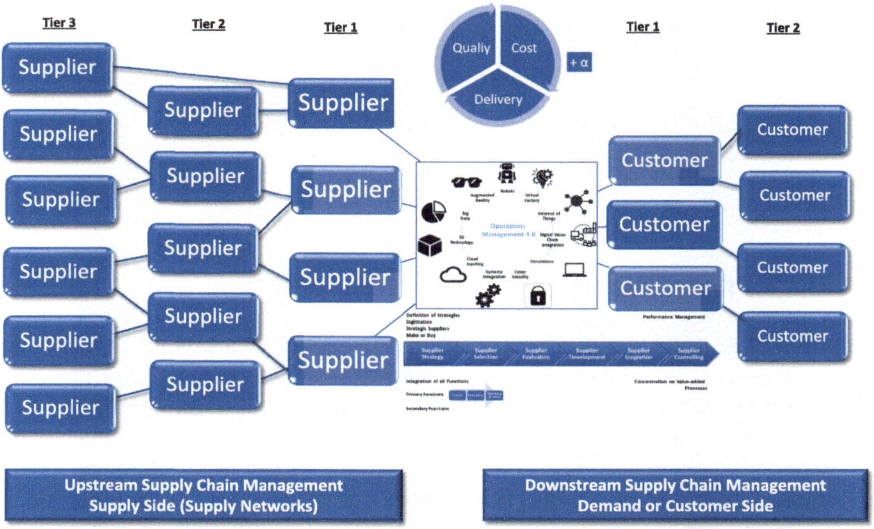

Fig. 7.2 Supply networks within the value chain. (Source: Author's source)

Infrastructure. As many companies have external value chains (purchase of goods, services) of more than 80 percent, supply management has here the most significant role in any enterprise. In many enterprises, functions are still working independently from each other, leading to a large amount of waste and inefficiencies. Many industries are currently faced by fierce competition. This is forcing manufacturing companies to concentrate on core competencies and to transfer the production of components, goods, and services to external suppliers (Aberdeen group, 2005). The number of value-adding activities has decreased constantly and now lies between 10 percent and 30 percent in this industry. The company Apple has no production and decided to outsource the manufacturing of iPads or iPhones to the company FoxConn. Such a development has had a great influence on the structure of supply chains and supplier relationships. Supply chains (the terms "supply chains" and "supply networks" are used synonymously in the literature) have become more complex and international, as pointed out by several authors Christopher and Peck see the level of complexity increasing in the upstream supply chain management of manufacturing companies in many industries, a trend which is characterized by the growing transfer of activities to suppliers and supplier networks, high numbers of supply chain layers (tiers), and the ongoing globalization of supply chains. As a consequence, vulnerability and risk exposure have risen significantly. The rapid increase in supplier activities therefore directly affects supply management, as emphasized by Emmett and Crocker (2009). In recent years, many companies have reduced their value-adding activities and implemented efficiency-oriented cost reductions, for example, outsourcing, single sourcing, low-cost country sourcing, platform concepts, lean management, design-to-cost approaches (Aberdeen group, 2005). Supply management has become more important in core and peripheral business areas (Trkman & McCormack, 2009) and is aimed at building resilient supply chains. Resilience is based on being able to anticipate, manage, and prevent supply chain disruptions at an early stage. On the other hand, supply risks have risen due to increased dependency on supplier networks (Fig. 7.3).

In their research "An Empirical Analysis of the Effect of Supply Chain Disruptions on Long-Run Stock Price," found that enterprises without operational slack and redundancies in their supply chains experience negative stock effects. The authors revealed the tremendous impact of supply chain disruptions on stock price performance and shareholder value. Supply disruptions can easily lead to high recovery cost, waste, and sharp decreases in sales. External customers become dissatisfied and internal core functions (e.g., assembly) are disturbed. In most cases, supply disruptions have negative impacts on brand image, sales figures, and the company's own financial situation as stressed by many authors writing about supply disruptions and resilient supply chains (Trkman & McCormack, 2009). Recent incidents in the media about disruptions caused by upstream supply management inefficiencies

Fig. 7.3 Porter's value chain. (Source: Authors source, adapted from Helmold et al. (2020))

from China show that the supply management excellence approach needs to tackle these issues in a proactive and sustainable way.

Supply management risks have mainly been investigated at the direct level of tier-one relationships, but consideration has not been fully extended to sub-suppliers, that is, tiers one, two, three, and beyond. The new concept of supply management therefore seeks to address these concerns by investigating how disruptions can be anticipated, prevented, and managed over the entire value chain including all tiers on the supply and demand side as shown in the figure by (Helmold & Terry, 2021). Recent supply disruptions show that current supply management organizations and supply management tools and concepts are not smart and resilient enough to avoid these supply chain discrepancies. Recent articles for example in the magazine "Automotive News" show that all car producers are facing severe problems due to suppliers´ problems. Not only the automotive industry but also many other industries face these issues.

The lean supply management concept was developed by (Helmold & Terry, 2021), who worked for Toyota Motors. It derived from a bundle of instruments which come from sophisticated production methods or supporting functions such as logistics. The ideal interplay and optimal combination of all instruments are essential for success. The vision of lean production is based on the just-in-time (JIT) philosophy and the Toyota Production System (TPS: Japanese = トヨタ生産システム) and focuses on the elimination of waste and the minimization of stock.

7.2 History of Supply Management 4.0

The history of supply management is shown in the Fig. 7.4. Supply management originated as a function, which was responsible for securing deliveries in supply management 1.0. Over the years, the supply management function has developed in most of the companies as primary and leading function, which utilizes digital tools to manage global supplier networks. Supply Management 4.0 focuses in this context on providing value-adding activities and processes throughout the value chain.

7.3 Supply Management Objectives

Supply side objectives are important. The seven rights (7R), which are the major objectives according to the lean supply management philosophy can be defined as:

1. Right products
2. Right quality
3. Right time
4. Right quantity
5. Right location
6. Right people

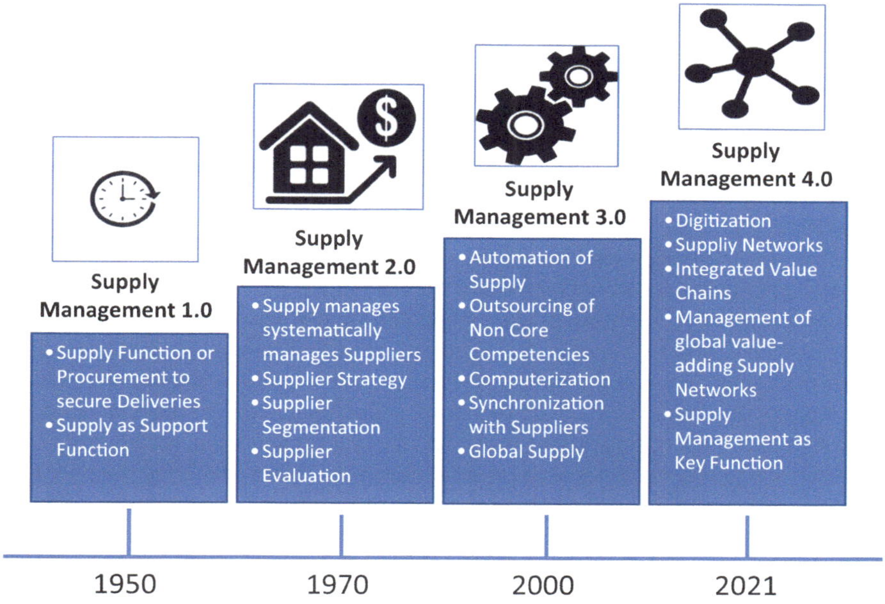

Fig. 7.4 History of Supply Management 4.0. (Source: Author's source)

7. Right cost

The right product refers to the right specification and requirements by the demanding customer. The products must have the required dimensions, layout, material, color, etc. The right quality means the clarification of all requirements in terms of quality and improvement measures to have the optimum quality levels. Quality is normally measured by hard factors such as non-conformities, field rejects, or defects at receipt (0 km defects). The right quantity is the placing of a specific order quantity triggered by internal and customer demands. Supply management has to transfer the customer and company demands to the supply networks. The right time means that products ordered have to be at the buyer's place in time, neither too early nor too late. Supply management has to recognize suppliers´ lead times. The lead time for any product starts from the order until the physical receipt of goods at the ordering party. The right location can be defined as the place, where the products are required. Shipment of products from China to Europe take more than 8 weeks, so that that the right location is closely linked to the lead time of products. The meaning of right people extends current definition of the five Rights (Emmett and Crocker, 2009) in line with the modern and lean philosophy of the new paradigm of supply management. Suppliers in global markets need to have the right sales people, project managers, and operators to meet the requested criteria. Project managers must have sufficient language skills and as well operators must be trained to produce good quality parts. People are becoming in a changing and global trade situation more and more important. Any product needs to have the right cost level; otherwise, it will not be demanded and bought.

7.4 Supply Management Process

7.4.1 Six Phases in Supply Management 4.0

Industries or companies which have outsourced a large scope of their products to global supply networks would especially benefit from such research in supply management, supplier relationship management, and supply networks. In conclusion, it is evident that proactive supply management requires a subset of principles: The principles can be described as follows: (1) Supply management is a function which is managing the entire value chain; therefore, supply management must be incorporated into the mission, values, and strategies of every organization. (2) Supply management best practices are focused on a multilayer approach, involving not only tier one, but also tier two and three levels; proactive supply management can only be introduced and executed if the corporate objectives are communicated and cascaded throughout the organization; the setup must be centralized as single point of contact to suppliers. (3) Advanced and innovative supply management has standardized tools and processes. (4) Supply management best practice companies have sophisticated B2B platforms/supplier portals in terms of quality, cost, and delivery and other suitable KPI. (5) Supply management and mitigation actions activities have to be preventive, proactive, and sustainable; activities have to be oriented long term. (6) Supply management requires a collaborative approach, including strategic alliances with suppliers. Such activities should be organized centrally. (7) Proactive supply management can be performed with a key account manager in terms of being a single point of contact for the supplier (customer). (8) Performance indicators have to be mutually agreed upon and may comprise both hard and soft factors. The assessment process should consist of quality, cost, delivery, and technological criteria. (9) The learning organization should, among other things, be characterized by the capability and competencies of coaching suppliers. (10) All the abovementioned principles should be combined with a philosophy of continuous improvement (Japanese: Kaizen) and reflection (Japanese: Hansei) to achieve a best practice model in supply management. Companies that want to distance themselves from their competitors through best-in-class supply management must implement the ten principles and adopt a collaborative approach in dealing with their supply base. Appropriate management of one's supply base can lead to competitive advantage. The strategic objective of supply management is the establishment, design, and management of supplier networks and the successful collaboration within these networks as the figure shows. The network consists of internal and external suppliers. The collaboration between supply partners and the management of the interactions is a key responsibility of the supply management function. A sophisticated information system is a pre-requisite for proper interactions (Fig. 7.5).

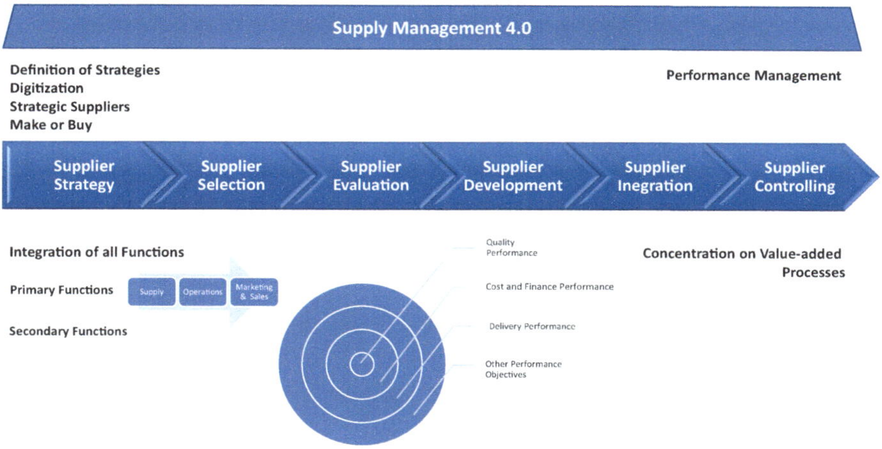

Fig. 7.5 Supply management process. (Source: Author's source)

7.4.2 Supplier Strategy

By shifting value-adding activities and non-core competencies to supplier networks that are in competition with each other, new performance concepts, strategies, and processes arise that have to be mastered. For a long time now, the focus in the future has not only been on increasing company-internal cost advantages, but much more on the exchange of information and the exploitation of global cross-company potential. In general, supplier management aims to provide a uniform method for analyzing potential and existing suppliers in order to make strategic decisions based on the results. At the operational level, this means making the performance of suppliers comparable, uncovering optimization potential, and reducing procurement costs. The strategic dimension of supplier management, on the other hand, aims primarily to define suitable procurement strategies based on a transparent basis for decision-making in order to reduce supply risks and dependencies and to increase procurement quality. The strategic goals of supplier management deal with the medium- to long-term optimization of the company's supplier base. Based on category or material group-specific procurement strategies, it is important to define precise development measures that enable a continuous increase in delivery quality or a reduction in procurement costs. The supply risk can be sustainably reduced, for example, through the collaborative optimization of cross-company processes. The early establishment of possible alternative suppliers and the targeted control of the procurement volume prevent the company from becoming dependent. Figure 7.6 shows the first of the six phases of supplier strategy. In addition, the relationship with strategically important suppliers that are difficult to substitute should be strengthened through cooperative and integrative measures. This ensures the competitiveness of your own company. Due to the long-term orientation, all measures to achieve the strategic goals should be regularly checked as part of a continuous process and

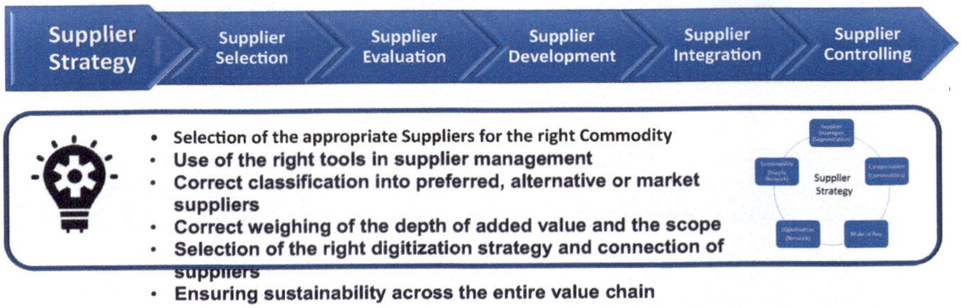

Fig. 7.6 Supply management process. (Source: Author's source)

Fig. 7.7 Elements of the supplier strategy phase. (Source: Author's source)

adjusted if necessary. Figure 7.6 shows the main elements in the phase of the supplier strategy with segmentation of suppliers, development of a material group strategy, feasibility studies on in-house or third-party production, the evaluation of degrees of digitization in supply chains, and the constant review of sustainability requirements of suppliers. The main tasks can be described as follows (Fig. 7.7):

- Choosing the right suppliers for the right material groups.
- Use of the right tools in supplier management.
- Correct classification into preferred, alternative, or market suppliers.
- Correct weighing of the depth of added value and the scope.
- Selection of the right digitization strategy and connection of suppliers.
- Ensuring sustainability across the entire value chain.

Supplier Segmentation

Every supplier strategy must be based on core elements such as classification, categorization, digitization, in-house or external production, digitization, and sustainability. Figure 7.8 shows these elements. As part of the supplier segmentation, the suppliers are grouped into company-wide classes according to preferred suppliers, alternative, benchmark, market, and other suppliers. Preferred suppliers are selected suppliers with excellent performance characteristics in terms of innovation, quality, costs, delivery reliability, sustainability, and processes. Preferred suppliers are given preferential treatment and are given specified volumes, order volumes, and procurement quotas. Preferred suppliers are usually involved in the development and product creation process of their own company at an early stage. The relationship is based on partnership. Alternative suppliers are suppliers who can be used alongside the preferred suppliers. Alternative suppliers are in the group of bidders, but their performance is not as good as the preferred suppliers in terms of quality, costs, delivery, and other characteristics, so they usually only receive smaller volumes and procurement quotas. The alternatives are followed by benchmark suppliers who serve as benchmarks and can be included in the group of bidders. Benchmarking in supplier management is a useful method for the systematic and structured acquisition of information and for the comparison of suppliers based on characteristics such as innovative strength, technological leadership, cost efficiency, or quality awareness. Benchmarking is thus a constant creative process to improve the supplier portfolio by determining and comparing the best-known services of existing suppliers and the comparison with new suppliers who show particularly strong performance characteristics (English: benchmark = the best; best practice). By adopting and continuously improving the identified best practice processes, the performance of your own area, competitiveness and ultimately customer satisfaction are improved. Seen in this way, a benchmarking project within the scope of a tender offers the possibility of comparison with the best solutions, reveals deficits

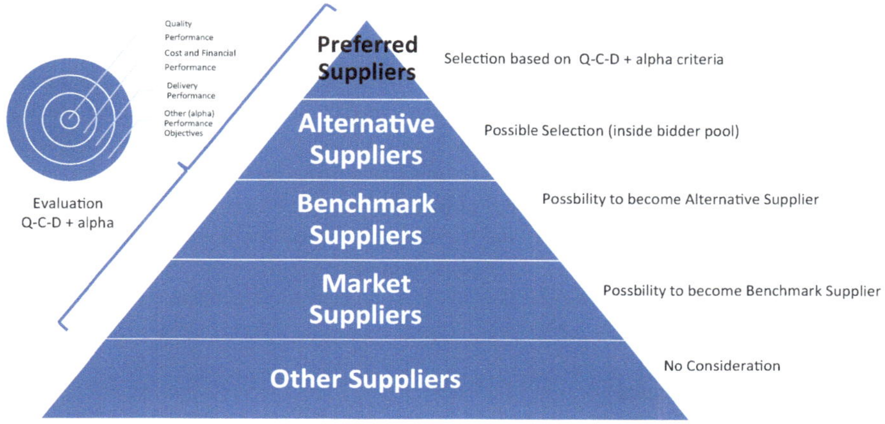

Fig. 7.8 Supplier segmentation and classification. (Source: Author's source)

and weak points, clarifies the need for action and can be used as an ideal tool for the development of new suppliers and constant competition. Benchmarking is not just a comparison of key figures or operations, but it is a comprehensive, holistically applicable process analysis for improving performance that can be used for all performance areas and the entire company. The benchmark suppliers are followed by market suppliers and all other suppliers. Market suppliers can be included in the group of benchmark suppliers if their supplier management has been qualified and evaluated. All other suppliers are not taken into account (Helmold & Terry, 2016).

Commodity Strategies

A material or product group or category (English: commodity or category) combines different individual parts or categories in a material group, which are usually made from the same basic material or raw material or can be divided into the same category. The differentiation of material groups can be freely defined and can be relatively coarse or fine, and this depends on the respective purpose. Examples of material groups: iron or ferrous metal, copper, plastic, rubber, leather, and wood. Other subdivisions are made, for example, according to electrical, mechanical, aluminum, or steel.

The primary goal for bottleneck materials is to secure the supply. To reduce the supply risk, one should look at the global procurement markets. As a rule, the local markets offer only inadequate sources of supply for shortage materials. By expanding the number of suppliers, the dependency on individual suppliers for bottleneck materials is reduced. The focus is not on the cost of the material, but on securing the supply. Since these are mostly low-value individual parts, product development is not very important. A reduction in the supply risk can be achieved by standardizing bottleneck materials. Figure 7.9 shows the possible material group strategies. This matrix is subdivided into strategic, lever, bottleneck, and non-critical material groups and market segments (suppliers). In the case of strategic material groups and market segments, it is advisable to enter into close ties with suppliers. This can take place through collaboration, joint or competitive development projects, collaborations or even company mergers (e.g., founding a new company or a joint venture). For leverage products, companies should bundle volumes and proactively approach potential suppliers in order to achieve the ideal strategy. Purchasing cooperations and alliances can also help to gain advantages in the market. In the case of bottleneck products, the strategy must be based on security of needs, so that long-term contracts prove advantageous. Global tenders or substitution are further strategies for ensuring security of supply. For standardized products, on the other hand, it is advantageous to regularly examine the market and exploit the potential. In this situation, B2B platforms or C-parts management from a single source or the bundling of requirements after a detailed market sutdy is recommend as appropriate strategy (Helmold & Terry, 2016).

Make-or-Buy Strategies

A make-or-buy decision addresses the in-house production or external procurement of a product. It is about producing a product (make) or buying it (buy). The operational function of production is always understood to mean in-house production.

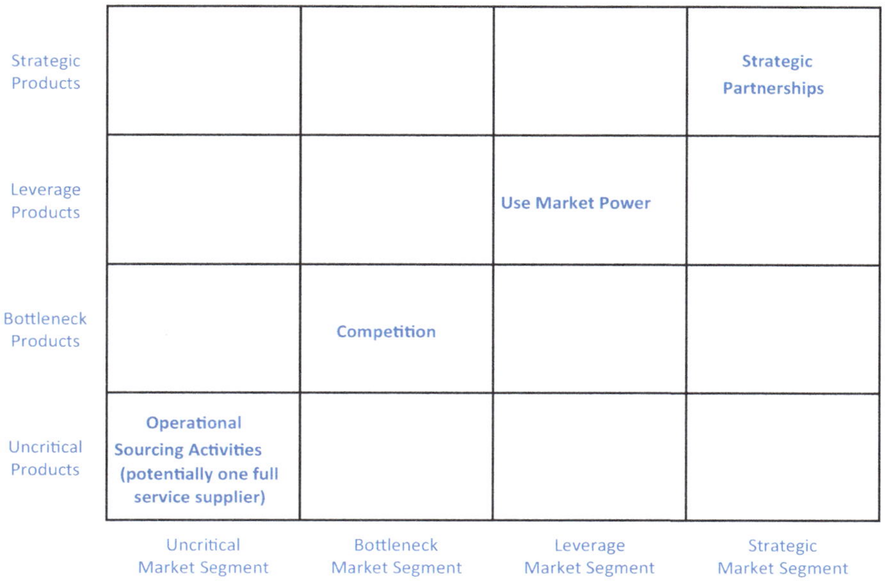

Fig. 7.9 Commodity strategies. (Source: Author's source)

Goods are manufactured with their own resources, employees, production factors, and production processes. In-house production means internalization, that is, the organization of economic activities and the production of a material group in your own company organization. External production, on the other hand, means that material groups and production volumes are outsourced to suppliers. In the case of external production, there are usually only variable costs. In the case of in-house production, the fixed costs are added. The difference between the two variable cost amounts is used to cover the fixed costs more with each piece (fixed cost degression) until they are completely covered. Figure 7.10 shows recommendations for action for companies according to the strategic importance and relevance of the material group on the Y-axis and skills and competencies for developing and manufacturing the material group on the X-axis. Companies must therefore concentrate on their own skills and competencies for the development and production of the material group and prefer a strategy of in-house production (make) in this segment, especially if the strategic importance and relevance of the material group is very high. With the same level of skills and competencies for a product group, but relatively low strategic relevance and value, a hybrid strategy with partial outsourcing can take place. However, companies must ensure that the knowledge for this material group remains in their own company. If your own company does not have competencies in a special material group that is of high strategic importance, we recommend cooperative partnerships with one or a few suppliers (external production or buy). Due to its strategic importance, it is worth pursuing long-term contracts, collaborations, or joint project developments with suppliers. With less relevant material groups and no

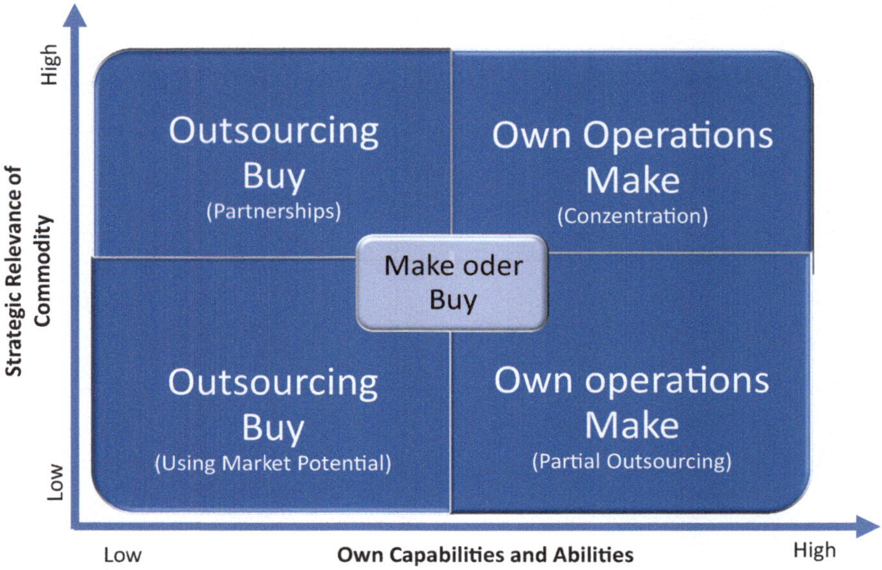

Fig. 7.10 Make-or-buy strategies. (Source: Author's source)

know-how in your own company, the market potential and competition can be fully exploited. The decision to purchase from a third party should therefore be carefully considered. It is therefore important to think about the basic advantages and disadvantages in advance. Some important ones are noted below.

The advantages of outsourcing are as follows:

- Concentration on core competencies and focusing of activities and resources on one's own core business.
- Possibility and opportunity to establish a proactive and preventive supplier management.
- Reduction of the vertical range of manufacture and transformation toward a lean production structure.
- Long-term optimization of the cost structure by reducing fixed costs and changing from fixed to variable costs.
- Improvement of the liquidity situation and, if necessary, improvement of the balance sheet ratios (e.g., by reducing the level of indebtedness if investments for which loans have to be taken out are not made).
- Flexible reaction to changes in demand is possible and part of the entrepreneurial risk is shifted to the supplier.
- Possibility of partnerships and the preservation of innovations that are not in one's own area of competence.

Disadvantages of outsourcing are as follows:

- Far-reaching cuts in existing structures in the event of outsourcing and unrest in the workforce.
- Loss of know-how and personnel with a possibly significant dependence on one provider.
- Long-term loyalty to suppliers' limits flexibility to actively react to market changes.
- The possibility that trade secrets will not be kept, especially in international business.
- Increasing coordination effort, especially in logistics and other departments that are involved in the value creation process.

ABC-XYZ Analysis

The ABC-XYZ analysis is a method in supplier management for the classification of material groups according to consumption, value, and according to the predictability of the consumption of procurement volumes in a company. The ABC analysis is often combined with the XYZ analysis for the procurement of products, the planning of production quantities, and other logistical issues. While the ABC analysis is primarily about the value and importance of customers, products, suppliers or purchased parts, the XYZ analysis analyzes their predictability and the possibility of making forecasts. It is made up of the ABC and the XYZ analysis as shown in Fig. 7.11. The classification looks like this:

ABC Article

- A-article: High value proportion of approximately 70% to 80%.
- B item: Average value share of approximately 15% to 20%.
- C-article: Low value share of approximately 5% to 10%.

XYZ Item

- X-articles: Articles with constant demand and high predictive accuracy.
- Y-article: Article with fluctuating demand and medium forecast accuracy.
- Z item: Item with irregular demand and poor forecast accuracy.

AX and BX articles have a high share of value and can be easily forecast in terms of consumption, as they are subject to uniform consumption. They are therefore relatively easy to control. AZ and BZ articles are to be regarded as problematic. They make up a high proportion of sales, but they are difficult to control due to their irregular needs. If too many articles in this category are stored, the storage costs increase. Insufficient storage can lead to bottlenecks in production.

		Value and strategic relevance		
		A High value product or material, mostly low-volume articles. Very high strategic importance.	**B** Medium value product or material, mostly low-volume items. Medium strategic importance.	**C** Low value product or material, mostly low-volume articles. Low strategic importance.
Predictability and consumption	**X** Relatively uniform, low consumption fluctuations. High forecast accuracy, very easy to plan.	•High share of value •Planned consumption •Detailed planning •Low or no inventory •Ensure fast availability at the supplier •JIT deliveries	•Average value share •Planned consumption •Detailed planning •Low or no inventory •Ensure fast availability at the supplier •JIT deliveries	•Low value share •Planned consumption •Low capital commitment •Uncritical treatment
	Y Inconsistent, absent or rising trend. Seasonal business with fluctuations. Medium prediction accuracy. Can be planned to a limited extent.	•High share of value •Irregular consumption •Detailed planning •Possibly. Create a safety reserve with the supplier •Ensure fast availability at the supplier	•Average value share •Irregular consumption •Detailed planning •Treatment like AY or BY •Ensure availability at the supplier	•Low value share •Irregular consumption •Consumption cannot be planned •Build up safety reserves as long as there is no bottleneck in the warehouse
	Z Inconsistent and absolutely irregular demand. Very low prediction accuracy. Difficult to plan.	•High share of value •Chaotic and sporadic consumption •Agree on a safety reserve with the supplier •JIT deliveries	•Average value share •Chaotic and sporadic consumption •Agree on a safety reserve with the supplier •Ensure availability at the supplier •Like AZ or CZ	•Low value share •Chaotic and sporadic consumption •Consumption cannot be planned •Build safety reserves

Fig. 7.11 ABC-XYZ analysis. (Source: Author's source)

Internationalization Strategies

Supplier management must ensure resilience in international transactions and business. In 2019, German companies imported preliminary products to the value of 606 billion euros, which made up a good 55 percent of Germany's total goods imports. Two thirds of the imported primary products came from other EU member states, a further 5.3 percent and 5.0 percent from the USA and China (Kolev & Obst, 2020). Supplier management must ensure through a clear structure and risk assessment that international supply chains are stable and do not lead to supply bottlenecks. The COVID-19 crisis, in particular, has shown that strategies for products from the health sector were not sustainable and good, so that supply bottlenecks, for example, masks or protective equipment has come (Helmold et al., 2020).

Sustainability and CSR Strategies

The primary task of classic supplier management is to create value-adding supply chains based on suitable criteria and strategies. This happens on the basis of the criteria quality, costs, delivery performance, and other significant aspects (QCD plus alpha). In times of political unrest, trade in an international context, climate change, stricter environmental guidelines, rising energy prices and enlightened, environmentally friendly consumers, supplier management has a key role in ensuring sustainable supply chains. Studies show "sustainability" as an integral part of the value chain offers companies good opportunities to differentiate themselves from the competition and thus increase sales. Sustainable (Fig. 7.12) includes

Fig. 7.12 CSR in operation and Supply Management 4.0. (Source: Author's source)

elements such as working conditions, environmental protection, human rights, anti-corruption, social standards, compliance with human rights, and respect for intellectual property.

Digitization Strategies

The digitization and linking of one's own company with the supply chain will, in the medium term, significantly increase the distance between companies that successfully apply this to their business model and those that miss this opportunity. Digitization also opens up an opportunity for smaller, faster, and more flexible companies to skip entire evolutionary stages of organizations, to overtake their competitors and to create their own markets. This also applies to supplier management or, in a broader sense, to the management of the supply chain. In the medium term, digitization will significantly increase the gap between companies that successfully apply it to their business model and those that miss this opportunity. Digitization also opens up an opportunity for smaller, faster, and more flexible companies to skip entire evolutionary stages of organizations, to overtake their competitors, and to create their own markets. This also applies to supplier management or, in a broader sense, to the management of the supply chain (Immerthal, 2017).

7.4.3 Supplier Selection

Every company has its specific strengths, the so-called core competencies, on which it must concentrate. Core competencies refer to skills, processes, technologies, knowledge advantages, or activities that a company can carry out better than the competition and has thus achieved a competitive advantage. Core competencies are the skills of a company to be able to do something better than others. This is a strategic competitive advantage. Core competencies are determined by four characteristics:

- Customer benefits.
- Imitation protection.
- Differentiation.
- Diversification.

The concept is a variation of the resource-based approach that has been opposed to the company's positioning in the market. When it comes to customer benefits, companies have to ask themselves whether sustainable added value can be provided for the customer based on their core competencies? The imitation protection, on the other hand, aims at exclusivity and unique selling points. Do the companies master the core competencies exclusively or can they be easily imitated by the competitor? Differentiation reflects the duration of the benefit. Does the core ability lead to a long-term and sustainable advantage over the competition? Diversification focuses on the markets and market segments. The key question here is whether the core capabilities offer potential access to new markets? Peripheral competencies, on the other hand, can be outsourced to suppliers, as these do not represent a competitive advantage. The relocation is called "outsourcing" and includes a corporate strategy that outsources individual product scopes, tasks, sub-areas, or even entire business processes to third-party companies. The selection of suppliers when relocating products, processes, and services is part of supplier management and the second phase after the supplier strategy, as Fig. 7.13 shows.

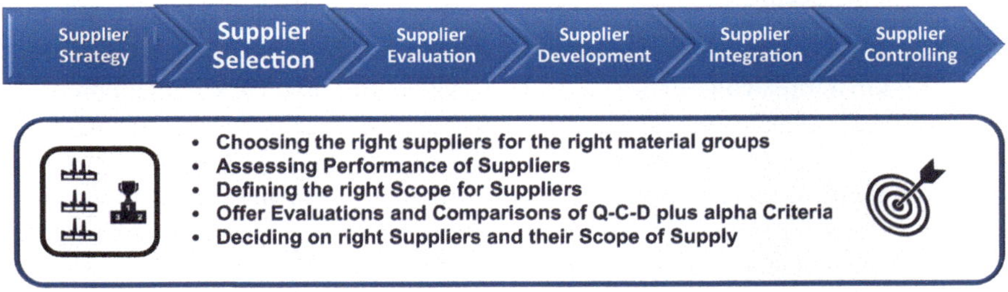

Fig. 7.13 Supplier selection. (Source: Author's source)

Supplier Selection Criteria

Before there can be a cooperation and a contractual agreement, a supplier selection must therefore take place on the basis of standardized selection criteria in a supplier selection matrix. Important criteria for the selection of suitable suppliers are shown in Fig. 7.14. One of the central criteria is the quality and nature of the products and services supplied. In addition, there are other important elements that need to be considered. An excellent supplier is not only characterized by high quality, low costs, and stable delivery performance, but also in other ways. The following criteria should therefore be considered when selecting a supplier:

- High quality of the goods and low error rate.
- A quality management system, for example, DIN EN ISO 90001: 2015.
- Distinct goodwill behavior on the part of the supplier if there are complaints.
- Constant readiness for delivery and high adherence to delivery dates.
- Strict adherence to promised delivery times or changes.
- Good accessibility and fixed contact persons at the supplier.
- High flexibility (enables quick reactions, e.g., to customer requests).
- Price guarantees (how long are negotiated prices promised).
- Few or well-founded or only moderate price increases in the past.

	of Supplier	Supplier 1	Supplier 2	Supplier 3	Supplier 4
1.	Quality - Delivery Quality - Field Quality - Warranty Processing	10	10	5	5
2.	Cost - Material Cost (Recurring) - Non-Recurring Cost - Cost Reduction Ideas	9	5	5	5
3.	Delivery - On-Time-Delivery (OTD) - Flexibility - Supply and Delivery Concepts, e.g. VMI	10	5	5	5
4.	Technology Leadership	5	5	0	5
5.	Relationship Management	10	10	0	5
6.	Innovation Capability	10	5	10	5
7.	Financial Strength	5	5	10	5
8.	Quality Management System, ISO 9001:2015	10	5	10	5
9.	Sustainability (CSR)	10	5	5	5
10.	Other Criteria	10	5	5	5
	Total Result	**89**	**60**	**55**	**50**

Fig. 7.14 Supplier selection matrix. (Source: Author's source)

- Financial stability and good credit ratings.
- Offer transparency (no hidden costs, fees, or minimum quantities).
- Sustainability and innovation.

Supplier Risk Management
Supplier selection includes measures that companies take before a need arises and a supplier is contacted. One of the main goals of supplier selection is to minimize risk. If a company chooses an unsuitable supplier, it is exposed to one or more of the following risks:

- Failure to perform the contract because a supplier is in financial difficulties.
- Poor performance of the contract.
- Supplier supplies poor quality.
- Lack of adherence to deadlines.
- The price for the services provided is too high.

Careful supplier selection is necessary in order to contain these risks. As part of the supplier evaluation, certain criteria are used to assess performance according to a defined system. In view of the trend that the integration of suppliers into company processes is becoming more and more important, the demands on suppliers are increasing. An ideal supplier portfolio is created when certain requirements are taken into account when making the selection.

- Selection of suppliers based on the supplier strategy.
- Cross-departmental supplier decisions and coordination processes.
- Selection based on objective and uniform evaluation criteria.
- Use of qualitative and quantitative criteria.
- Transparent, cost-, and time-efficient selection process.
- Selection of the most innovative and best supplier based on the selection criteria.

Quality management systems such as DIN EN ISO 9001:2015 also refer to a selection of suppliers taking into account central elements such as the selection and evaluation of suppliers. The standard indicates that the processes, products, and services provided meet the requirements and that the companies must determine and apply criteria for selection and evaluation.

7.4.4 Supplier Evaluation

The third phase in supplier management is the supplier evaluation. The instrument of the supplier evaluation comparable systematic assessment, which is to evaluate the performance of suppliers or service providers on the basis of previously defined characteristics, is mainly used for continuous and preventive supplier monitoring. During observation, the delivery services are regularly monitored in order to

Fig. 7.15 Supplier evaluation. (Source: Author's source)

identify changes in performance at an early stage. The supplier evaluation helps to an objective and systematic supplier selection, to the development of an optimal supplier portfolio, and to a continuous improvement process. The supplier evaluation is carried out with the help of certain evaluation criteria that are important for the evaluation of the supplier. Evaluation criteria are static and dynamic factors. Figure 7.15 shows an example of a supplier evaluation with internal and external company data.

Appropriate Selection of Evaluation Criteria

Depending on the complexity and industry spectrum, the departments of quality, purchasing, production, logistics, sales, data processing, finance, or research and development can be included in the process. Supplier management takes on the coordination of this interface between the company and its suppliers. The result of the supplier evaluation is recorded in the form of a holistic degree of fulfillment and can later be used for the strategy derivation and selection. The criteria used to evaluate suppliers should be defined and weighted appropriately for the company. The basis for determining the criteria are the goals that the company pursues in cooperation with the supplier, as well as special requirements for the supplier or for the product or service to be delivered. The assessment criteria are best determined with the help of a requirements analysis. Depending on the exact requirements a company places on the supplier and its product or service, the evaluation criteria can also be different and, above all, their weighting can be different. However, there are some criteria that must be considered in most cases when evaluating a supplier. These include the following:

- Quality of the product/frequency of errors.
- Costs and pricing conditions.
- Delivery time, delivery reliability, and logistics.
- Terms of payment.
- Capacity.
- Reliability/risk of delivery failure.
- Location and transport.

- Flexibility.
- Sustainability.

The most important methods for supplier evaluation are point evaluation methods, profile analysis, and price structure analysis. A point evaluation method for supplier evaluation is a relatively simple way of evaluating and comparing suppliers based on the allocation of weighted points or grades. A point evaluation procedure based on measurable key figures has the best informative value. As part of a profile analysis for supplier evaluation, supplier performance profiles are juxtaposed and compared. In this way, a profile analysis reveals the advantages and disadvantages of the individual suppliers. The biggest difference between the point evaluation method and the profile analysis is that the individual criteria are not weighted in the profile analysis and are also not combined into a single performance value. The price structure analysis is primarily about the criterion of the costs that a supplier causes. For the price structure analysis, the price criterion is therefore broken down into the supplier's cost and profit components. Material costs, hourly rates, purchase costs, etc., are to be named here as sub-criteria.

Supplier Evaluation as Predictive and Preventive Tool
These categories can be performance of the delivery, price evolution, production capacity, quality of management, technical capabilities, and service. Once there is a mechanism in place to periodically collect performance data from suppliers, the next step is to review the performance data. Ideally, the format that the data is in should lend itself to comparison and analysis. The data should also be in a format that can be quantified and scored. Many companies use a supplier evaluation or scorecard for this. Moreover, data from different types of assessments such as internal surveys, external surveys, and site visits should be incorporated into the analysis. Since most large organizations have many strategic suppliers and lots of data, it is almost impossible to obtain, organize, and review data from assessments effectively on a large scale without automation or software. When evaluating supplier performance data, the two things to look for (besides the obvious) are large changes in the performance metrics and overall trends. By identifying trends, a company can make projections about where the performance data will be in the future and can take action accordingly. Downward trends and deterioration in performance can signal a problem. Moreover, an abrupt change in performance metrics might signal an imminent problem. However, there could be another explanation. In this case, it makes sense to obtain more data from the supplier and to dig deeper to find the source of the problem. It may be a one-time anomaly or it could be something more. Monitoring supplier performance proactively can ensure that exceptions to policies are tracked and personnel and resources are assigned to address the problem quickly. Alerts and notifications can provide up-to-the-minute information to company personnel letting them know of changes in supplier performance.

Having a system that can take the assessment/scorecard data and can output it in a report or other format is helpful because members of the team can all access and review the information quickly and easily. The performance evaluation of Daimler

Fig. 7.16 Supplier evaluation tool. (Source: Author's source)

shown in Fig. 7.16 is an example of a supplier evaluation. For a supplier the performance is very bad, so that immediate actions have to be taken. Once there is sudden drop in supplier performance or a downward trend, it is important to take action quickly. Quick action can reduce the risk of disaster significant loss and gives the company the ability to take steps to prevent bad outcomes. Some actions that can be instigated include communicating with the supplier, conducting further evaluations, developing an improvement plan, or finding an alternative supplier. The actions taken may depend on many factors. These include the supplier's past performance, level of current performance, strategic importance, possible damages, and overall risk. One of the first things to do is to contact the supplier and find out what went wrong and why. The results of the performance assessment should be provided to the supplier and can create a basis for discussions.

The poor performance could have been the result of something outside of the supplier's control. It could have been a problem with process, personnel, a supplier, or something else. By communicating with the supplier, personnel can determine the cause of the problem and try to work with the supplier to make changes to bring the supplier performance back into compliance with the contract or with company policies. If the vendor does not have a good explanation or understanding of why the problem occurred, this may be a sign of trouble. Once the causes of a problem or set of problems have been identified, the next step is to devise a supplier improvement plan. The plan should be specific to the problem, should involve both company personnel and supplier personnel, and should involve a timeline for addressing the problem or bringing the performance into compliance. This process should also be a collaborative process and should be aimed at improving the overall supply chain. Even if a supplier's performance is acceptable, the company may wish to invest time and resources in developing suppliers and improving suppler performance. If the problem is too severe, cannot be fixed in a timely manner, or poses too great of a risk, the company may wish to stop doing business altogether with the supplier. This means that the company should carefully find an alternative source of supply and, if possible, reduce its reliance on the supplier in question. Emmett & Crocker (2009) and Dust et al. (2010) also propose using such criteria for evaluating the performance of suppliers. Interestingly, the interviews revealed that many companies have created sub-criteria of Q-C-D-SF according to their own needs. Regarding the question of how often manufacturing companies in the European transportation industry measure supplier performance, what they do internally with the data, and how they communicate the results to suppliers, several different answers were given. In the best case, data was updated on a weekly basis and made available to suppliers through a web-based tool. Concerning the evaluation of supplier performance, all interviewees outlined three to four categories, like traffic lights:

- Category one (green): acceptable with minor deviations and without conditions.
- Category two (yellow): acceptable with conditions.
- Category three (red): not acceptable.

In category one (green), the evaluation is approved and accepted with minor deviations. In category two (yellow), the evaluation is accepted with conditions. Conditional acceptance means that any subsequent action plan has to be approved by the supply management department. If a supplier shows severe deficiencies and is categorized three (red), the evaluation is not accepted. This can mean that a new supplier is not allowed to supply parts. In cases where category three is measured during serial production, specific supply management actions (e.g., management escalation, supplier audits, dual-sourcing) might be the consequence. Some of the challenges associated with supplier evaluation may be mitigated by the use of appropriate tools. For simple projects, a spreadsheet can be used. But as evaluations become more complex or more frequent, data management and data integrity issues become significant. Web Electronic RFP/ Tendering systems are often used for initial selection projects. Some products provide functionality for combining both initial selection and ongoing evaluation and benchmarking. Without few exceptions, there is no evaluation model which considers the maturity and level of relationship with suppliers. The doctoral thesis "Establishing a best practice model of supplier relationship management (SRM) for multinational manufacturing companies in the European transportation industry" makes suggestions for this aspect. There is also an M.B.A. thesis available, which includes the assessment of the Guanxi for supply management in China. Wider, within established supply management evaluation methodologies, the Carter 10 C's model is an internationally recognized approach (Emmett and Crocker, 2009). This model looks at aspects which should be evaluated before contracting and as part of the ongoing supplier performance appraisal. The ten categories can be summarized as the following:

1. Capacity (Does the organization have the capacity and capability to deliver the order?)
2. Competency (Is the organization, its people, or its process competent?)
3. Consistency (Does the organization produce a consistent output?)
4. Control of process (Can the organization control its process and offer flexibility?)
5. Commitment to Quality (Does the organization effectively monitor and manage quality?)
6. Cash (Has the organization got a strong enough financial base?)
7. Cost (Is the product or service offered at a competitive price?)
8. Culture (Are the supplier and buyer cultures compatible?)
9. Clean (Is the organization ethical, funded legitimately, and does not engage child labor?)
10. Communication efficiency (Does the organization have support technology of information integration?) to support collaboration and co-ordination in the supply chain.

Supplier Evaluation as Management Tool

As an essential component of supplier management, the supplier evaluation contributes to the control of supplier relationships, the development and maintenance of suppliers, and to improved quality and logistics performance. In order to achieve these goals in the best possible way and to get a global picture of the supplier's performance, an assessment is necessary, which not only focuses on so-called hard facts such as adherence to deadlines and quantities, but also on "soft facts" such as communication skills. Furthermore, the supplier evaluation is carried out globally according to the same standards and criteria, thus allowing a location-based evaluation and comparability of supplier performance. By expanding the evaluation criteria, we want to optimize future cooperation with our suppliers at all essential interfaces and reward constructive cooperation. The supplier evaluation is often carried out digitally using real-time data, but it can also be carried out monthly, quarterly, or semi-annually.

7.4.5 Supplier Development

Supplier development is the fourth phase in the supply management process as shown in Fig. 7.17. The term "supplier development" describes the activities and improvements of close, partnership-based and long-term relationships between customers and supplier networks within the value chain (Helmold & Terry, 2016). Hofbauer et al. (2016) describe supplier development as a continuous process to improve current or new suppliers. The basis of the development is the results of the supplier evaluation and key figures, which were described in the previous chapter. Emmett and Crocker (2009) define supplier development as a support process through direct or indirect measures. Here, too, the primary goal is to improve supplier performance (Emmett and Crocker, 2009). Figure 7.18 shows three categories,

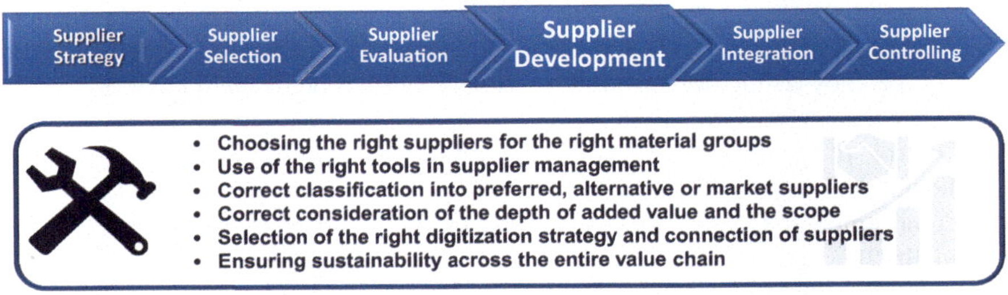

Fig. 7.17 Supplier development phases. (Source: Author's source)

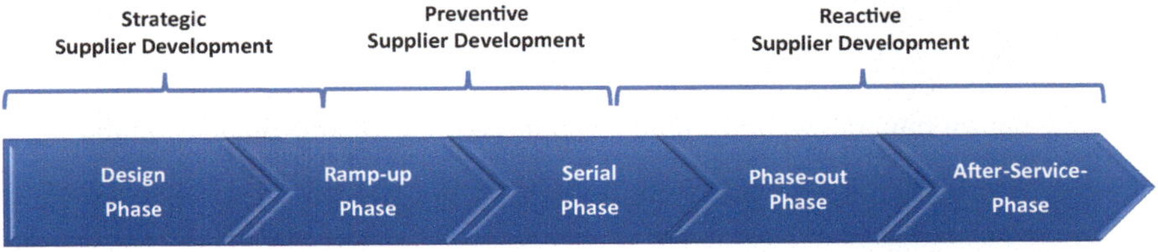

Fig. 7.18 Supplier development. (Source: Author's source)

strategic, preventive, and reactive supplier development, of supplier development in connection with the life cycle of a product. Product phases can be divided into development, start-up, series, phase-out, and after-service phases.

Strategic Supplier Development

The strategic supplier development already takes place in the development phase. Measures are usually transferred to the start-up phase of a product. The strategic approach to supplier development aims at the long-term, conscious, and continuous (further) development of the supplier's performance (potential). Strategic supplier development is initiated proactively to maintain competitive advantages over the long term. An essential difference to the merely reactive supplier development lies in the conscious search and selection of fields for development measures. The strategic supplier development is basically carried out through the direct participation of the buyer, who invests in supplier development measures and thus also in the suppliers themselves. An essential feature for the application of direct supplier development is a strategic partnership with the supplier, as amortization of the development activity over the relationship life cycle is required. The ability of a supplier to develop in the strategic sense means the creation of scope for action through options for the customer.

Preventive Supplier Development

Preventive supplier development aims at the early and forward-looking improvement of the suppliers on the basis of performance characteristics (performance characteristics) by the supplier management. Preventive measures are intended to prevent poor performance in the areas of quality, costs, or delivery performance and usually have a longer time horizon. The need is not yet acute, but sensors and early alarm systems (audits, supplier evaluation, incidents) show deviations in the performance of the suppliers. In the best-case scenario, preventive measures are defined at the start-up of a product before series production.

Reactive Supplier Development

Supplier development includes measures taken by the customer as a merely reactive improvement in the event of short-term deterioration in performance of a supplier in series, discontinuation, or after-service. It is usually caused by a current, specific problem in the exchange of services with the supplier (poor performance). The development measure has a short-term time horizon. The necessity arises from problems of the supplier, for example to deliver on time (security of supply in operations) as well as quality defects of the product or the service itself. With reactive supplier development, suppliers only become aware of the buyer when acute problems arise, so that are very short-term countermeasures (Troubleshooting). Often suppliers are encouraged to adhere to target agreements (based on key figures), the deficits of which have emerged from the supplier evaluation in the categories of quality, costs, or delivery performance.

7.4.6 Supplier Integration

Supplier integration means the integration of the supplier into the company's corporate structures and processes so that processes and systems are synchronized in order to be able to work together more effectively and successfully, as Fig. 7.19 shows. In the case of supplier integration, independent companies work together to optimize their processes and structures in order to coordinate them as well as possible to increase success. This can sometimes be a difficult undertaking, not just for the purchasing department. With a goal-oriented implementation, however, ideally a win-win situation arises for the market partners involved. Supplier integration begins where the company's own boundaries end. A prerequisite for a functioning integration of external actors in one's own process chains is therefore an opening to the selected partners. Likewise, there must be a willingness to change internal work

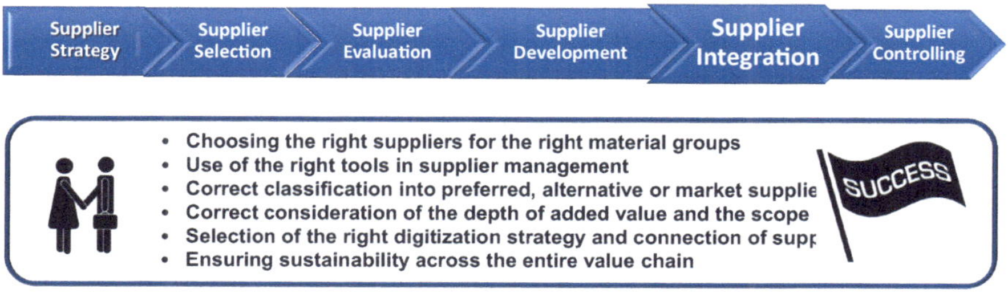

Fig. 7.19 Supplier integration. (Source: Author's source)

processes, ways of thinking, and also the key figure/bonus systems. Depending on the industry, there are numerous opportunities for close, long-term cooperation with suppliers. Important processes that need to be taken into account when integrating suppliers include the following areas:

- Research and Development: Even further ahead in the value creation process, the involvement of external partners starts in the research and development area. In this way, suppliers and customers can each contribute their specific know-how in joint project teams, bundle knowledge, and achieve synergy effects in the development of new products.
- Purchasing: Often a supplier integration starts due to the naturally existing contacts in the purchasing area, for example with the agreement of specific delivery windows or packaging units up to the fully responsible warehouse management by the supplier. For example, this requires the forward-looking provision of medium to long-term production and sales plans.
- Production: If supplier integration extends into the company's production processes, so-called supplier parks are often created in the direct vicinity of the customer, for example to implement just-in-time production.
- IT: An optimal exchange of information can only be guaranteed through IT standards and the joint use of corresponding IT applications.

Supplier Coaching

Supplier coaching is the systematic, collaborative improvement of supplier competencies through the measures carried out by supplier management together with the supplier. Coaching measures can be carried out with suppliers, distributors, and sub-suppliers, with external providers, in a (supplier) academy or in the seminar room. Coaching measures require special coaching competencies of the employees in supplier management. Coaching activities usually cover a specific subject area within the supply chain (project management, quality management, methods of lean production, etc.). No matter whether accompanying the project in the planning phase, accompanying series production or in the after-service phase, coaching measures lead to rapid improvements. In coaching, the focus of supplier management is on increasing product and process quality. Many companies have set up their own supplier academy (Porsche, ZF Friedrichshafen, Bosch). These help your own company to develop or coach new suppliers or high-risk suppliers to the required degree of maturity with regard to standards or quality requirements. The goal is the sustainable quality improvement of your suppliers. The most relevant factors are quality, time and costs. Actions must, for example the reduction of scrap and rework must be lean, flexible, efficient and innovative. Experts or supplier development coaches (Eng.: trainers, consultants) must ensure in all actions within the supply chain consider comprehensive quality, project and series support. This incorporates manufacturing and administrative processes of supplier parts. In addition, standardized supplier management programs and concepts also support the warranty and gurantee cost processes. The required requalification, qualification measures and upgrading measures in quality or complaint management actions must always focus on sustainability. All measures must focus on sustainability. Coaching in supplier management requires methodological and training skills through analysis and qualification.

International Purchasing Offices

International purchasing offices or global supplier management centers are part of internationalization and the change in the concept of supplier management. Multinational corporations such as Volkswagen, Daimler, Siemens, Bosch, or Bombardier have purchasing offices in regions such as China, India, or Eastern Europe that offer savings potential or are geographically distant from the parent company. Only in November 2015 did Deutsche Bahn open an international purchasing office in Shanghai. On the purchasing side, companies like Bombardier have more than six locations in China. Meanwhile, the added value share of Chinese products in sectors such as the automotive or rail industry is more than 20% to 30%. In terms of network-oriented supplier management, this is referred to as Best Cost Country Sourcing (BCCS). Traditional companies use terms like Global Sourcing (GS) or Low Cost Country Sourcing (LCCS). Of course, international purchasing or supplier management offices involve costs. For a purchasing office in China, you can get around EUR 50 thousand to EUR 80 thousand p.a. calculate, which makes up a full-time position in terms of full costs (1 full-time employee including salary and fringe benefits, office space, travel expenses, training, etc.). The costs for this have to be amortized through savings. It is not only large companies that benefit from international factor costs. Not only multinational corporations but also medium-sized companies have the opportunity to move on the international stage. The German Centers in China provide office space and production capacity in key industries / processes available. In addition, international purchasing cooperations can be set up in which the fixed costs for a purchasing office are shared. International offices in supplier management are centers of excellence and should not be confused here with the so-called "shared service" centers (SSC) that are increasingly emerging.

7.4.7 Supplier Controlling

Its origin has the controlling concept in practice. It was formed by Deyhle in analogy to the term "marketing" and is closely related to the tasks of controllers. The scientific discussion of the term "controlling" began on a broader scale in the 1970s. The first basic understanding of controlling in terms of time assigns it the task of providing business information for management purposes. In this sense, controlling should fulfill a business transparency function. Controlling is then concerned with the systematic definition and assignment ("breaking down") of the goals to be pursued, measuring their achievement, determining deviations between target and actual values, and developing measures to eliminate them. In other words, controlling aims to lead the company through and with the help of planning and the

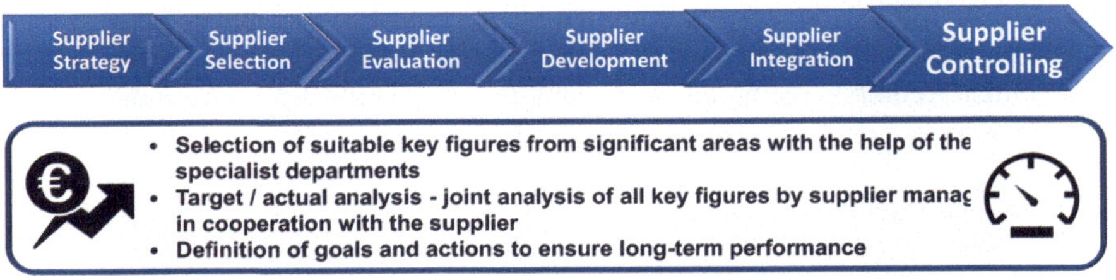

Fig. 7.20 Supplier controlling. (Source: Author's source)

resulting plans. The latter run through the entire company, from strategic to operational planning. Controlling in this sense can also be understood as a cybernetic process that is illustrated with the control loop of planning and control.

As the last phase in supplier management, supplier controlling assesses supplier performance, forms the basis of objective key figures, and forms the basis for supplier control and supplier management (Fig. 7.20). Typical key figures are the adherence to quantities and deadlines for the delivery of goods as well as the rate of complaints. Which key figures are used in individual cases depends on the selected supplier management scenario. There are differences, for example, between central, group-wide supplier control on the one hand and local, plant-related control on the other. The informative value of the key figures depends directly on the quality of the data that is included in the key figure calculation. In industries with little vertical integration, supplier controlling based on key figures is crucial for the success of your own products. The quality of supplier controlling is only as good as the quality of the underlying data. Four case studies from the automotive industry show the state of practice in supplier controlling and form the basis for an integrated architectural design. The architecture for data quality management in supplier controlling identifies the essential design elements and their relationships with one another.

The basis for performance measurement, the definition of goals, and the review of results in strategic and operational supplier management are a traceable system of indicators for each supplier. A key figure system consists of various key figures from different areas, which on the one hand can be calculated from the "hard" factors available in the system and, on the other hand, are determined from objectified subjective assessments, that is, "soft" factors. Excellent key figure systems enable the procuring company to carry out a 360-degree analysis through which preventive measures can be taken. The influence of the various key figures on an overall key figure results from their weighting. The key values determined in an evaluation cycle and thus the degree of target fulfillment form the basis for measures to further develop the supplier relationship in strategic and operational supplier management. The key figures that are calculated from automatically determined "hard" factors include quality data such as delivery quality, complaint rate, defects (measured in parts per million, PPM), cost and financial figures, delivery information, quantity reliability, sustainability factors, or innovation figures. Key figures can be kept in a supplier file, which contains important information about the supplier. Figure 7.21 shows key figures in supplier controlling.

Supplier Controlling KPI Dashboard	Quarter 1 Actual-Plan	Quarter 2 Actual-Plan	Quarter 3 Actual-Plan	Quarter 4 Actual-Plan
Purchasing Spend - Frame Contracts (Euro) - Savings (%) - Usage of Frame Contracts (%) - ...				
Process KPI - Quantity of Orders (Euro and %) - Quantity of Frame Contracts (Euro and %) - Quantity of Deliveries (# and %) - ...				
Quality - Delivery Quality (%) - Field Quality (%) - Warranty Process and Cycle Time (Time/Case) - ...				
Cost - Material Cost (Euro) - Non-recurring Cost, e,g. Design (Euro) - Cost Saving Initiatives (Euro and %) - ...				
Dellivery - On-Time-Delivery (%) - Flexibility (Change of Quantity, Dates etc.) (%) - Additional Deliveries (%) - ...				
Financial KPI - Turnover (Euro) - Profitability (%) - Productivity (%) - ...				

Fig. 7.21 Supplier performance dashboard. (Source: Author's source)

7.5 Control via Digital Supplier Dashboards and Cockpits

A supply or supplier dashboard (or cockpit) provides management with an at-a-glance awareness of the status of certain performance indicators such as inventory and supply operations (see Fig. 7.22). Thus, it is possible to respond to challenges before any incident is happening. The supplier dashboard is showing key operational indicators and trends like NCG, OTD, outgoing quality, and sub-supplier performance. Indicators can vary from case to case. A supplier dashboard or supplier cockpit is a one-page summary of the supplier's critical performance indicators as shown in the example above. The dashboard is supposed to give managers a quick overview of deteriorations and status on quality, delivery or other critical issues. It enables the supply manager to take immediate actions based on a graph or a coloring.

7.6 Case Study: Apple's Outsourcing Strategy

Apple's commercial triumph rests in part on the outsourcing of its consumer electronics production to Asia. Drawing on extensive fieldwork at China's leading exporter, the Taiwanese-owned Foxconn, the power dynamics of the buyer-driven supply chain are analyzed in the context of the national terrains that mediate or even

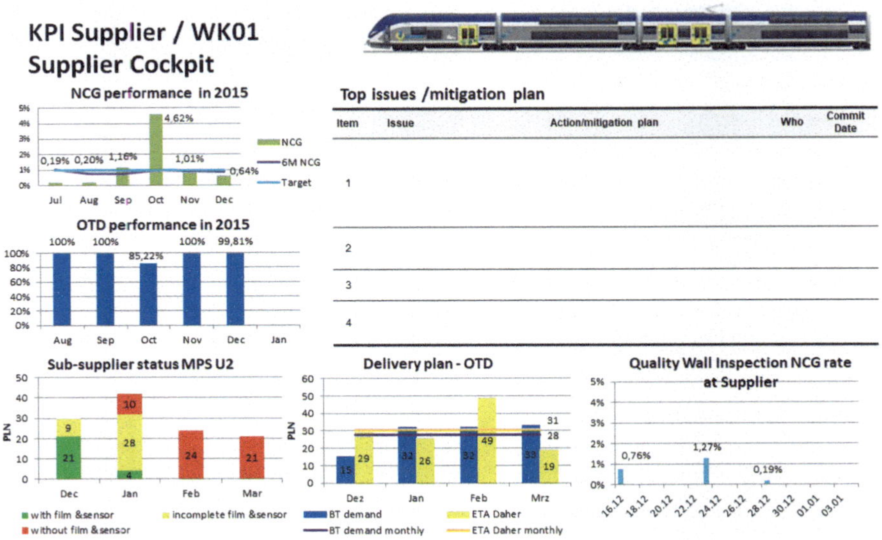

Fig. 7.22 Supplier dashboard. (Source: Helmold and Terry (2016))

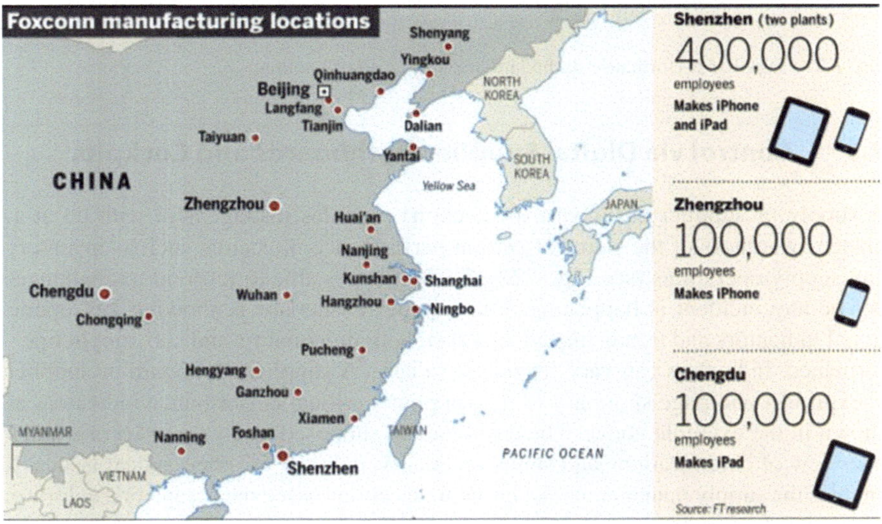

Fig. 7.23 Foxconn's manufacturing sites for Apple

accentuate global pressures. Power asymmetries assure the dominance of Apple in price setting and the timing of product delivery, resulting in intense pressures and illegal overtime for workers. Responding to the high-pressure production regime, the young generation of Chinese rural migrant workers engages in a crescendo of individual and collective struggles to define their rights and defend their dignity in the face of combined corporate and state power. As the principal manufacturer of products and components for Apple, Taiwanese company Foxconn currently employs 1.4 million workers in China alone. Arguably, then, just as Apple has achieved a globally dominant position, described as "the world's most valuable brand", so too have the fortunes of Foxconn been entwined with Apple's success, facilitating Foxconn's rise to become the world's largest electronics contractor. Figure 7.23 shows the employees and the location of factories in China for Apple iPhone and iPad production.

References

Aberdeen Group. (2005). *Assuring supply and mitigating risks in an uncertain economy*. Supply Risk Management Benchmark. Boston. 11/2005.

Dust, R., Gleiser, M. & Gürtler, B. (2010). Total Supplier Risk Monitoring. Lieferfähigkeit präventiv absichern. MQ, Magazine for Quality and Management, 1–2, 27–29.

Emmett, St. & Crocker, B. (2009). Excellence in Supplier Management. How to better manage contracts with suppliers and add value. Best practices in Supplier Relationship and Supplier Development. Cambridge: Cambridge Academic.

Helmold, M., Einmahl, R., Rassmann, K., & Carvalho, L. (2020). In IUBH Discussion paper. Lessons from the COVID-19 Situation: Rethinking Global Supply Chain Networks and Strengthening Supply Management in Public Procurement in Germany. Abgerufen 31.10.2020. https://www.iubh-university.de/wp-content/uploads/DP_Logistik_Helmold_4_2020fin.pdf.

Helmold, M., & Terry, B. (2016). *Lieferantenmanagement 2030. Wertschöpfung und Sicherung der Wettbewerbsfähigkeit in digitalen und globalen Märkten*. Springer Wiesbaden.

Helmold, M. & Terry, B. (2021). *Operations and supply management 4.0. Industry insights, case studies and best practices*. Springer: Cham.

Hofbauer, G. et al. (2016). Lieferantenmanagement: Die wertorientierte Gestaltung der Lieferbeziehung (Betriebswirtschaftslehre kompakt). Oldenbourg München.

Immerthal, L. (2017). Lieferantenmanagement im Wandel. Die Digitalisierung im Lieferantenmanagement beginnt mit guter Kommunikation. In Beschaffung aktuell. Abgerufen 31.10.2020. https://beschaffung-aktuell.industrie.de/einkauf/die-digitalisierung-im-lieferantenmanagement-beginnt-mit-guter-kommunikation/.

Kolev, G., & Obst, T. (2020). Die Abhängigkeit der deutschen Wirtschaft von internationalen Lieferketten. Institut der deutschen Wirtschaft. IW-Report Nr. 16. 23. April 2020. Abgerufen 31.10.2020. https://www.iwkoeln.de/studien/iw-reports/beitrag/galina-kolev-thomas-obst-die-abhaengigkeit-der-deutschen-wirtschaft-von-internationalen-lieferketten.html.

Trkman, P. & McCormack, K. (2009). Supply chain risks in turbulent environments – a conceptual model for supply chain network risk. International Journal of Production Economics, 119(2), 247–258.

8 Financial SCRM and Mitigation Management

Enable Action by removing barriers.

—*John Kotter*

8.1 Financial Performance in Supply Chain Risk Management

Financial performance is a subjective measure of how well a firm can use assets from its primary mode of business and generate revenues. This term is also used as a general measure of a firm's overall financial health over a given period of time and can be used to compare similar firms across the same industry or to compare industries. There are many different ways to measure financial performance, but all measures should be taken in aggregation. Line items such as revenue from operations, operating income, or cash flow from operations can be used, as well as total unit sales. Furthermore, the analyst or investor may wish to look deeper into financial statements and seek out margin growth rates or any declining debt. Financial performance analysis includes analysis and interpretation of financial statements in such a way that it undertakes full diagnosis of the profitability and financial soundness of the business. The financial analyst program provides vital methodologies of financial analysis.

M. Helmold et al., *Supply Chain Risk Management*, Management for Professionals, https://doi.org/10.1007/978-3-030-90800-3_8

8.2 The Balance Sheet, Income Statement, and Cash Statement

8.2.1 The Balance Sheet

The balance sheet is a financial statement that reports a company's assets, liabilities, and shareholders' equity at a specific point in time and provides a basis for computing rates of return and evaluating its capital structure as shown in Fig. 10.1. It is a financial statement that provides a snapshot of what a company owns and owes, as well as the amount invested by shareholders. It is used alongside other important financial statements such as the income statement and statement of cash flows in conducting fundamental analysis or calculating financial ratios. It provides an overview of how well the company is managing assets and liabilities. Analysts can find information about long-term vs. short-term debt on the balance sheet. They can also find information about what kind of assets the company owns and what percentage of assets are financed with liabilities vs. stockholders' equity (Fig. 8.1).

8.2.2 Income Statement

The income statement provides a summary of operations for the entire year. The income statement starts with sales or revenue and ends with net income. Also referred to as the profit and loss statement, the income statement provides the gross profit margin, the cost of goods sold, operating profit margin, and net profit margin. It also provides an overview of the number of shares outstanding as well as a comparison against prior year performance. Figure 10.2 outlines the P & L statement with a loss (red) or a profit (green) (Fig. 8.2).

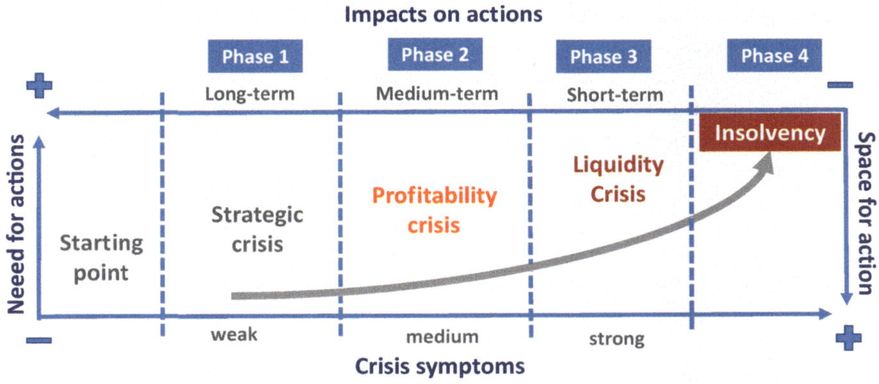

Fig. 8.1 Balance sheet. (Source: Author's own figure)

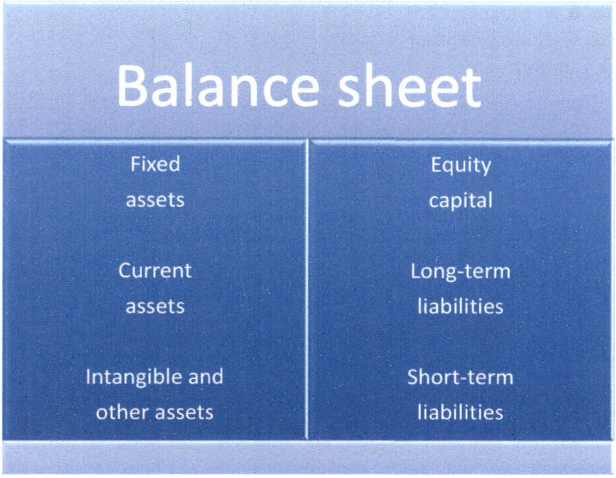

Fig. 8.2 P & L account. (Source: Author's own figure)

8.2.3 Cash Flow Statement

The cash flow statement is a combination of both the income statement and the balance sheet. For certain experts, the income articulation is the most vital monetary statement since it gives a compromise between total compensation and cash flow. This is where analysts can see how much the company is spending on stock repurchases, dividends, and capital expenditures. It also provides the source and uses of cash flow from operations, investing, and financing. Financial analysts often assess the firm's production and productivity performance (total business performance), profitability performance, liquidity performance, working capital performance, fixed assets performance, fund flow performance, and social performance. Various financial ratios analysis include the following:

1. Working capital analysis
2. Financial structure analysis
3. Activity analysis
4. Profitability analysis

8.2.4 Financial Ratios

Financial PM ratio analysis is the process of investigating the relationship between various balance sheet, income statement, and cash flow statement accounts. Analysts may use ratios to investigate these relationships across multiple time periods through what is commonly called a trend analysis or between various alternative target companies in what is traditionally labelled or a cross-section analysis.

Fig. 8.3 Financial PM ratios. (Source: Author's own figure)

- Profitability ratios: measure a company's ability to generate profitable sales from its assets
- Liquidity ratios: measure a company's ability to meet its short-term obligations
- Solvency ratios: measure a company's ability to meet its long-term obligations
- Activity ratios: measure how efficiently a company performs day-today tasks, for example, collection of receivables
- Other ratios: measure other important elements in financial PM (asset turnover or growth rate) (Fig. 8.3)

8.2.5 Financial Crisis Symptoms

Financial distress or related financial emergency is a term in finance, and it is a situation in which an organization faces extreme budgetary issues and battles in satisfying money-related commitments, for example, obligations, credit installments (Gabler Wirtschaftslexikon, 2018). The term is utilized to show a condition when guarantees to loan bosses of a company are broken or respected with trouble. In the event that money related misery cannot be relieved, it will ultimately prompt indebtedness. Financial distress is typically associated with certain expenses to the organization. These are known as expenses of financial distress. Financial distress refers to a condition in which a company cannot meet, or has difficulty paying off, its financial obligations to its creditors, typically due to high fixed costs, illiquid assets, or revenues sensitive to economic downturns. Recent examples like the company Jack Wolfskin show that companies must anticipate and prevent a situation, which puts the company under stress (Handelsblatt, 2017). A financial crisis can be prevented and involves immediate actions and related negotiations with stakeholders like banks, employees, suppliers, or investors (Helmold et al., 2019). A company under financial distress can incur costs related to the situation, such as more expensive financing, opportunity costs of projects, and less productive employees. Employees of a distressed firm usually have lower morale and higher stress caused by the increased chance of insolvency, which threatens them to be forced out of their jobs (Helmold et al., 2019). There are often alarm signals indicating the upcoming crisis as outlined by various authors (Schmuck, 2013; Müller, 1986). Alarm signals like decreasing revenues, high operating cost, and low profits usually indicate that a company is not in a good financial health situation (Schmuck, 2013). Struggling to reach profitability targets over a longer period indicates a business cannot sustain itself from internal funds and needs to raise capital externally (Helmold et al., 2019). This raises the company's business risk and significantly lowers its credit rating with banks, lenders, suppliers, or investors (Schmuck, 2013). Limiting access to funds typically leads to liquidity issues and results often in a company failing as shown in Fig. 8.4 (Four phases model of Müller; Müller, 1986). Poor sales growth or decline indicates the market is not positively receiving a company's products or services based on its business model. When extreme marketing activities result in no growth, the market may not be satisfied with the offerings, and the company may close down. Likewise, if a company offers poor quality in its products or services, consumers start buying from competitors, eventually forcing a business to close its doors. When debtors take too much time paying their debts to the company, cash flow may be severely stretched. The business may be unable to pay its own liabilities. The risk is especially enhanced when a company has one or two major customers (Helmold et al., 2019). Müller describes four phases from a strategic crisis, the profitability crisis, the liquidity crisis to the insolvency (Müller, 1986; Helmold et al., 2019). The four phases of a financial crisis are described Müller by the strategic crisis, the profitability crisis, the liquidity crisis, and the insolvency. Müller describes the strategic crisis as threat to the potential and substance of a company, which occurs due to inadequate strategies in terms of differentiation, knowledge, innovation, or cost advantages (Schmuck, 2013). In this strategic phase, market needs and elements are not fully taking into account, so that the

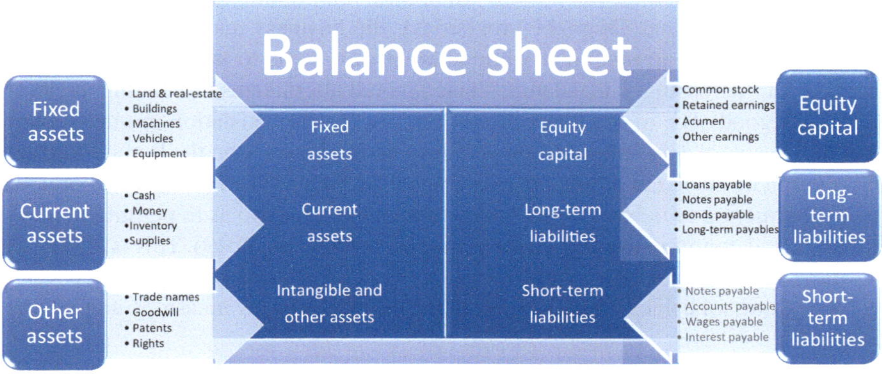

Fig. 8.4 Phases to financial insolvency. (Source: Helmold et al., 2019, adapted from Müller's four phases model. Müller, 1986)

foundation of the company is gradually weakening (Helmold et al., 2019). In this situation, the symptoms are weak, the corrective actions are long term, and the need for actions is rather low compared to the following phases (Müller, 1986). The strategic phase is followed by the profitability crisis, which is characterized by signs of a weak financial performance in terms of revenues, cost, cash, and profitability (Schmuck, 2013). Signs in this phase are stronger, often resulting in a loss, struggling to achieve targeted financial ratios or non-achievement of profit targets (Schmuck, 2013). The third phase is the liquidity crisis, in which a company is not capable of meeting its financial obligations anymore (Schmuck, 2013). This situation is severe as the cash situation and balance is not sufficient to pay the debts. As the credit rating decreases in this phase, companies tend to borrow money with higher interest rates or to prolong payments to suppliers, employees, or banks where possible (Helmold et al., 2019). The last phase of the model by Müller is the insolvency (Müller, 1986). Insolvency is the state of being unable to pay the money owed, by a person or company, on time. Those companies in a state of insolvency are said to be insolvent. There are two forms: cash-flow insolvency and balance-sheet insolvency. Cash-flow insolvency is when a person or company has enough assets to pay what is owed, but does not have the appropriate form of payment. For example, a person may own a large house and a valuable car, but not have enough liquid assets to pay a debt when it falls due. Cash-flow insolvency can usually be resolved by negotiation. For example, the bill collector may wait until the car is sold and the debtor agrees to pay a penalty. Balance-sheet insolvency is when a company does not have enough assets to pay all of their debts. The person or company might enter bankruptcy, but not necessarily. Once a loss is accepted by all parties, negotiation is often able to resolve the situation without bankruptcy. A company that is balance-sheet insolvent may still have enough cash to pay its next bill on time. However, most laws will not let the company pay that bill unless it will directly help all their creditors. For example, an insolvent farmer may be allowed to hire people to help harvest the crop, because not harvesting and selling the crop would be even worse for his creditors. In some jurisdictions, it is illegal under the insolvency laws for a company to continue in business while insolvent. In others (like the USA with its insolvency law and Chap. 11 provisions), the business may continue under a declared protective arrangement while alternative options to achieve recovery are worked out. Increasingly, legislatures have favored alternatives to winding up companies for good. The major focus of modern insolvency legislation in many countries and business debt restructuring practices no longer rests on the liquidation and elimination of insolvent entities but on the remodeling of the financial and organizational structure of debtors experiencing a financial crisis so as to permit the rehabilitation and continuation of their business (Helmold et al., 2019). This is known as restructuring, business turnaround, financial crisis mitigation, or business recovery. Implementing a business restructuring plan includes various measures and can be described.

8.3 Restructuring and Turnaround Actions

8.3.1 Definition of Restructuring

Restructuring or financial turnaround actions (mitigations) are sets of corporate activities taken when significantly modifying the debt, operations, or structure of a company as a means of potentially eliminating financial harm and improving the business. These mitigations require communication and negotiations with all affected stakeholders as outlined by Helmold et al. (Helmold et al., 2019). When a company is having trouble making payments on its debt and financial commitments, it will often restructure to pay its debts and to improve financial and operational performance (Helmold et al., 2019). A company restructures its operations or structure by cutting costs, such as payroll, operations, supplier's cost, or reducing its size through the sale of assets. Restructuring is often linked to external experts who help the company to restructure its operations, performance, and financials. Restructuring means to have the appropriate actions and leads to many discussions and negotiations with stakeholders like employees, suppliers, or customers to fundamentally improve the financial situation of a company (Schmuck, 2013; Helmold et al., 2019). Due to the vital significance, restructuring plans must be designed, executed, and controlled by top management (Helmold et al., 2019). Restructuring involves top management and negotiations with stakeholders. (Source adapted from Helmold et al., 2019.) The four types of restructuring can be outlined as shown in Fig. 8.5:

- Strategic restructuring
- Structural restructuring
- Restructuring for profit improvements
- Financial restructuring

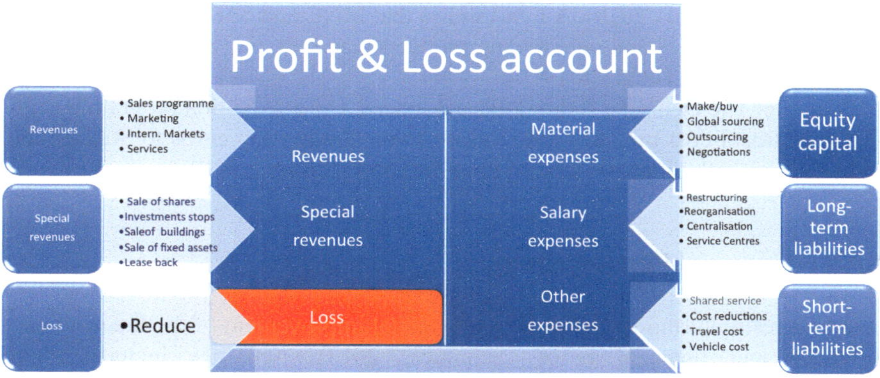

Fig. 8.5 Restructuring ways for financial turnaround. (Source: Author's own figure)

8.3.2 Strategic Restructuring

Strategic restructuring means to redefine the strategy of an enterprise from top to down. The strategic restructuring will result in a new strategic pyramid including elements like mission, vision, and strategic objectives.

8.3.3 Structural Restructuring

Structural restructuring targets the structure of a company and has an impact on organization and the existing structure. Aligning the organization and re-align operations lead to more efficient and effective processes (often central, decentral, or a hybrid form) with smoother roles and responsibilities. Structural restructuring is often pursued from a polycentric management toward a matrix organization and requires systematic and suitable information systems and controlling structures (Helmold et al., 2019).

Example: Volvo Truck re-aligned is organization to a brand-centric organization, thus improving efficiency and effectiveness (Deal, 2016).

8.3.4 Restructuring for Profit Improvements

Restructuring for profit improvements target the revenues and expenses (Helmold et al., 2019). Actions comprise anything that will increase revenues like a special sales program, increased focus on cash cows in sales, or deletion of unprofitable products or services. In addition, the company will take drastic actions in order to minimize expenses and cost. This is normally all areas of expenses. Companies are often tackling cost drivers like material, personnel, or operating cost by global sourcing, outsourcing to shared service centers, or the implementation of lean principles (Helmold et al., 2019). A trend shows that MNC and SME are concentrating on core competencies and outsourcing products, services, and activities to foreign companies (Helmold et al., 2019).

Example: The Deutsche Bahn (DB) announced a cost reduction program by cutting operational cost by 300 million euros from 800 million euros to 500 million euros to drastically improve financial performance (Reuters, 2018).

8.3.5 Financial Restructuring

Financial restructuring includes the fundamental improvement of the financial performance and financial ratios (Schmuck, 2013). Activities include assets Improvements, which can be seen in the balance sheet (see Fig. 13.3), the review of elements in the profit and loss sheet, and cash initiatives. Cash improvements can be realized through pulling ahead customer payments, advanced revenue income, and as late as possible outflows of payments to employees, suppliers, banks, or other stakeholders (Olfert, 2013, 2015). Late payments to suppliers and other stakeholders can be negotiated through the agreement of extended payment terms (normally from 30 days to 60 or 90 days).

Example: The Company Zalando introduced an initiative to extend payment terms to suppliers to minimum 90 days in order to improve the cash situation (Zalando, 2019).

8.4 Financial Effects on Balance Sheet, Income Statement, and Cash Flow

8.4.1 Financial Effects on Balance Sheet

The balance sheet is a statement of the financial position of a business which states the assets, liabilities, and owner's equity at a particular point in time. In other words, the balance sheet illustrates your business's net worth. The balance sheet may also have details from previous years so you can do a back-to-back comparison of two consecutive years. This data will help you track your performance, and will identify ways in which one can build up your finances and see where you need to improve. One can also use the balance sheet to determine how to meet the financial obligations and figure out the best ways in which you can use credit to finance the company's operations. The balance sheet is the most important of the three main financial statements used to illustrate the financial health of a business. Figure 8.6 illustrates the areas of mitigation actions and how the actions influence the situation of the balance sheet (Olfert, 2013, 2015). A standard company balance sheet has two sides: assets, on the left and financing, which itself have two parts, liabilities and ownership equity, on the right. The main categories of assets are usually listed first and typically in order of liquidity. Assets are followed by the liabilities. The difference between the assets and the liabilities is known as equity or the net assets or the net worth or capital of the company and according to the accounting equation, net worth must equal assets minus liabilities. Another way to look at the balance sheet equation is that total assets equals liabilities plus owner's equity. Looking at the equation in this way shows how assets were financed: either by borrowing money (liability) or by using the owner's money (owner's or shareholders' equity). Balance sheets are usually presented with assets in one section and liabilities and net worth in the other section with the two sections "balancing." In a financial crisis, companies will sell unnecessary fixed assets like land and real estate, buildings, or machines in order to obtain additional revenues and cash. Investments with a high

Fig. 8.6 Balance sheet. (Source: Author's own figure)

amount of funding must be limited to necessary purchases; in some cases, it is possible to lease instead of purchasing. Second, inventories and supplies (assets) must be evaluated. Inventories must be reduced or fully eliminated, so that any associated cost of working capital can be reduced. A recommendation in this context is the agreement of vendor-managed inventories (VMIs), in which the suppliers (vendors) take care of their inventories. Vendor-managed inventory (VMI) is a supply chain management (SCM) and logistics tool, in which a supplier of goods, usually the manufacturer, is responsible for optimizing and managing the inventory held by himself or a warehouse attributor (Helmold & Terry, 2016). VMI requires a communication link, usually typically electronic data interchange or internet platforms, that provides the supplier with the customers' sales figures and forecasts. Based on forecasts the suppliers keep and own the inventory until the goods are called off by the customer. The benefits of a vendor-managed inventory system include better inventory accuracy, forecasting, and service (Helmold & Terry, 2016). Other assists like patents, intellectual proprietary rights, or brand names might also help to improve the financial situation can be liquidated into cash. An example is the Ford Motor Company, which faced financial distress in 2006. Ford had to get a life-saving loan by providing the rights of the Ford logo to investors to receive money (Vlasic, 2012). The other side of the balance sheet contains equity capital, which are shares and loans. In this area, companies have to negotiate with investors on additional investments or shares. The banks play an important role when negotiating on loan conditions, repayments, or shifting short-term debts into long-term debts (Helmold et al., 2019). In many cases, companies also pay their invoices from suppliers or salaries later in order to improve the balance sheet (Helmold et al., 2019).

8.4.2 Financial Effects on Income Statement

The profit and loss account (P & L statement or account) or company statement is a financial statement that summarizes the revenues, costs, and expenses incurred during a specified period. The P & L account provides information about a company's ability or inability to generate profit by increasing revenue, reducing costs, or both. Some refer to the P & L statement as a statement of profit and loss, income statement, statement of operations, statement of financial results or income, earnings statement, and expense statement. Figure 8.7 shows a P & L account including revenues (left side) and cost or expenses of the company (right side) (Olfert, 2015). Revenues contain sales or special revenues from activities that are not directly linked with the business of the company. Expenses normally include material expenses, salary expenses, and other expenses (Olfert, 2015). The trend to concentrate on core competencies lead in many organizations to a high portion of material expenses.

Figure 8.8 outlines the way restructuring is aimed at improving the revenue situation with a parallel reduction of expenses in order to become profitable (profit in green). Cost reduction initiatives targets elements, for which the customer is not willing to pay. These elements are described as waste and must be eliminated or

Fig. 8.7 P & L account with improvement actions. (Source: Author's own figure)

Fig. 8.8 Profit improvements. (Source: Author's own figure)

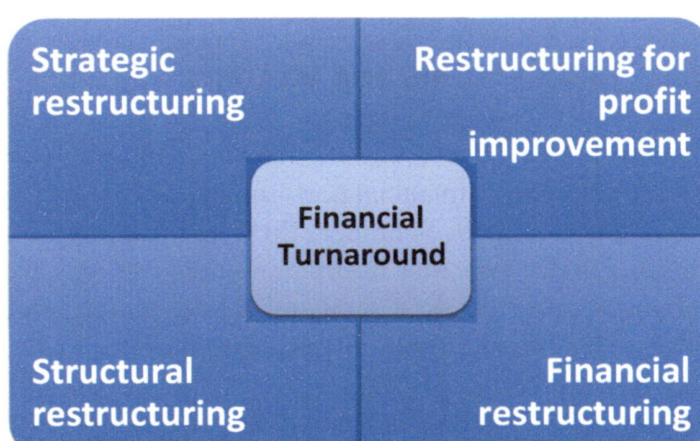

reduced. The cost emphasis focuses therefore on the efficiency of the firm's processes. General cost reduction efforts (e.g., lean management, downsizing) do not necessarily improve efficiency, but quality efforts that reduce costs always do. Successful programs tend to increase the productivity of quality efforts by reducing the input (labor and materials) required to produce a unit of output. These improvements can be incremental (continuous improvement) or discontinuous (process reengineering). In either case, the focus is internal and the goal is to reduce costs.

Customer satisfaction improvements are sought only indirectly, through such results as increased reliability or lower prices. Cost reduction programs thus transfer their savings to the bottom line directly and can be applied to all areas of the value chain.

Actions for profitability improvements can contain numerous activities throughout the value chain of a company. Most effective actions normally occur in the area of material, design, sales, or personnel cost as outlined in Tables 8.1 and 8.2.

Revenues must be increased by the sales and marketing function through negotiations with suppliers.

8.4.3 Financial Effects on Cash Flow

The cash flow statement is a tool which shows the movements of cash and cash equivalents in and out of the business. Companies must have a good cash situation as chronic negative cash flows are symptomatic of troubled businesses (Olfert, 2013, 2015). On the sales side, it is recommended to negotiate on advanced and early payments via marketing and sales management, whereas on the supply side the procurement function must negotiate standard and longer-term payment terms, for example, 60 or 90 days after receipt of goods. In severe cases, it also possible to negotiate with banks, investors, or employees on later payments of repayments, dividends, or salaries (Helmold et al., 2019). All actions need to be thoroughly taken into account, including positive and negative effects (Schmuck, 2013).

8.5 Recommendations for Turnaround

8.5.1 Restructuring and Strategy

Restructuring the business offers many advantages to companies to achieve successfully a turnaround in financial performance as outlined by Helmold et al. or Schmuck (Helmold et al., 2019; Schmuck, 2013). A company can face new opportunities by realigning and restructure business models and organizations. A restructuring plan must incorporate detailed financial ratios, which affect positively balance sheet, profit and loss account, and the cash situation.

An integral part of restructuring is the process to bring in all key stakeholders as necessary to increase the effectiveness of the turnaround plan (Helmold et al., 2019).

8.5.2 Specialist Involvement

Restructuring necessitates knowledge and the urge of actions which improve the financial side of the company quickly (Schmuck, 2013). If a company struggles with debt management issues or serious cash flow pressures of any sort as a business, then it is strongly recommended by various authors to get external support to get specialist advice on the most essential subjects at key moments. Impartial expert

Table 8.1 Cost reduction initiatives

Cost area	Action and area of negotiation	Generic strategy
Material and purchase cost	Material cost savings through commercial negotiations	Commercial savings
Material and purchase cost	Material cost savings through global sourcing	Global sourcing
Material and purchase cost	Material cost savings through economies of scale and bundling	Economies of scale
Material and purchase cost	Material cost savings through improved logistics management	Logistics optimization
Material and purchase cost	Material cost savings through value engineering	Value engineering
Engineering and design cost	Engineering offshoring to best cost countries	Outsourcing, offshoring
Engineering and design cost	Optimum design and target costing	Design-to-cost
Operational and production cost	Lean production services	Just-in-time (JIT) production system
Operational and production cost	Shifting production to foreign operations	Internationalization
Operational and production cost	Deciding to outsource labor intensive processes	Make or buy
Operational and production cost	Increasing efficiency through machines and robots	Automatization
Personnel cost	Reducing total amount and budget of salaries and wages	Optimization of work force
Personnel cost	Reducing head count reduction	Organizational alignment
Personnel cost	Shifting services to shared service centers	Outsourcing, offshoring
Marketing and sales cost	Reducing marketing and advertising cost	Advertising
Marketing and sales cost	Optimization of distribution cost	Distribution
Marketing and sales cost	Closing unprofitable niche markets	Downsizing
Stationaries	Suspension of any new orders	Elimination
Training cost	Eliminating all training cost. Introducing train-the-trainer concept	Train-the-trainer
Energy cost	Reducing waste, recycling, and disposal cost	Sustainability
Inventories	Shifting to inventory to suppliers and customers	VMI
Cost for buildings and maintenance	Selling buildings and leasing back	Lease back

Source: Author's own table, adopted from Helmold et al. (2019)

Table 8.2 Revenue increase initiatives

Revenue increase	Action and area of negotiation	Strategy
Sales programs	Approaching existing customers to buy more	Sales promotion
Additional products and services	Adding new products and services	Value add extension and growth
Adding new products and services	Designing and selling new products	Diversification
Entering new markets	Moving to foreign markets like China	International market growth
Approaching new target groups	Considering new customer groups	Market growth and customer segmentation

Source: Author's own table, adopted from Helmold et al. (2019)

advice is always available and for companies in distress, third-party support and guidance for directors can make a huge difference for the better (Schmuck, 2013).

8.5.3 Taking all Financial Options

Even if your company's credit rating is not great or you have been rejected for loans by mainstream lenders, there are other finance options available that might be able to help you overcome your funding problems.

Increasingly popular alternative funding solutions include invoice factoring and discounting, while asset financing and refinancing are other options well worth considering. Crowd funding and peer-to-peer lending are also major growth areas at present, with both markets adding valuable variety to the funding equation for small companies with big ideas.

8.5.4 Liquidation

When your business is facing up to significant financial problems, then it could be that you will need to take drastic action. Liquidating assets that are not fundamental to the way your company operates can help raise cash and open up the prospect of satisfying creditors and overcoming the worst of your debt-related issues.

It is important to be clear in understanding precisely what is and is not essential to your business in terms of tangible assets. Arriving at decisions on these points will likely require careful consideration but by liquidating equipment, tools, vehicles, inventory, or property assets, you can give your company a potentially vital lifeline as you look to climb out of debt and move toward sustainability.

8.5.5 End Non-essential Relationships

In reality it is necessary, that tough and significant decisions have to be made in the longer-term interests of a business on a higher management level, when the company is under financial pressure and when liabilities or debts are increasing.

It could be that long-serving employees have to be let go and relationships with trusted suppliers have to end. From the perspective of directors, this is can be a difficult process but, where the alternative is your company going out of business entirely, it is preferable and advisable to take that kind of tough choices before they are out of your hands entirely.

8.6 Case Study: Tesla and Its Financial Strategy

For any organization, performance management plays an important role in monitoring and ensuring that the organization meets all of its prescribed goals and targets, as well as in communicating these achievements effectively to its key external stakeholders. In the case of Tesla, the company imposes various techniques and measurement to keep track of the company's performance, which is primarily based on productivity. For example, the company measures its manufacturing performance based on the number of cars produced a day; for the customer service division, it considers the number of inquiries resolved, emails answered, and complaints handled. In addition, Tesla also establishes Key Performance Indicators (KPI) to monitor its production, inventory, and generally assess the success of achieving the goals within the predetermined duration. In fact, for prospective managers at Tesla Inc., familiarity and experience with applying and monitoring KPIs for a particular area are not just huge advantages but also part of job responsibilities. Tesla's key stakeholders include its investors, directors, employees, suppliers, shareholders, partners, the government, financial institutes, and the public. Communicating performance to these entities is not limited to disclosing the company's financial reports but also informs them about the company's visions, strategies, targets, milestones, key issues, and major accomplishments.

Tesla Motors Inc. has maintained regular and efficient communication with its stakeholders. The company publishes its annual report on its website, disclosing key financial data, the company's strengths and values, potential risk factors, its products, services, network and infrastructures, and other important information. The company also communicates with its stakeholders by organizing annual meetings for its stockholders with webcasts for those who cannot attend in person, Q&A conference calls to share the company's quarterly financial results, and factory tours for those who want to have a closer look at the company's manufacturing and operations. The company also manages its own blogs and official pages on social media websites including Facebook and Twitter to keep stakeholders abreast of the company's latest developments and achievements.

In case some major crisis happens, the company also responds very promptly to keep the crisis under control. For example, when a video showing a Tesla Model S catching fire went viral on YouTube in 2013, Elon Musk, Tesla's CEO, quickly shared a post on the company's blog to explain the reasons behind the accident, regain customers' trust in Tesla's vehicles, and reaffirm the company's potentials with the investors.

There are various financial data a company can reveal to the public and its stakeholders, communicating different aspects of its financial performance and financial viability. As for Tesla, with regard to the market niche of electric vehicles, all of its vehicle models released so far have remained the best-selling electric car models around the world. In December 2016, Tesla sold nearly 190,000 electric vehicles in all markets, making Tesla the second largest global pure electric car manufacturer across the globe. The forthcoming Tesla Model 3, which is expected to come out in 2018, promises another successful product for Tesla with more than 400,000 pre-orders through sales on the company website. Tesla conducted its IPO on NASDAQ exchange in 2010 with an initial price per share of USD 17, and it sold out more than 13 million shares almost overnight. As of today, its share price skyrocketed to USD 325, up nearly 20 times compared to its starting price.

As impressive as its increasing trend of its share price and sales revenue, Tesla Motors Inc.'s financial statement for the year of 2016 showed that the company experienced a loss of USD 674 million, resulting in negative earnings per share of USD −4.5. Similarly, its estimated P/E ratio for the year 2017 is USD −42.71.

That these two important ratios are negative might raise serious concerns among Tesla's investors. Nonetheless, the company attributed most of its loss to its enormous spending on research and development to achieve its ambitious growth and production plan, and it expected to recoup these investments soon.

References

Deal, L. (2016). *Volvo Group restructuring to brand-centric organization*. Retrieved 5.1.2019. https://www.successfuldealer.com/volvo-group-restructuring-to-brand-centric-organization/

Gabler-Wirtschaftslexikon. (2018). *Unternehmenskrise*. Retrieved 26.5.2018. https://wirtschaftslexikon.gabler.de/definition/unternehmungskrise-49331

Handelsblatt. (2017). In: Handelsblatt. 13.01.2017. Finanzielle Zukunft Gläubiger verschaffen Jack Wolfskin Luft für Verhandlungen. Die Verhandlungen über die Zukunft Jack Wolfskin haben begonnen. Um die zu vereinfachen, verzichten die Banken vorerst auf die Rückzahlung von Krediten. Finanzinvestor Blackstone bangt um die Kontrolle des Unternehmens. Retrieved 26.5.2018. http://www.handelsblatt.com/unternehmen/handel-konsumgueter/finanzielle-zukunft-glaeubiger-verschaffen-jack-wolfskin-luft-fuer-verhandlungen/19247752.html?ticket=ST-874329-5m5EZ42jWMfXaeA6SVbH-ap2

Helmold, M., & Terry, B. (2016). *Liefeantenmanagement 2030. Sicherung der Wettbewerbsfähigkeit durch Wertschöpfung in globalen und digitalen Märkten*. Springer Wiesbaden.

Helmold, M., Dathe, T., & Hummel, F. (2019). *Erfolgreiche Verhandlungen. Best-in-Class Empfehlungen für den Verhandlungsdurchbruch*. Springer Gabler Wiesbaden.

Müller, R. (1986). *Krisenmanagement in der Unternehmung: Vorgehen, Massnahmen und Organisation*. Peter Lang Verlag Bern.

Olfert, K. (2013). *Investition*. 13. Auflage. NWB Verlag Herne.

Olfert, K. (2015). *Finanzierung*. 15. Auflage. NWB Verlag Herne.

Reuters. (2018). *Deutsche Bank 2018 restructuring costs to rise to 800 mln from 500 mln on new cuts*. 26.4.2018. Retrieved 5.1.2019. https://www.reuters.com/article/brief-deutsche-bank-2018-restructuring-c/brief-deutsche-bank-2018-restructuring-costs-to-rise-to-800-mln-from-500-mln-on-new-cuts-idUSF9N1L900W

Schmuck, M. (2013). *Financial distress and turnaround. An empirical analysis oft he automotive supplier industry*. Springer Wiesbaden.

Vlasic, B. (2012). Prized Logo Is Returned to Ford. The blue oval is back home. *New York Times*. Retrieved 6.1.2019. https://www.nytimes.com/2012/05/23/business/a-prized-logo-is-returned-to-ford.html

Zalando. (2019). *Zalando SE General Conditions of Purchase for Indirect Purchase*. Retrieved 5.1.2019. https://eprocurement.zalando.com/wp-content/uploads/2017/04/Zalando-SE-General-Conditions-of-Purchase-for-Indirect-Purchase.pdf

SCRM in the Aviation Industry: "Risk Management Strategies to Resilience ReTake-off" 9

Without data, you're just another person with an opinion

– W. Edwards Deming

9.1 Resilience ReTake-off

We live in a period which tests the resilience of both organizations and individuals as we constantly experience dynamic changes and transformations. In such an environment, the aviation industry must be flexible to improve business performance and organizational resilience, manage risks, and adapt innovations to its products and services.

Resilience is the risk that ranks on top in the agenda of today's business managers. The conditions created by the pandemic test the resilience of businesses and organizations. The aviation industry is a resilient industry being a leader in managing often simultaneous challenges in operational, environmental, and social areas. Causes, business models, and management systems based on the pandemic are being reshaped according to the pandemic environment. Supply chain risk management, one of the main components of the sustainability in the aviation industry, is also one of the areas that has been reshaped.

The ability of organizations in the aviation industry to manage risks that threaten their sustainability, to address difficult conditions, and to be prepared for unexpected situations, depends on their endurance. Thus, it is predicted that businesses with institutional resilience above a certain level can survive.

Aviation provides the only rapid worldwide transportation network, which makes it essential for global business. It generates economic growth, creates jobs, and facilitates international trade and tourism (ICAO, 2019).

By its nature, aviation requires organizations and businesses in many different disciplines to work together. The aviation industry is facilitated by many and diverse

M. Helmold et al., *Supply Chain Risk Management*,
Management for Professionals, https://doi.org/10.1007/978-3-030-90800-3_9

product and service sectors in order to offer its services to its customers. The existence of organizations and businesses from such different disciplines in aviation has caused aviation to have a complex structure. All these businesses and organizations come together to form the aviation supply chain that depend on each other directly or indirectly. Although having organizations and businesses from different disciplines offers advantages, it also presents many risks.

As in all supply chains, the main purpose of the aviation supply chain is customer satisfaction. All businesses have certain standards and controls to ensure customer satisfaction. Thankfully, these controls enable the minimization of the risks that may arise during the production and provision of services and products, and the severity of their consequences.

Supplier businesses are businesses that provide the inputs, raw materials, goods, and services required in the process of the provision of goods and services to the end consumer, by the enterprises in the aviation industry. Therefore, suppliers are one of the determining organizations in aviation, in managing the risks affecting the intangible and tangible values to be obtained through goods and services.

9.2 Introduction to Air Transportation

The aviation industry includes numerous and diverse organizational groups which allow all kinds of transportation to be provided by air vehicles manufactured by humans. The aviation industry involves all kinds of actions related to aircraft, carried out by both industries and institutions. Aviation is comprised by two main segments, namely, civil aviation and military aviation. Military aviation can be examined under the subheadings of reconnaissance, providing security and exercises for military purposes. Civil aviation has three subgroups, grouped according to their aim of actions: commercial aviation, aerial work, and general aviation.

Air transport is a driver of global trade and e-commerce, allowing globalization of production. Aviation provides the only rapid worldwide transportation network, which makes it essential for global business. It generates economic growth, creates jobs, and facilitates international trade and tourism (ICAO, 2019) (https://www.icao.int/sustainability/Documents/AVIATION-BENEFITS-2019-web.pdf).

In the aviation industry, specific international and national institutions manage, supervise, and provide permits and compliance: ICAO—International Civil Aviation Organisation, EASA—European Aviation Safety Agency; ACI—Airports Council International, IATA—International Air Transport Association are leading institutions both intergovernmental and non-governmental. These institutions also set the standards and legal obligations that organizations in the aviation industry must comply with.

The provision and presentation of products and services in air transport is based on the supply chain. Therefore, sustainable provision of aviation products and services requires a risk management-based system.Supply chain in aviation is evaluated as a whole consisting of stakeholder organizations involved in all processes including the delivery and recycling of aviation service-related products (such as aircraft, spare parts, and catering) to the manufacturer and/or customers.

More than one organization must interact and work together in order to provide a service in aviation and to offer this service to users. Let us consider, for example, a flight service. In providing the most basic flight services, there is a need for airport services, flight crew, transportation, and tracking of passenger baggies to get on a plane and a plane. Therefore, in order to provide the flight service, airlines are always in interaction with various companies and various suppliers, in an ongoing process, product, and personnel services. It can be seen that there is a process and flow. When the potential of these interactions to affect the service positively and negatively is analyzed, the effect of suppliers on ensuring and maintaining safety, which is a fundamental element in aviation, will be better understood.

Organizations in the air transport industry prefer to work with suppliers and mostly outsource, due to the cost-effective strategies they adopt in their managerial approach and in order to gain competitive advantage. For example, airline companies, aircraft manufacturers, and airport operators cooperate with many suppliers to provide products and services to their customers by purchasing services or parts or equipment.

Developments in transportation modes and integrated use globally have enabled suppliers to cover large geographical areas in the aviation industry and to work with suppliers from many and various parts in the world, since with the integrated and advanced modes of transportation, the mobility and speed of both people and products and services in the world have increased.

Airline companies work in cooperation with many suppliers in the process of first obtaining a service and then providing the service component they have created to their customers. The air transport supply chain starts with aircraft manufacturers, charterers, air navigation service providers (or ANSPs), travel agents, and shipping brokers and continues with providers of other services. Other services include computer reservation systems (or CRS), catering, ground handling and maintenance, repair and overhaul (or MRO), operators, vendors, airlines, authorities, catering services, retail, regional, etc. In addition, the equipment, raw materials, and materials needed by operators, ground handling, consultants, and OEMs are supplied from supplier manufacturers.

All the airline suppliers generate higher returns compared to airlines, the returns varying for each business partner. Computer reservation services providers, travel agents, and freight forwarders are the most profitable ones with returns more than double than the cost of capital. The bargaining power of aircraft manufacturers is high, due to a limited number of suppliers. The major portion of the world's demand for aircraft requirements is accommodated by four top manufacturers: Boeing, Embraer, Bombardier, and Airbus. Cessna, Piper, Diamond, Mooney, Cirrus Design, and Raytheon are some of the leading small aircraft manufacturers. They mainly serve based on private aviation and flight training in the general aviation market. In addition, many airports and ground handling companies are local monopolies. General Electric and Rolls-Royce are the two largest aircraft engine manufacturers in the world. Clearly, continuity of workflows in air transport depends on the management of supply chain risks (Fig. 9.1).

Fig. 9.1 Fundamentals of a sustainable supply chain. (Source: Author)

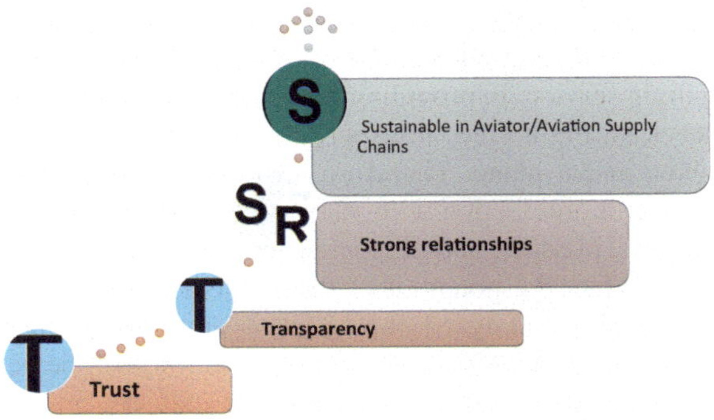

The air transport supply chain consists of aircraft manufacturers, charters, air navigation service providers (or ANSPs), travel agents, and shipping companies. The supply chain also includes providers of other services such as computer reservation systems (or CRS), catering, ground handling and maintenance, repair and overhaul (or MRO), as well as regional operators, ground handlers, consultants, aircraft parts manufacturers, equipment manufacturers, software companies, propeller manufacturers, aircraft engines manufacturers (Rolls-Royce and General Motors are leading companies to produce aircraft engines), aviation headsets manufacturers, landing gear manufacturers, chip manufacturers, aviation class hardware, consumables, composite materials companies, aircraft body parts producing companies. In essence, it includes a broad stakeholder group that includes the products and services required for an aircraft and aviation service, such as companies that manufacture electrical components. In this context, establishment of trust in the stakeholder group and the soundness of relationships stand out as critical elements in terms of sustainable supply chain, which are also important to seizing opportunities in supply chain for all stakeholders.

There is a limited number of suppliers in the aviation industry. Hence, supplier characteristics should be especially taken into consideration in the management of the aviation supply chain market. Moreover, aviation organizations consider these supplier structures while developing their strategies. Clearly, relations with suppliers play a critical role in terms of products and services to be purchased from them. Therefore, stakeholder relations are the leading risk source considered in the supply chain. Market structure aircraft manufacturers have high bargaining power. For example, most of the world's demand for aircraft requirements is met by Boeing and Airbus manufacturers. Apart from this pivotal role of aircraft manufacturers in supply chain management, many airports and ground handling companies also have a local monopoly. As a result, the limited number of suppliers affects the market structure and shapes the strategies.

Supply chain management is one of the risky issues in view of sustainability of production processes, since there are complicated interrelations among airports, airlines, and ground handling organizations. Notably, aviation industry with many commercial engagements and alliances between airports, airlines, and their suppliers of ground handling agents (GHAs) operate in a business environment, which is more global and complicated. Current operational environment in aviation industry requires more focus on safety and security issues and requirements for compliance with laws and regulations. Managing risks in stakeholder interrelations in supply chain requires needs to become a more integral part of managing safety and security risks in airports, airlines and ground handling agents, besides other suppliers, such as spare parts suppliers or maintenance repair organizations (MRO) (Adapted from Foster, 2016, https://www.bsigroup.com/en-US/blog/supply-chain-blog/security/airline-industry-supply-chain-threats/).

Toward managing supply chain-based risks timely and holistically, implementation of supply chain risk management should be established in organizations after being tailored according to organizational characteristics, aims and objectives, as well as qualifications of organizational resources. Thus, SCRM will indirectly contribute to the identification of risk sources, handling risk, and, thus, reduction in damages, incidents, and injuries of personnel, besides managing supply-related issues.

Supply chain risk management refers to a network system that mediates between supplier and customer and manages and establishes the organization. It is essential to manage the flow of information and materials between stakeholders, cooperating within the scope of procurement, without interruption and in a cost-effective manner. An effective supply chain risk management will also ensure customer satisfaction, and this will contribute to the development and continuity of stakeholder relations and of the level of cooperation. Therefore, a holistic approach should be envisaged for all components involved in the aviation industry, namely, suppliers, service providers, consumers, and other support providers.

Since product and service components are complex in air transportation, the supply chain is also complex. This process, which includes the manufacturer and the service provider, is a high-cost yet high-profit, technology, safety, and quality-oriented network fabric. Clearly, strategic planning should be included in management to eliminate the complexity of this network fabric. The goal is always to add more value to the customer. As it is a dynamic and complex process, it is very important to be properly and successfully managed.

> **AIRBUS:** "*Airbus, partners and suppliers are part of an extended family, and they play a crucial role in the common business success. Around 80% of Airbus' activity is sourced. The company works with more than 12,000 suppliers worldwide that provide products and services for flying and non-flying parts.* (AIRBUS, Be an Airbus supplier, Retrieved at April 16, 2021 from https://www.airbus.com/be-an-airbus-supplier.html)"
>
> ***BOEING:*** *"The 787 Dreamliner has about 2.3 million parts per airplane. They include everything from "fasten seatbelt" signs to jet engines and vary in size from small fasteners to large fuselage sections. Some parts are built by Boeing, and others are purchased from supplier partners around the world. Suppliers have been part of the Boeing Production System since the company was founded in 1916. William Boeing Sr. procured finished assemblies such as engines and materials such as the "very best Irish linen" as covering for the wings of his first airplanes. (BOEING, World-Class-Supplier-Quality retrieved at april 16, 2021 from* https://787updates.newairplane.com/787-Suppliers/World-Class-Supplier-Quality"

The Airbus supplier structure illustrates the complex nature of the supply chain in the aviation industry. As seen above, suppliers are a critical part of production. Therefore, the number and diversity of the procurement risks of such a complex process will be understood more clearly, as well as the importance of their management. This management process includes material requirements and ordering. Thus, many aviation companies prefer to work with an intermediary institution that will perform supply chain management on their behalf in line with their needs. These institutions help the procurement process to run smoothly by providing the connection and communication between the manufacturer, customer, and supplier. Thus, in this dynamic structure, the intervention process for any problem that may be experienced in supply is minimized.

Airbus has different suppliers for direct procurement, grouped in the following commodities for flying parts (AIRBUS, 2021):

- Aerostructures
- Equipment and systems
- Material and parts
- Propulsion
- Specialized IT and services

Airbus and Boeing are the only players in the wide-body market, dominating the narrow-body segment as well. In the medium term, opportunities for new players in this market are unlikely, due to the duopoly of Boeing and Airbus (https://blog.satair.com/ten-risk-in-aviation-industry).

This supplier structure also explains the diversity and number of risk areas. Each supply area includes risks as a cooperation area and may require specific strategies. Common values, transparency, and trust stand out as determining factors in the selection of suppliers for aviation organizations. Airbus clearly states this as a prerequisite for both its partners and suppliers. Aviation organizations are aware that suppliers play a pivotal role in providing quality and qualified service to their customers.

The tendency to outsource supply and logistics activities in the supply chain process is preferred by many organizations due to the advantages it provides. It is emphasized that the selection of the suppliers to cooperate with in order to obtain these advantages is a critical element with both risk and opportunity components. In aviation, suppliers may be seen in the following contexts (Adopted from Espesito, 2007):

- Raw material suppliers
- Other components and parts suppliers
- Equipment suppliers
- Major structure suppliers

Supply chain management is one of the risky issues in terms of sustainability, due to the complex relationships between stakeholders such as aircraft manufacturers, aircraft parts manufacturers (accessories, electrical, rotables/components) airports, airlines, and ground handling companies. Most importantly, the aviation industry is becoming more global and complex, with many business links and alliances between airports, airlines, and ground services representatives (GHAs) suppliers. The current operational environment in the aviation industry requires a greater focus on safety and security issues and compliance with laws and regulations.

As it is a service sector, the provision of products and services in aviation requires a series of complex activities, high costs and high level of specialization, qualified and licensed personnel, the use of advanced technological applications, and cooperation for the supply chain in accordance with the aforementioned. Effectively managing the risks of the supply chain becomes important in reaching the users of the products and services of the industry's stakeholders, such as aircraft manufacturers, airport operators, airlines, navigation service providers, air traffic control service providers, and ground service providers.

Supply chain risk management is the minimization of sustainability threats of a network and capturing opportunities of organizations cooperating between suppliers and customers (risk is considered in its dual nature: threat and/or opportunity).

The aviation industry includes the design and manufacture of aircrafts and the design and production of technologies related to these aircrafts. Furthermore, the aviation industry produces services using aircraft. This aviation industry requires huge and extensive investments and financing in terms of both design and production and maintenance capabilities and infrastructural needs. Moreover, the aviation industry is a specific and compromised field that uses advanced and intensive technology, has a research and development basis, and has very different market dynamics. In addition, technologies developed in this field have significant direct and indirect benefits to the economic and social development of countries, and of sectors in these countries. For the sustainability of aviation investments and benefits, it is predicted that supply chain risk management should be implemented systematically and with a strategic approach.

As is known, air vehicles consist of thousands of sub-parts and systems. Both equipment and software are required for these systems in aircrafts to work properly and uninterruptedly. In addition, there are special standards and certification requirements, depending on the legislation, for almost each of these systems and subsystems. Accordingly, the supplier structure also changes. The interaction of the design and production stages of the final products developed in the aviation industry can be fully and accurately understood with the supply chain structure and supply needs formed depending on this. The supply chain can be used as the final platform of products as well as for the subsystems and intermediate products to be integrated into the final platform (Adapted from SATAIR, 2021(https://blog.satair.com/ten-risk-in-aviation-industry).

9.3 Hybrid Risks in the Aviation Industry and Business

By its nature, the aviation industry is a source of considerable economic activity, creating jobs that directly serve passengers at airlines, airports, and air navigation services providers. These include check-in, baggage handling, on-site retail, cargo, and catering facilities. Moreover, aviation directly enables jobs in the manufacturing sector (those companies that produce aircrafts, engines, and other vital technologies) (ICAO, 2019). Within the scope of this economic catalyst, many and diverse fields of this activity are exposed to diverse and multiple interactive risks.

The structure and resilience of suppliers working with organizations operating in air transportation, such as airports, airlines, ground service providers, navigation service providers, flight training academies, aircraft maintenance organizations, may vary from region to region. High-impact risks, such as economic and pandemic-related risks, affect the resilience and sustainable business level of suppliers. In the pre-pandemic period, suppliers, who are at the forefront of capacity planning and strive to keep up with high demand, are currently developing new strategies for reproduction planning and performance management.

IATA states that a resilient supply chain is critical in the "Resource Wars" scenario, where there is increased conflict. In this context, IATA predicted that airlines will need to maintain robust, redundant supply chains to protect themselves from global wide-scale disruptions (IATA, Future of The Airline Industry 2035, https://www.iata.org/contentassets/690df4ddf39b47b5a075bb5dff30e1d8/iata-future-airline-industry-pdf.).

Due to the pandemic, both economic and social changes have started to occur in the business environment. These sharp changes are testing organizational resilience. Business models, customer demands, business styles, and business environments have begun to change and transform. Even flight networks and airport hubs have begun to change. Aviation stakeholders and flight networks are being restructured due to the dynamic business environment and evolving framework of ownership. In effect, this means an opportunity for radical restructuring in terms of risk management. Hybrid systems are highlighted in our pandemic agenda. It would be safe to predict that hybrid systems will be applied more in both business and social life in the future. Since there will be more hybrid applications in aviation, hybridization is expected in risk types and the structures of existing risks.

Each of the risks faced by the aviation industry and businesses may have multiple sources, or they may combine to create a new risk. Therefore, risks in aviation fall within the hybrid risk concept. This new concept also updates the risk management strategies and emphasizes that the risks should be handled on the basis of performance. Hybrid risks create business continuity risks for organizations in the air transport industry. Thus, SCRM in aviation considers hybrid risks in a high-level integrated business environment within supply chain.

The momentum of development and change is constantly changing; the business continuity of organizations in the air transport sector depends on the high level of flexibility, adaptability, ability to produce better products, and cost-effective performance levels. Supply chains are one of the conditions for achieving these goals.

Moreover, suppliers require cost-effective operations and high-level integration with aviation industry.

Toward effective management and decision-making, according to supply chain-based risks in the aviation industry, the level of integration within the air industry supply chain should be well understood by managers of stakeholders in the supply chain. Integration level may be shaped and/or tailorized according to aviation organization structure and aims. For example, maintenance organization may enable low degree integration, but aircraft manufacturer companies may prefer a more integrated supply chain for their operations.

"Managing the Supply Chain" Risk

Managing the supply chain is considered one of the leading risks in the air transportation industry. Due to high demand, supply chains should ensure these high volumes with improvements their performance and capacity. According to IATA (2018), drivers are assessed as having greater than average impact and uncertainty. An integrated supply chain allows manufacturers to look into business processes across multiple suppliers and disparate platforms to follow materials, components, and people wherever they are. The importance of emerging markets, economic growth, and the appetite of developing countries for natural resources may boost global prices and make it trickier to configure supply chain assets (IATA, FUTURE OF THE AIRLINE INDUSTRY 2035, https://www.iata.org/contentassets/690df4ddf39b47b5a075bb5dff30e1d8/iata-future-airline-industry-pdf.). Thus, the supply chain framework may change according to changing fundamentals in market and economic conditions.

Supply chain risk management aims to deliver products and services to customers at the right time, at the right place, and at the right price, in a cost-effective manner. Thus, aviation organizations will be able to achieve their corporate goals within the integrated system, by seizing both financial optimization and good quality delivery level. It is predicted that the investments made and to be made in this direction will improve corporate value in both medium and long term.

In order to keep up with the changing technological environment and to meet the new needs that arise, flexibility, adaptation, speed, and openness to innovations and continuous monitoring of innovations should be considered as part of the supply chain risk management process. Since the business environment and business dynamics are in a state of constant change and development, the functioning and management of the supply chain is also in a state of constant development.

One of the aims of AviSCRM is to make the complex supply chain process manageable and controllable by dividing it into groups according to risk sources. Thus, SCRM also supports strategic planning and management. Clearly, the application and handling of the process specified at each stage will vary, according to the institutional objectives and the activities of the enterprise. These process—group concepts—should be considered from strategic and operational perspectives. In the strategic stage, the execution method of the stages in the process is designed according to the risk map. Decisions are made regarding the methods to be used to carry out the stages in the processes from an operational perspective.

In supplier relations risk management, the emphasis is on mutual gain of the stakeholders and the trust-based relations between them. In cases where one of the stakeholders fails to meet their expectations from the supply-based relationship, there is a possibility of a disruption. In order to manage supply chain-based risks, such as equipment failure, quality-based problems, miscommunication, information system failure, changes in customer demand, economic crises, political issues, supply problems of raw materials from different countries, and changed law and regulations, it is one of the principles of SCRM that suppliers also participate in the process of product development and commercialization. Thus, optimization can be achieved in the process of introducing the product or service to the market.

The AviSCRM (ASCRM) model is also important for aviation organizations with its strong and proactive internal control system, as the continuous monitoring of supply-related operations and related resources ensures that the potential weaknesses and strengths of the system are noticed in a timely manner. Thus, the performance of procurement risk management will always be high, and it will serve as a guide for decision-makers. As the performance of supply chain risk management increases, the operational performances of the self-stakeholder enterprises will be monitored and areas that can be improved will be noticed. Therefore, risk management also supports all stakeholders in improving their performance and capabilities with a win-win approach.

A large number and variety of parts and materials are used in the production of an aircraft. In addition, since the certification of each material and part is a specific usage standards and system, the suppliers in the aviation sector have different qualifications depending on the product.

It would be advisable to look at system dynamics to understand the increasing need for integration in the supply chain. In the aviation industry, it is necessary to procure many subsystems and parts, to produce and supply major systems, then assemble and then create the final product and service. Avionic (electrical and electronical) systems, power units/systems, air frame (structures) and control surfaces, electric subsystems, avionic equipments, cockpit, air conditioning, cabin systems, fuel systems, landing gear systems, and hydraulic systems may be given as examples of major and subsystems. This comprehensive and complex chain of processes requires integrated supply chain implementation and management of hybrid risks. The supply chain management system has different structures and conditions for each of the components of the aviation industry's sub- and main systems.

Since operating costs are high in the aviation industry, organizations operating in the sector need effective supply chain management to develop their processes and process related activities for their products and services, and to develop their strategies toward increasing both cost-effective practices and quality.

The service and product components in the aviation industry have their own characteristics and requirements; thus, each of the components of the supply chain management system has different structures. Moreover, the supply chain is a critical factor in delivering products and services to customers; it also has the potential to add a high level of value to product and service components in aviation. In that aspect, supply chain risk management also has a strategic meaning. Therefore, the supply chain is playing a determinative role in achieving the goals in strategic management. Therefore, the supply chain is one of the main parts of the value chain. In the aviation industry, as in other sectors, it is accepted that the value chain starts with suppliers due to its potential to directly affect customer satisfaction and quality. Moreover, supply chain risk management in aviation contributes to the increase of quality by promoting cost-effective practices and business continuity. Besides, SCRM accelerates the adaptation process to the changing market by creating an environment that supports flexibility and the use of high technology.

Thanks to aviation supply chain risk management (AviSCRM), cooperation between businesses is increasing, and there is an information-sharing network established with stakeholders that is developing. Besides, correct and timely use of resources is possible with risk management. Production performance also increases as businesses will work to support each other's objectives with the common risk culture. Since the supply chain risk management system produces optimized solutions by identifying risk sources and risks, it guides managers in planning, coordination, and resource allocation and increases awareness of opportunity-based investment areas. As it supports more agile and dynamic business environments, it has the potential to contribute to employee performance and motivation levels. Therefore, supply chain risk management is a fundamental part of the aviation industry and its business strategy.

AviSCRM (ASCRM) improves the level of cooperation in line with this strategy and supports the creation of a climate of trust among organizations. In this environment of cooperation and trust, risks can be shared, communication increases, and the adaptation speed of organizations to changing situations and flexibility to innovations increases.

AviSCRM (ASCRM) supports the coordination of multiple functions both within the organization and among supplier stakeholders. In addition, AviSCRM (ASCRM) considers strategic, operational, and tactical levels in the development of coordination areas in organizations.

In a successful and effective AviSCRM supply chain risk management, processes and stages of processes are designed as integrated and flexible at the same time. All steps in this process are established to be dynamic, up to date, and based on expertise and technological competence, in order to understand the effects of all existing and potential risk sources with the potential to affect the supply chain and the effects of risks on each other and the interaction between them. In this respect, it is considered one of the decision-making support systems. According to risk management-based approach, supply chain management is considered to be a holistic system in which each component is designed to fulfill multiple functions and coordinates the relevant elements.

9.4 New SCRM Model for Aviation: Conceptual "AviSCRM" Framework

In the civil aviation sector, the supply chain is important as a global network in the sustainable competition of the manufacturers and in providing quality products and services to their customers and even reaching them. In this global supply chain network, which spreads to a wide geography with different regions and localities, problems may arise due to risks.

All activities of an organization involve risk. Organizations manage risk by identifying it, analyzing it, and then evaluating whether the risk should be modified by risk treatment in order to satisfy their risk criteria. Throughout this process, they communicate and consult with stakeholders and monitor and review the risk and the controls that are modifying the risk in order to ensure that no further risk treatment is required (ISO 31000:2009(en)Risk management — Principles and guidelines).

It is suggested that the Flexible Supply Chains facility, sought in aviation, should be handled with a risk management-based approach. In this respect, newly designed and proposed AviSCRM (ASCRM) model provides reasonable assurance for businesses in the supply chain to increase their resilience in a business environment with variable and uncertainties.

Newly designed conceptual framework model for AviSCRM enables supply chains to be more flexible and more responsive. With the integration of the proactive and reactive approach, the risks related to every situation can be addressed with the contingency approach. AviSCRM provides the opportunity to identify both risk sources and the risks in these areas and potential events that will affect the sustainable supply chain. Every system in aviation has a backup; when a system fails, the alternative system is activated. Moreover, it creates alternatives to ensure that the supply chain is not interrupted and is sustainable with risk management. Working through scenarios, risk management helps them improve preparedness by strengthening the business for potential events in both strategic and operational resilience areas. Thus, in times of crisis, the hesitations and disruptions due to the crisis can be kept to a minimum in these enterprises. Therefore, operational efficiency and corporate performance also support risk management.

Stakeholders are partners in the supply chain, and one of the biggest risks in this partnership, as in other partnerships, is the abuse of the trust relationship between the parties. For this reason, it is very important to maintain and implement a mutual trust relationship.

The new AviSCRM model provides considerable advantages as follows:

(i) Flexible and agile configurations of supply chains.
(ii) Control before taking a proactive approach.
(iii) Improving strategic resilience: via shared information, trust-based collaboration, strategic alignment, identifying sources of risk and potential risks.
(iv) Including backup systems such as aviation systems so that activities in the supply chain are not interrupted.
(v) Collaboration among supply chain stakeholders B2B.

(vi) Consolidation and cooperation.
(vii) Creating common benefits.
(viii) Establishing a strong framework to encourage and support the development of regional companies and stakeholder organizations.
(ix) Coordinated management of both information and resources.
(x) Together to create new markets with new projects, products, and services. Also, they can react to events in a short time by making accurate and timely decisions.
(xi) Allocation of limited resources for emergencies.
(xii) Company culture and practices should be in a way that support the critical role of employees in maintaining company resilience.
(xiii) Developing multi-criteria decision-making skills and creating an environment that support learning organization culture.
(xiv) Continuous monitoring of opportunity and threat components of risks both reactively and proactively with an integrated approach.
(xv) Determination and implementation of managerial approaches suitable for risks.
(xvi) Increasing organizational resilience with a flexible management style.
(xvii) Increasing operational resilience: increasing preparedness for changes and crises, establishing a crisis management system, determining roles and responsibilities, improving situational awareness.
(xviii) Managerial decision-making processes that will ensure performance optimization.
(xix) Developing resilience with a workplace environment that supports learning and continuous innovation.
(xx) Improved flexibility, improved resilience, preparedness for contingency situations.

Holistic and systematic corporate-wide risk management implementations in supply chain may improve corporate performance. Leading organizations are aware that risk management-based systems contribute to gaining a competitive advantage. These organizations, which manage their risks more effectively, reveal their potential and add value to all their stakeholders. In this view, our risk management-based viewpoint has been reflected at supply chains (adapted from Deloitte https://www2.deloitte.com/tr/services/risk.html). Supply chain risk management systems, designed in accordance with the contingency approach and system approach, are designed dynamically and flexibly, and are always updated in changing business conditions.

Aviation supply chain risk management (AviSCRM) is both a dynamic model and a disciplined system. AviSCRM helps to ensure risks that prevent organizations from reaching their goals and opportunities that facilitate the achievement of goals are recognized and managed in advance. The system, which started with private sector applications, has also been adopted by public institutions. The main purpose of enterprise risk management is to support profit-increasing practices in the private sector and to help improve the benefit factor in public institutions.

Supply chain risk management in the aviation industry is considered a holistic management system designed to optimally manage the risks arising from the input of the process carried out for the production. The process has economic, operational, human, and social factors. Therefore, the sources of risk are determined by considering the human, organizational, and operational environments and their costs. With the proposed model, determining risks from risk sources in the aviation industry operating environment, which includes variables and uncertainties, and managing them by making timely decisions, can help collaborative organizations in the supply chain structures to increase their resilience and act in a more flexible and dynamic manner.

The AviSCRM Conceptual Framework:

1. *Initial step*:
   (a) Internal environmental analysis: organizational factors-based risk sources
      (i) Management attitude
      (ii) Communication level
      (iii) Collaboration policy and strategy
      (iv) Corporate risk culture and organizational culture
      (v) Human resource qualifications: age, graduate, positions, personality
      (vi) Corporate/organizational aims
   (b) External environmental analysis: economical factors-based risk sources
      (i) Volatility in the geopolitical and economic environment (https://blog.satair.com/ten-risk-in-aviation-industry)
      (ii) Stakeholder expectations
      (iii) Competition
      (iv) Globalization
      (v) Volatile business environment
      (vi) İnformation technologies and systems
      (vii) Regulations and laws
      (viii) Competition
2. *Risk assessment: Identification, analyses, evaluation, prioritization, risk mapping*
   (a) Identification of SC risks (*have potential impact on supply chains*)
      (i) Organizational risks
      (ii) strategic risks
      (iii) Economical risks
      (iv) Operational risks
      (v) Environmental risks: sustainability-based approach
   (b) Risk Analysis
   (c) Prioritization
   (d) Risk mapping: handle strategies for prioritized risks
      (risk mapping for supply chains according to operation fields in aviation)
3. *Strategy development/strategic decision-making:* Strategic decision-making for stakeholder relations of SCRM
   (a) Identification of potential partnership with suppliers and supply resources
   (b) Selection of best strategy and their implementations

   (c) Buyer-supplier partnership
   (d) Supplier evaluation process: Supplier selection and their assessment
4. *Risk treatment*: Decision-making on risk handling options:
   (a) Risk acceptance and taking: taking risks and seizing potential opportunities
   (b) Risk transfer
   (c) Risk avoiding
   (d) Risk mitigation: keeping the risk under control by minimizing it
   (e) Risk sharing and cooperating/collaboration with the risk-related stakeholder/s to manage them
   (f) Risk-based positioning as both operational and organizational context

These options may be implemented individually or combined with others. The interactions of may require a combination of several management options. For example, it may be the case that a risk is taken because the opportunity appears to be worthwhile, and, at the same time, the risk is shared with a supplier. In this case, a strategic decision is taken, and two management options are applied.

5. *Information integration*
6. *Monitoring, control, and reporting*: Both results and ASCRM performance
7. *Performance optimization and continuity*
   (a) Improving strategic resilience
   (b) Improving operational resilience
   (c) Continuously improving and developing RM system as loop

This model has 7 main steps and their substeps as shown in the following figure

Steps with their brief explanation

Step 1 is the initial step in this model which includes analyzing of both internal and external business environments in view of their risk capacity and also their potentials.

Developing new business models in the supply chain aviation industry, improving supply chain stakeholder relations, and using smart systems, digital applications, and technology-intensive systems in supply processes have both diversified and increased the risks. ASCRM (or AviSCRM) is the determination of risk sources in this ever-changing risk environment making optimum managerial choices according to the interaction of risks with each other and their impact and severity. Changes in risk sources as internal and external create the need for new approach to their management. Some examples of changing risk sources are the following:

(i) Changes in the material structures and production techniques used in the production of products and services in the aviation industry
(ii) Changes in stocking methods and requirements due to the changing characteristics of the products

(iii) The spreading of the field of activity to wider and different regions and locations
(iv) Production resources that have been changed due to sustainable growth goals increase the quantity and quantify of risk resources in the supply chain
(v) Changing economic conditions and economic volatility
(vi) Pandemic-based changed business models, changed human resource management style in organizations
(vii) Changing customer needs and demands
(viii) Digitalization in process of both aviation and supply chains

Organizations need to be more adaptive to change. They need to think strategically about the management of the increasing volatility, complexity, and ambiguity of the world, particularly at the senior levels in the organization and in the boardroom where the stakes are highest (COSO, 2017). Supply chain risks can be internal or external. The location of the resource affects its controllability. This, in turn, affects which of the managerial options for them will be used. In this view, the diversity and multitude of risk sources show how vital supply chain risk management is in the aviation industry. Risks may be classified according to their sources, as follows:

(a) Organizational risk factors: Management approach and attitude, investment decisions
(b) Operational risk factors: Damages, human factor, operational process, human-machine interface; lack of human resources to use digital systems and advanced technology systems; capability and competency problem
(c) Environmental risk factors: Pandemic, stakeholders, changing customer demands and needs
(d) Financial risk factors: Budget, economic volatility in business environment, sector-based restrictions and contractions in aviation sector

The sustainability of the aviation industry is directly proportional to the success of risk management. Risk management is of great importance especially for the aviation industry, because the losses incurred are not only large-scale financial losses but can also include loss of life. The cost of an accident or an incident in aviation is particularly high from an economic, social, and legal perspective.

AviSCRM (ASCRM) includes determination of risk sources and potential risks in these sources, preparation of risk scenarios, prioritization of risks according to their impact severity and probabilities, preparation of risk map, and making management decisions regarding risks, according to the risk map.

Step 2 is risk analysis level in process which involves developing an understanding of the risk. Risk analysis provides an input to risk evaluation, to decisions on whether risks need to be treated, and on the most appropriate risk treatment strategies and methods. Risk analysis can also provide an input into making decisions where choices must be made, and the options may involve different types and levels of risk (*AS/NZS ISO 31000:2009*).

It is the evaluation of the potential risks that may arise in the steps taken by the enterprise, in the direction of the strategies of the enterprise, and the preparation of risk scenarios. Institutional resources are allocated according to these scenarios. Strategic decision-making is made according to risk analysis results. Being prepared for the future, taking precautions in a timely manner, keeping the damage to a minimum, and seizing opportunities can be achieved through risk-sensitive strategic decision-making. Monitoring of both risk-related possibilities and risk scenarios have vital impact on strategic and operational decisions. Strategies developed according to the risk map support businesses to make the right decisions in a timely manner to achieve their goals. COSO stated that ERM accommodates evolving technologies and the proliferation of data and analytics in supporting decision-making (COSO, 2017)

Step 3 includes strategic decision-making about the stakeholder map of the supplier. Partner selection is vital decision-making. Partnerships based on a win-win Business-to-Business (B2B) approach on trust and cooperation are one of the critical determinants of optimum management of supply chain risks. According to COSO (2017), strategy selection is about making choices and accepting trade-offs. So, it makes sense to apply enterprise risk management to strategy as that is the best approach for untangling the art and science of making well-informed choices (COSO, 2017, p.8).

Step 4 is about decision-making on risk handling options to seizing opportunities and minimizing threats achieving business objectives in ASCRM.

Step 5 is based on integration information about both risk sources and risks, which have potential to make an impact on achieving objectives in supply chain. Detailed identification with sound techniques is carried out in this process.

Step 6 includes both results according to risk handling performance and new arising and/or changing risks. This step also includes the updating of related systems according to the contingency approach.

Final step 7 is about optimization to organizational resilience, in view of both strategic and operational aims. Well-designed and soundly implemented ASCRM may give convenient and smart assurance to achieving organizational aims of supply chain. Risk management framework in this model considers, evaluates, and optimally manages all risks related to procurement from a corporate perspective. In essence, it is a process that has both proactive and reactive integration, applied throughout the life of the business in a systematic and continuous cycle, being one of the essential parts of management.

According to COSO (2017), ERM enhances alignment between performance and enterprise risk management to improve the setting of performance targets and understanding of the impact of risk on performance (COSO, 2017). In line with COSO, an SCRM maximizes the achievement of organizational goals only if integrated with strategy and performance.

All activities in aviation consist of integrated business processes. In order to realize operational services, many products, equipment, and systems need to be supplied. It is a critical element for uninterrupted service to provide the products that are needed advantageously, with multiple transportation modes, and to integrate them into operations and operating processes at the right time. Thus, mode optimization is an area of competition. An optimization involving different transportation corridors is achieved in order to take advantage of transportation advantages with multiple modes. At this point, airports have transformed into logistics bases with the integration of transportation modes. Furthermore, airports have considerable qualifications for supply chain, such as large passenger and cargo capacity, the presence of large storage areas, high quality in infrastructure and ground services, and the ability to load and unload multiple cargo aircrafts.

Organizations may gain a competitive advantage via mode diversity optimizations. Aviation is a very resilient industry, familiar with dealing with many operational challenges. But pandemic-based causes are starting to be addressed as part of normal daily network planning and operations in airlines, airports, and ground handling operations, but some may lead to more systematic permanent changes. Thus, business models and management systems may be expected to reshape according to the pandemic environment (Fig. 9.2).

The absence, the limited, or insufficient operation of one chain can generate significant risks in the output of the whole industry. The aviation industry is set on chains to maintain their productions and services. Hence, AviSCRM (or ASCRM) is a fundamental management issue in both the aviation industry and civil aviation management.

Organizations in aviation industry are working in a large supplier chain. With such a huge network of suppliers, small mistakes and little delays may cause a chain reaction and, as a result, budgets and schedules could spin out of control. Ernst & Young notes that there is also a risk that companies will have disputes with suppliers or subcontractors related to work specifications, quality of supply, or customers concerns (Adapted from https://blog.satair.com/ten-risk-in-aviation-industry).

According to Lufthansa report, Risk-based business partner due diligence is intended to ensure the integrity of suppliers and service providers. During this process, compliance screenings are conducted by the responsible employees in order to identify at an early stage any compliance risks that could arise from cooperation with external business partners. Depending on the result, various measures, including the avoidance or termination of a business relationship may be necessary for dealings with the business partner. https://investor-relations.lufthansagroup.com/fileadmin/downloads/en/financial-reports/annual-reports/LH-AR-2020-e.pdf

According to their investment relations report that Lufthansa has a holistic and systematic risk management approach. and they look at both identify supply chain-based risks and after that integrate them into the corporate risk map. Lufthansa has accomplished the identification of all supplier risks according to their type and levels. every product group manager has accomplished risk assessment for their supplier. the procurement units responsible for product groups carries out a risk assessment for the suppliers. risk assessment results are included in their Group risk management. their risk analyses are based on all direct suppli-

Fig. 9.2 New AviSCRM model: conceptual framework for aviation

ers on both expenditure and country. they develop actions plan for Suppliers in "extreme risk" countries. and they are working with the advisory company to make a risk analysis. they are assessing their supplier risks. also, the procurement units responsible for product groups carry out a risk assessment. https://investor-relations.lufthansagroup.com/fileadmin/downloads/en/financial-reports/annual-reports/LH-AR-2020-e.pdf

9.5 Industry Manufacturers: Aircraft and Aircraft Spare Parts

The aviation industry requires a flexible, secure, sustainable, and fast-running supply network due to its scope and the structure of aviation operations.

Companies that manufacture aircrafts and their parts collaborate with airlines. They supply in line with the demands of the airline companies in the market. Clearly, the production of the aircraft and its parts, which is the most basic element of aviation before the fleet formation process of the airline companies, is the beginning of many processes.

When an airplane must stay on the ground due to technical malfunctions (AOG), high costs may be incurred. Missing even a single part can halt an entire production or maintenance process. Nobody wants a delayed flight to be further delayed or worse, a malfunction during the flight. At this point, although the passengers are flying under the security of the captain pilot, in fact, everyone on the aircraft can be present to the extent that the supply and logistical facilities allow. Every single creature in the aircraft is flying under relative assurance of supply, and this is a huge responsibility. When it comes to servicing aircraft in service, nothing is more important than speed and reliability. Every minute that aircrafts are on the ground (AOG) translates into loss of revenue.

The supply of aircraft and spare parts cover the procurement process of all kinds of materials and parts belonging to the whole aircraft, from the largest aircraft parts to the most sensitive and smallest components.

It is very important for everyone to be able to supply these parts as quickly as possible in case of a potential malfunction at the airport. Meanwhile, for a safe and timely flight, each of these parts and components must be well preserved.

In this view, highly important parts and components such as airframe parts, assembly parts, engines, helicopters and helicopter parts, brakes, landing brakes, and hoods are carried with the highest safety precautions. Parts put into circulation upon customer demand are delivered to their intended destination on time. During the management of the process, packaging, shipping, and storage conditions are met in line with customer demands.

To understand the aviation industry's supply chain, a holistic understanding of all relevant stakeholders of the industry and their interactions with each other is required. This interaction is the necessary initial step for identifying risks and risk sources and, therefore, developing risk management strategies. Considerably, value is created by chains in aviation industry. Thus, value-based management implications support corporate sustainability.

Air transport involves more than merely moving people from one place to another. As already demonstrated, it incorporates many services. Therefore, it needs different organizations and businesses in order to obtain these services. Examples such as financing, advertising, legal affairs, flight operations, personnel, engineering, maintenance, and catering services can be considered. Thanks to the presence of each of the abovementioned, the airline travel chain can be completed.

The source of the acceleration of aviation development is the rapid follow-up of technological innovations and its rapid adaptation to the industry. In addition, for sustainable competition, the use of developing technologies, ensuring timely use, integration into systems, and continuous use are among the vital needs. In this context, it is a prominent requirement that air transport is the most flexible sector in the human-machine interface. Clearly, it brings along the unique risks of flexible systems and situational approaches in managing these risks.

Increasing mobility around the world has made aviation activities the preferred means of transportation. Until the restrictions caused by the pandemic, the industry has experienced a very rapid growth and development momentum in the last 50 years. Sustainable development will not be possible to be achieved without a compatible supply chain management.

While products and services are produced in aviation, businesses purchase materials, equipment, software, spare parts, and services from both domestic and foreign companies. This requires considering the risks in the areas of import, export, and customs clearance in supply chain management. In this respect, it may be useful to create a supply portfolio in terms of resource dependency in the aviation industry, oligopoly market, and scale economy-based features and associated risks. However, in some cases, there may not be an alternative supplier due to technical reasons or agreements. Thus, when determining supply chain risk management strategies, risk sources are also considered. Strategies are developed with the goal of optimization, according to risk sources. Optimization covers the areas of meeting the required products and services to the competitive environment cost-effectively, with appropriate quality and in the right amount at the right time.

The air transport industry has an oligopolistic structure. Oligopoly refers to the fact that a large number of buyers purchase from a small number of sellers, and that the companies in the industry consider the activities of other companies while carrying out their activities. In addition to the entry barriers in the industry, there are also features, such as the economies of scale, that concern the economic dimension of airline transport; growth through mergers, interdependence, being a capital-intensive sector; high cash flow, being a labor-intensive sector; low profit margins; and changing demand according to the seasons (Kocak, 2016).

Accelerated changes and technological innovations in the business environment have led to noticeable structural transformations in business approach, business models, and their processes. Accordingly, businesses adapt risk management-based practices in order to optimally ensure the supply of product and service production factors, and the delivery of services and products to customers. In this context, they have started to include the issues of which risks they face, which ways they will follow in determining the sources of these risks, and how they will manage the identified risks in their decision-making processes. Therefore, supply chain risk management supports cost-effective adaptation to current conditions by improving the level of flexibility. It also ensures the correct identification of investment areas, the use of communication and monitoring systems that improve the level of institutionalization, the development of sustainability-based resource dependency strategies, the implementation of cost-effective risk management solutions, and the continuous monitoring of performance. Thus, supply chain risk management includes factors that support sustainability for aviation businesses as it ensures that the right product is kept in the right amount, in the right place, with high flexibility, and in a low cycle time.

The effectively managed supply chain supports the business to rank higher in the sustainability index. In this connection, sustainability is evaluated in four dimensions. Supply chain risk management supports organizations to achieve their economic, social, organizational, and environmental sustainability goals. This support creates competitive advantage and increased market share opportunity for organizations and/or businesses. In this respect, the stakeholders to be included in the procurement system should be carefully determined.

Air transport is a large industry and its preference can be increased by being in harmony with the organizations and businesses it hosts and by optimizing reliable, safe, and quality services. Considering the maintenance part in this chain, an airline business must be able to get the confidence it expects from its maintenance and repair service. Airplanes are made up of quite a few components. For example, a missing screw can endanger the safety of flight. As regards safety, the aircraft maintenance team is equally important with the pilots. The training and experience received by technicians working in aircraft maintenance companies play a pivotal role. Theoretical, simulative, and practical training should be offered to employees. Moreover, all processes need to be progressed quickly and flawlessly. In parallel, the planning of maintenance is another equally important factor. Maintenance should be carried out properly and on time, and proceed in accordance with aviation laws. Simultaneously, the tools and liquids needed for these phased maintenance operations should be of high quality, reliable, and suitable for use. It is the maintenance and repair company that needs to obtain these from suppliers. At the end of the day, the maintenance and repair area are vital parts of sustainable and/or uninterrupted aviation activities and operations.

In the air transport industry, companies that produce aircraft and parts, airlines, airport companies, maintenance enterprises, food (catering) businesses, ground services, fuel companies, technical enterprises, flight training companies, and air traffic enterprises closely collaborate. In this working process, there are areas where they interact with each other in terms of supply. Thus, it is also necessary for businesses to strengthen their relations with each other and to develop cooperation based on trust in order to manage supply chain risks in the desired way. For example, The Lufthansa Group's expectations of its suppliers in terms of social and ecological responsibility are summarized in the Supplier Code of Conduct. P.114 https://investor-relations.lufthansagroup.com/fileadmin/downloads/en/financial-reports/annual-reports/LH-AR-2020-e.pdf.

Companies that manufacture aircrafts and their parts cooperate with airlines. Special alloy materials, motors, electronics, and support systems that are not used in most other industries are used in aviation. Extraordinary applications in many engineering fields, from high-speed aerodynamics, resistance to very harsh environmental conditions, to the design of high strength with very light structures, are carried out in the aviation industry (Republic of Turkey Presidency, Strategy and Budget Directorate, 2020).

Airport operators ensure that airline companies carry out their transportation operations safely, by fulfilling the necessary standards. They collaborate closely with airlines at the point where aircrafts pass from ground to air and from air to ground. On the other hand, maintenance services, ground services, food (catering) services, and fuel companies also find work areas for themselves in the centers of airport operations.

Spare parts are items that can be exchanged, that are kept in the inventory to repair or replace the defective part. Clearly, spare parts have a great role in the supply chain and they should be tracked with information systems. The inventory management of spare parts is an important issue to be considered, as some of them break down frequently while others fail frequently. The supply of spare parts may not be economical in some cases for the following reasons: (Wikipedia; http://en.wikipedia.org/wiki/sparepart).

(a) It is possible that parts are not used.
(b) Failure to properly store parts may result in malfunctions.
(c) Requires incurring inventory costs.
(d) Parts may not be available from the supplier when needed.

Airline companies make one of the most important contributions to this process with fleet formation. The fleet, which is very costly and the basis of air transport operations, is formed by airlines, and interaction with other businesses takes shape at the airline's headquarters. It should not be overlooked that aviation operations are interdisciplinary work. Each business has a very important role. However, having customer finance and aircraft are essential for a breakthrough in the industry.

Maintenance businesses are directly related to airlines and technical businesses. Aircraft airworthiness is formed by the cooperation of maintenance and technical operations. On the other hand, they are indirectly related to the airport operation. Provision of the area where maintenance is performed is arranged by the airport management in a coordinated manner to ensure security. Fuel businesses are directly related to airlines and airport businesses. Fuel companies, which take the task of transporting the fuel from the center to the aircraft, can position their fuel-filled vehicles close to the aircraft, by paying to the airport operators whose area they use for rent. Food (catering) services are associated with airlines and ground handling services. These businesses, which are among the customer targets of airline companies, also cooperate with ground services, which also include passenger businesses.

Flight academies and flight schools are also indirectly associated with airlines and maintenance businesses. In effect, this sector covers more airline companies that provide training within its scope. The training and individual skills of the flight or maintenance personnel they have trained will indirectly affect the organizations in these fields. Indeed, they are directly related if we consider the effect of the human factor during the flight operation.

Aviation is a globally developing and very comprehensive industry. Many areas are essential for this industry to form. In simple terms, the aircraft factory and hundreds of engineers and technicians are needed for aircraft production. In parallel, supply companies should step in for raw material and parts requirements. For the aircraft to take off and land, the airport, air traffic control (ATC) units, and the operation of these places are required. Air law contains strict clauses, and they are all rules that must be followed. A different service is required for the maintenance of the aircraft. Moreover, personnel recruitment and training is required to ensure flight. Furthermore, advertising is required to gain customers. Different organizations are needed for the health, safety, and comfort of the passengers (insurance, catering, seating). In addition, we come across many aspects and procedures involved such as flight schools, trainings given to technicians, the engineering required for airport construction, the way the raw material is obtained, the financing of the airline, legal transactions, and website management for the training the personnel receive.

The fleet structure, planning, and the variety of aircraft in airlines vary according to the type of aviation business, the customers it will serve, and the flight network. For airlines to establish their fleet, aircraft manufacturers are indispensable and vital suppliers, since no airline can design and therefore manufacture its own aircraft. Airline companies should procure aircraft from aircraft manufacturers in order to start their activities and to continue these activities. There are very few suppliers in the world related to the production of aircrafts with very high costs. In parallel, manufacturing aircrafts requires an advanced technical expertise. While the production of aircrafts is of great importance for airline companies, it is a direct factor for customers, because when airline customers are segmented by marketers, the customer segment is of a serious size, with less price sensitivity but high sensitivity to quality, comfort, and convenience. Therefore, it is important that the aircraft be produced by aircraft manufacturers that meet the expectations of this customer segment and directly affect airline-customer relations. Another key factor to be considered is safety and security. The high risks of air travel make some issues more important for customers. Thus, the first issue that customers pay attention to safety and security is how the aircraft is used and the aircraft quality. In terms of airline business, the fact that the aircraft is new and built by a well-known manufacturer is advantageous to the customer, and, in this respect, it directly affects the customer.

Aircraft engine production and aviation industry is considered as a field that has no application in other industries and requires very deep experience and production technologies. Therefore, aviation industry investments require economic, capacity, and technology usage skills. Hence, there are very few aircraft engine manufacturers in the world. Entering the aircraft engine field and achieving success is difficult for the reasons listed above.

Aircraft engine requires unique, multi-disciplinary technologies and some specialized knowledge. This information is difficult to know and master in other branches of industry, and its areas of use are extremely narrow.

Rolls-Royce Holding that manufactures commercial engines also manufactures for military aircraft and ships. The number of aircraft engine manufacturers is very limited. The main ones include Pratt & Whitney (1925, USA), General Electric (1892, USA), Rolls-Royce (1904, UK), Japanese jet engine manufacturer IHI, NPO Saturn (1916, Russia). Usually, an engine flies for an average of 20–30 years in an aircraft. As a result of the slightest mistake, social and economic bills are high and the effects of that continue for many years. Therefore, intensive studies are carried out in order to avoid moral and material losses, to make full and reliable production, and to minimize the risks. The amount of resources—time, financing, research and development work—where aircraft engine malfunctions or technical errors need to be corrected can be very high and require a lot of time.

"The A&D sector is experiencing a significant growth in demand. The growth in demand increases pressure on the production capacity for OEMs and their suppliers. In the case of critical parts and assemblies, the number of available suppliers is small. For such parts, the risk of production disruption due to supply failure is even greater," says Bill Colbert, Partner, Advisory—US, Ernst & Young, in the report (SATAIR, 2021, https://blog.satair.com/ten-risk-in-aviation-industry).

There are many product and service suppliers in the aviation industry. There is more than one supply chain of airline companies, ground handling companies, and aircraft manufacturers that first receive services in many areas, such as maintenance repair, flight planning, operational services, aircraft allocation, personnel recruitment, and customer service, and then offer this service component to the customer. Although they provide a service in some areas from their own internal resources, they generally turn to external resources due to the high cost in the industry and the fact that they are in a competitive market. These external sources can be national organizations, aircraft suppliers, cargo services, security services, catering providers, ticket vendors, and fuel suppliers. Although suppliers have an important place in the aviation industry, they have to keep up with the technological developments in the industry. For example, CORNEA Havacılık Sistemleri Sanayive Ticaret A.Ş is a company that provides technological systems in the aviation industry. It produces in-cabin entertainment and internet service provider systems for air vehicles. Capable of producing many in-cabin entertainments equipment, Cornea's products include wireless IFE, seat-back IFE, and tablet base IFE. Another example is GE Aviation. The center, which focuses on the design and technology development of GE Aviation's commercial and military aircraft, vessel, and industrial engines, contributes to new designs and technologies used in aircraft flying around the world with engines produced by GE and the joint venture company CFM International.

Airline companies need aircrafts and parts production, maintenance, airports, airport terminals, catering, ground, fuel, technical, and air traffic businesses in order to maintain their assets and activities. Airports, airport terminal companies, airlines, ground handling companies, catering service providers, maintenance and repair organizations operating in the aviation industry all interact with and depend on each other to continue their activities safely, fully, and accurately. Airlines obtain their spare parts from aircraft manufacturers, such as Airbus and Boeing. Each aircraft has its own manual handbooks. Handbooks which clearly mention when the parts need to be replaced. This is also included in regular maintenance planning. Since it is not known when unaccounted errors or electronic parts will break down, each airline must keep extra spare parts in their warehouses by calculating them. Otherwise, any unforeseen breakdown may cause the plane not to be flown for days as parts need to be delivered to airlines.

Suppliers are vital business partners for Airline companies. Airline companies are collaborating with suppliers in their all operations and activities as following areas: the service production and provision processes; allocation of the aircraft to be used in their fleets; maintenance and repair services for the aircraft in their fleets; permits required from the competent authorities to continue their activities; network planning; marketing and advertising activities; catering services; handling services; obtain products and services; personnel employment; other operational services; ticketing and reservation systems and services; establishment of risk management systems; capacity building; personnel and manager training; customer services. Although their own internal resources are used in the services to be provided in some areas, due to the high costs and competition in the industry, they adopt an outsourcing strategy in some areas such as education, establishment of quality systems, and risk management systems and catering services. Thus, it is possible for airline companies to produce and offer products and services thanks to the suppliers. Therefore, the suppliers they collaborate with are in the position of business partners and stakeholders for airline companies.

"Safety First!"

Safety and security are key priority in aviation. Therefore, supply chains must be built on transparency, trust, and reliability. In evaluating the effect of airport operations on airline companies in terms of safety, the concept of security will emerge. Airport businesses provide security services. In this respect, it is vital that security risks are fully and accurately managed so that the flights are carried out as planned.

The procurement process in the systems of organizations in aviation starts with the emergence of the needs for the system and ends with the activities until the system is removed from the inventory. Supply chain risk management should be established and implemented, in order to add value to the supply value chain. Therefore, the airline's economic, social, and environmental sustainability depends on its ability to meet changing demands in a volatile business environment, to compete, to establish supply chains based on cooperation and trust, and to optimally manage supply chain risks. In general, the supply chain and risk management systems that aviation organizations need to establish are shaped by their long-term managerial strategies and resources, tactics in the medium term, and daily operational decisions in the short term. Collaborative relationships with their suppliers also provide aviation businesses with advantages in terms of cost-effective results and better delivery time. From this point on, the successful management of a supply chain in aviation depends on the dynamic, trust-based, and cooperative relations of the stakeholders forming the chain. Supply chain risk management also guides aviation organizations on how to improve their relationships with their suppliers.

9.6 Multi-criteria Decision-Making Problem: Supplier Relations in the Aviation Industry

Different organizations work in cooperation with aviation and that has the potential to affect each other directly or indirectly as they are in a continuous and affecting relationship with each other at every stage of the flight. These services are included under the main categories of security services, catering, aircraft maintenance, financial service, tour operator, airport services, terminal management, aircraft rental, hotel management, information technology management, insurance management, and store management. By the way of illustration, airline companies obtain support services that are outside of their area of expertise from ground handling companies. Moreover, ground handling companies provide the necessary external resources for the realization of flight operations by presenting the works of their own to airline companies. Thus, each organization aims to achieve sustainable financial and operational success by focusing on its core competence. For airport services that can respond to the increasing demand for air transport, these organizations must carry out their activities in a healthy way.

Supplier evaluation process is a critical decision-making process that requires taking many facts into consideration in order to effectively manage the supply chain. The most popular criteria, considered by decision-makers in supplier selection, are quality, delivery, price/cost, production capability, service, management, technology, research and development, finance, flexibility, reputation, relationship, risk, safety, and environment. Since supplier selection decisions involve the evaluation of different criteria, this process emerges as a multi-criteria decision problem. Regarding this concept, Turkish Airlines could serve as an example. The Turkish Airlines group includes 17 companies. This means that they have companies which are also suppliers in aviation such as catering, oil, and maintenance fields. The main services received by Turkish Airlines and the supplier partners providing these services are as follows:

(i) *Fuel: Thy OpetHavacılık Fuels A.Ş.*
(ii) *Maintenance and Repair: TürkHavaYollarıTeknik A.Ş.*
(iii) *Catering: THY DO&CO İkramHizmetleri A.Ş.*
(iv) *Cabin: TCI Cabin Interior Systems San. ve Tic. A.S.,UçakKoltukÜretim San. ve Tic. A.S.*
(v) *Education: Thy Flight Training and Airport Management Inc. (TAFA)*

(source: Turkish Airlines (2021) Group Companies, https://investor.turkishairlines.com/tr/hakkimizda/grup-sirketleri)

Aircraft manufacturers are heavily dependent on demand from the air transport industry, either directly or through leasing companies. Air transport is linked in terms of both the level of activity and strategic decisions regarding airports and aircraft manufacturing. The change in passengers' behavior following the COVID-19 crisis, travel restrictions, and the ensuing economic crisis has led to a dramatic decline in demand for airline services. Through cross-industry linkages, this uncertainty affects the entire aviation industry (OECD, 2021, 1 http://www.oecd.org/coronavirus/policy-responses/covid-19-and-the-aviation-industry-impact-and-policy-responses-26d521c1/).

Aircraft asset values have decreased. As a result of this coup, many aircraft had to retire early and leave. In December 2020, consulting firm Ishka estimated that the valuations of 15-year-old aircraft had dropped between 20% and 47% since the beginning of the year. While cargo conversions mitigate further devaluation, other analysts forecast a 50% reduction in aircraft valuations. It is estimated that there are more than 5000 aircraft in the system. Supply for parts already exceeds demand, and as a result, aircraft will retire and begin to break apart at a higher rate than we have seen before, although not all, to avoid a complete market crash (https://armac-systems.com/optimizing-component-availability-sourcing-post-covid-19/).

Five hundred sixty-six aircraft were delivered by Airbus in 2020. This number is 34% less than 2019. While 1131 net commercial aircraft orders were received in 2019, 383 net aircraft orders were received in 2020 (AIRBUS, 2021, https://www.airbus.com/aircraft/market/orders-deliveries.html#results).One hundred fifty-seven commercial aircraft were delivered by the Boeing company in 2020. This number is 380 in 2019. While 246 net commercial aircraft orders were received in 2019, 184 net commercial aircraft orders were received in 2020 (https://www.boeing.com/commercial/). Today, the 2021 fleet has more than 23,700 aircraft, while by 2031 the fleet is estimated to be more than 36,500. However, it is still far from pre-COVID predictions, making the 2021 global fleet 28,800 and the 2030 fleet more than 39,000. None of the three segments—airlines, aviation, and MRO—are expected to meet pre-COVID predictions by the end of 10 years. For MRO companies, a smaller fleet means less business. The demand is expected to be 33 percent, or $ 60 billion, below combined pre-COVID estimates for 2020 and 2021. As the market begins to recover, the long-term MRO growth trend is currently about half of pre-COVID expectations. Cumulatively, demand for MRO is expected to be $ 95 billion lower over the forecast period (https://www.oliverwyman.com/our-expertise/insights/2021/jan/global-fleet-and-mro-maket-forecast-2021–2031.html?utm_source=forbes&utm_medium=referral&utm_campaign=mro-forecast&utm_content=2021-jan&utm_id=cmp-10984-x9y4v0).

In the next decade, 4700 aircrafts, which were put into production at the beginning of 2020, will no longer be built. This is the equivalent to 2.5 years of production lost almost overnight. Most suppliers quickly increased capacity to support overflowing orders from leading aerospace manufacturers in 2018 and 2019. At present, they find themselves in an idle capacity and cannot pay the debt of this investment. Aircraft cancellations and delays related to COVID-19 are catching up with production schedules: 1800 planned deliveries or 55% of the expected number will not end in 2020. The slowdown will continue until 2021, when production will be 30 percent lower and deliveries will decrease by about 20 percent compared to pre-COVID estimates. By 2021, the fleet will be 18% smaller than the beginning of 2020. By 2030—almost a decade later—a fleet of approximately 34,300 aircrafts will be 12% below pre-COVID estimates for that year (https://www.oliverwyman.

com/our-expertise/insights/2020/nov/covid-19-closures-in-aerospace-supply-chain.html.). The level of fleet inactivity will worsen before it improves, resulting in more aircraft that never return to active service. Additional capacity demand will remain quiet, lease extensions and placements will become more difficult, and OEM production rates may not return to 2018–2019 levels before 2025 (https://www.pwc.ie/reports/aviation-industry-outlook-2021.html).

9.7 Risks and Sources of Risk Under Supply Areas in the Aviation Industry

Performance, cost, and certification requirements are of paramount importance for aircraft and supply chains to remain competitive in the industry. Engines are one of the costliest components of aircrafts, and their life cycle cost is also quite high. Moreover, engine suppliers are limited worldwide. Most of the engine subcomponents have a short life cycle and heavy maintenance costs.

In today's supply world, competition is no longer between competitors but between supply chains, in which these companies are also included. Only those who provide the fastest, best performing, best solutions, most cost-effective, products/services of the described quality, will be able to increase their share of the cake by gaining competitive advantage. It is clear that in the defense aviation industry, which is the driving force in the political, commercial, and military relations of our country as well as the world, it is clear that effective and efficient supply chains should be established as a basis for effective resource management in terms of cost, time, and labor (Öçlü, 2015).

Airlines need aircraft maintenance services. Organizations operating in this business are called MROs. Airline companies receive comprehensive services from these organizations, such as calibration, line maintenance, base maintenance, AOG services, NDT, engine and APU, component maintenance, engineering services, landing gear maintenance services, and in-flight maintenance services. In order for these services to be applied to commercial airline aircrafts, the organization must be certified by the national and international aviation authorities. Clearly, obtaining such technical services from approved and regularly audited institutions will have a positive contribution to safety. Operational safety has reached the highest level thanks to the aircrafts, which are regularly maintained by trained, qualified, and experienced personnel.

Enterprises in aviation should collaborate with a wide supplier network for the production of products and services. Potential errors and delays in this vast network could cause a chain reaction and consequently budgets and programs could get out of control. In these respects, Ernst & Young points out that there is a risk that companies may have disputes with suppliers or subcontractors regarding job specifications, supply quality, or customer concerns. Since this risk of conflict can damage the trust and partnerships between aviation companies and their suppliers, it also poses a risk that threatens sustainable production

In their study, SATAIR points to three additional challenges and types of risks in the aviation industry that could pose a threat to the efficiency of the supply chain as follows (SATAIR, 2020):

(i) *Niche parts and processes pose a greater risk to on-time delivery:* For some parts, such as composite components and wing skins, MROs and airlines depend on a small number of suppliers, leaving them with few options in case of failures or disruptions. This challenge can be somewhat mitigated by working closely with the supplier to understand the stability and detect potential disruptions before they develop into full-scale disasters.

(ii) *Further risks associated with low-cost countries:* As the demand for air travel rises in emerging economies, OEMs, airlines, and MROs are establishing new connections with local suppliers. Though working with local suppliers has significant cost benefits, it, too, could expose this part of the aviation industry to critical issues, such as IP violations, delays, and quality issues.

(iii) *Investment to fund new programs and technologies:* Implementation of new programs and technologies ties up significant capital. The cost to develop new initiatives, such as additive manufacturing, must be recouped on volume production, but the investment might initially leave companies more financially exposed, thus posing a risk to the entire aviation supply chain.

(Source: SATAIR, 2020, The top 10 risks the aviation industry is facing, compliance, Jan 1, 2020, Retrieved at March 2021 fromhttps://blog.satair.com/ten-risk-in-aviation-industry)

In conclusion, supply chains, which play a decisive role in the production of products and services in the aviation industry, must have a high and sustainable performance level for their corporate sustainability, maintain their cost-effective activities, and maintain a relationship based on trust and set cooperation.

Aircraft Maintenance

The need for maintenance, repair, and renovation as airline transportation is rapidly increasing, and with this, the (MRO) sector is growing at a great pace in the same direction. Maintenance and repair activity require a very good supply chain system and its management. Therefore, the development and continuous growth of the aviation repair and maintenance sector at the same pace with the development acceleration of aviation are important for managing the sustainability risk of production in aviation.

Turkish Technique serves as an example. This company, which serves many airlines, also serves Turkish Airlines and Pegasus. Airlines do not prefer to establish their own maintenance services due to the high costs. It is more appropriate to receive services by specialist care companies. Aircraft Maintenance Organizations have their own fees at the airports and operate there.

Risks Associated with Purchasing Spare Parts

Spare parts supply is one of the critical risks affecting sustainability in terms of both time and quantity. The main condition for the provision of products and services in the aviation industry is the production of spare parts in sufficient quantity, the supply of these parts without damage with correct shipping, the stocking and use of the supplied parts are the main stages of the process, and the risks of each phase affect the products and services (Fig. 9.3).

Spare parts concern the airline in terms of stock and finances. In addition, the timely and sufficient supply of all kinds of consumables used by the aircraft (hydraulic oil, engine oil, etc.) affects the flight schedules and the duration of the aircraft on the ground (Yont & Bugdayci, 1998).

Airlines obtain their spare parts from aircraft manufacturers such as Airbus and Boeing. Each aircraft has its own manual handbooks. It is written when the parts need to be replaced. This is also included in regular maintenance planning. Since it

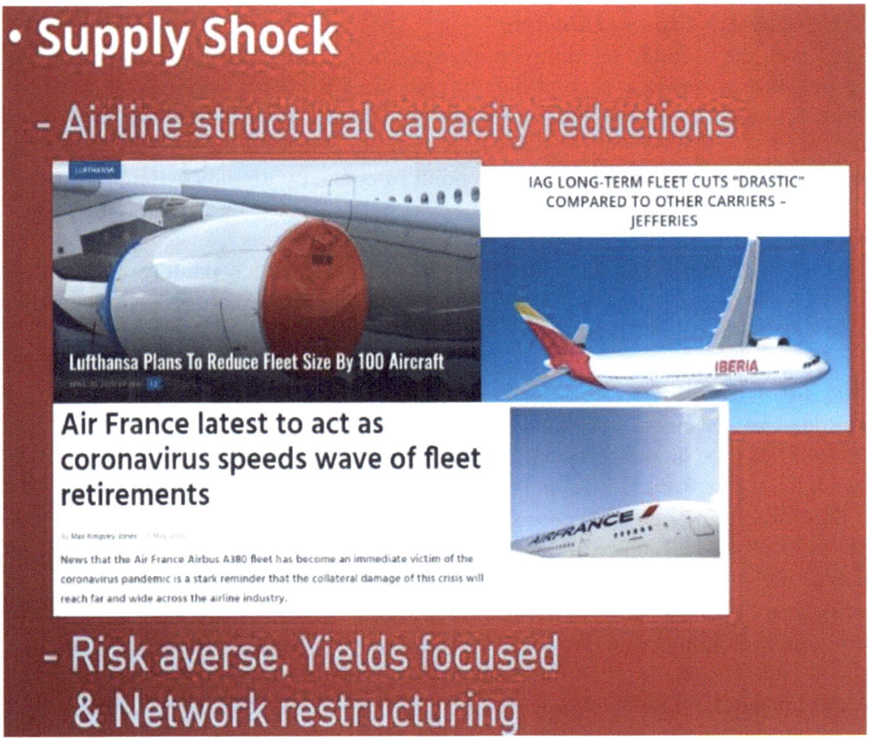

Fig. 9.3 Supply shock—Airline structural capacity reductions—Risk averse, Yields focused & Network restructuring. (Source: Olivier Jankovec Director General,ACI_EUROPE, State Of The European Airport Industry, Cappadocia University « Fore-sight of the Next Decade, 16 March 2021. https://kapadokya.edu.tr/MediaUploader/Documents/ACI_EUROPE_Keynote%20Speech_16.03.21.pdf)

is not known when unforeseen failures or electronic parts will break down, each airline must keep extra spare parts in their warehouses by calculating themselves.

Risks Associated with Software Purchase
HititYazılım, which sells software to airline companies, can serve as an example. In the recent past, Hitit software has also started to sell software to foreign airlines. By trusting experts, airlines buy a less costly and better-quality service. The service is provided on the online web.

Risks Related to Receiving Catering Service
LGS Sky Chefs, Gate Gourmet, and Servair are companies that provide different catering services around the world. Do-Co catering company was established in partnership with Turkish Airlines. It serves more than 60 airlines. Other airlines outsource this service, as well. The main reason is that the establishment costs are high.

Risks Related to Ground Handling
There are many ground handling companies such as Havaş, TGS, and Çelebi. The airlines wish to provide ground handling services to their customers. It is known that it is at a very critical point and any error will cause customer loss. Ultimately, costs are less when outsourcing. Ground handling companies are located at the airport. This is very important as it is the point of contact with the customer.

Aircraft Receiving: Aircraft Supply
Generally, airplanes are procured from two major vendors, namely, Boeing and Airbus. The rate of Airbus in the fleet of airlines in Turkey is increasing steadily. Turkey is increasing its relations with Airbus steadily due to regional reasons.

Risks Involved in Staff Training: Training provision
Training services and training documents may be obtained from internal and national sources or international and external sources. Turkish Technic receives training services from Eskişehir Technical University. Outsourcing is preferred due to the limited number of licensed expert trainers in the field. Airlines make purchases, such as fuel, catering, and spare parts. Combustible and heavy materials, such as fuel, are transported from one point to another by cargo vessels. Spare parts products are also delivered by sea transportation if there is no emergency. In case of emergency, products are delivered by air transport from manufacturers such as Airbus and Boeing, too. Purchases made in this respect with digital and electronic stock control of the companies.

Airline transportation and supply chains management concept have undergone changes and innovations with the COVID-19 pandemic. In freight transport, two types of transport stand out in the airline industry. The first is the operations of large transport aircrafts by air cargo companies, the second is the operations carried out by using the spaces left from the passenger loads in the lower-check section of the passenger transport aircrafts. Air cargo has become more prominent due to the decrease in passenger transportation, due to the pandemic. In this view, air cargo companies continued to work by increasing their assets without being damaged during the pandemic period. Moreover, they analyzed the growing market well and there were companies that proceeded to strategy changes.

9.8 In the Shadow of the Pandemic Perspective to Aviation Industry Supply Chain Management/ Pandemic-Based Analysis

COVID-19 is constantly making changes in lives in both peoples and business. We have met new mandatory changes in all social lives and business lives, with dramatic losses. All economies and lives are reinvented. Thus, sharp changes create challenges for all business sectors with national economies.

"Business Continuity Risks"

One of the biggest impacts has been the reduction in passenger transport demand, due to a combination of government lockdowns and fears of contracting and spreading the virus when using mass transport modes. While freight transport has also been reduced, the drivers of freight activity during the current crisis are complex, driven by both supply- and demand-side factors, and in the latter, by the need to keep essential services operating. In contrast, passenger transport (for both leisure and business travel) is often optional, and more influenced by people's decision-making processes (IEA International Energy Agency (2020), Changes in transport behaviour during the Covid-19 crisis, Jeremy Sung and Yannick Monschauer, https://www.iea.org/articles/changes-in-transport-behaviour-during-the-covid-19-crisis).

One of the biggest impacts has been the reduction in passenger transport demand, due to a combination of government lockdowns and fears of contracting and spreading the virus when using mass transport modes. While freight transport has also been reduced, the drivers of freight activity during the current crisis are complex, driven by both supply- and demand-side factors, and in the latter, by the need to keep essential services operating. In contrast, passenger transport (for both leisure and business travel) is often optional, and more influenced by people's decision-making processes. The focus of this chapter is therefore on passenger transport (IAE, 2020, (https://www.iea.org/articles/changes-in-transport-behaviour-during-the-covid-19-crisis).

Aviation industry is a high-tech, knowledge-intensive, and expensive industry both qualitatively and quantitatively, and it is a pioneering sector that requires very well-trained manpower and large financial resources. Therefore, it is clearly observed that it plays a "locomotive" role for other industrial branches, while contributing to economic development, providing employment for educated workforce, reducing dependency in critical technologies and systems, and improving international trade.

The aviation industry has experienced tremors before, such as the oil crisis of the 1970s and September 11; but none have done as much damage as the COVID-19 pandemic. The annual number of passengers, which has increased over the last 10 years, has dropped so drastically that it seems as if the person drawing the chart fell asleep. According to the report of the International Civil Aviation Organization dated June 5, in 2020 the number of passengers worldwide will experience a decrease of between 2.3 billion and 3.1 billion—40%–53% of the total number of seats. This will cause a loss of 300–400 billion in turnover (GE Turkey Blog, https://geturkiyeblog.com/havacilik-endustrisinin-daha-hizli-toparlanmasina-yardimci-olabilecek-uygulama/).

We are experiencing extraordinary times due to the pandemic. Aviation is among the sectors that are most affected by the pandemic, due to the restrictions on flights between countries, yet it adapts the fastest to new regulations. In view of this, it is considered safer than other indoor daily activities such as grocery shopping or dining out.

As the pandemic affected every industry, it diversified the sustainability risks in the aviation industry and made it difficult due to resource constraints. Compared to the previous year, more than 60 percent decrease was observed in air traffic, and flights came to a halt. Companies have suffered financial losses as the planes need to be maintained even when they are not flying. Many companies have faced bankruptcy. At the same time, problems arose for those working in airlines, they lost their jobs, or could not receive their salaries. Airline companies that do not hire employees have adopted the principle of working part time. They worked 2 days per week and paid half the wage. Due to the lack of new recruitment during this period, many new graduates became unemployed. Flight schools could not graduate students as they could not conduct flight training activities. At the same time, aircraft manufacturers were in a difficult situation, and even leading companies such as Boeing and Airbus experienced a decrease in the number of employees. If one considers the losses of big companies:

(i) Lufthansa lost approximately 3 billion euros in the first half of 2020. It has been heard that there is an excess of 22 thousand personnel and it is thought that 100 aircraft should be removed from the fleet.
(ii) Ryanair experienced a turnover loss of 95 percent in April and June compared to the same time period last year. It suffered a loss of 185 million euros.
(iii) International Airlines Group's turnover fell to 5.3 billion euros.
(iv) It has been heard that 12 thousand personnel working at British Airways will be dismissed.

Aviation is primarily an industry that provides transportation services and, therefore, an area where people need to work and be in close proximity with each other. As such, it is very vulnerable to the pandemic. First of all, the most noticeable effect was the decline in passenger demand, which affected airline revenues to a great extent, and subsequently one of the important details, the problems in the areas of supply, maintenance and repair, and spare parts production, which are considered to be the cornerstone of aviation.

> *The year 2020 entered the history books as a year of great changes due to the COVID-19 epidemic. The volume of global aviation dropped to almost zero during this period, as aviation authorities completely stopped international flights in the second quarter of the year to slow the spread of the virus. The flight restriction measures taken in the second quarter were slightly eased in the third quarter and accordingly, TAV Airports experienced a strong recovery period in international passenger traffic in the third quarter of 2020. However, restrictions on commercial travel still persist between most countries, including the geographies where TAV operates. In most countries that allow commercial travel, passengers are expected to experience a quarantine period in their destination country and document a COVID-19 negative test result before boarding. As a result of these practices, unrestricted reciprocal travel opportunities still exist among very few countries. The number of passengers we serve in 2020 has decreased by 70% compared to 2019, due to travel restrictions applied to different degrees throughout the year. All components of the industry, consisting of airport operators and airlines around the world, have also gone through a similar year. The industry expects commercial flight restrictions to be lifted towards the second half of the year, as vaccination, which started in December 2020, exceeds a critical threshold in 2021.* (https://webcmstavairports.tav.aero/files/1615449193_Faaliyet%20Raporu%20 2020%20TR.pdf)

The aviation industry is one of the sectors most affected by the pandemic caused by the SARS-CoV-2 virus. Due to the inward closure of countries, flights between countries have decreased critically. In this respect, to address this situation, airlines have adopted ways such as flight cancellation and delay. In order to take the necessary precautions in domestic flights, the necessary tests and social distance practices have been implemented. In the pandemic reality, which people have not encountered before and which has been very difficult in terms of finding solutions, the demand rate has decreased considerably as people prefer to use their own private vehicles as a means of in-country transportation. The fact that the aircraft that are grounded are parked in suitable environments has created a large amount of extra cost for airlines. According to pre-pandemic plans, airline companies, in employing personnel are turning to methods such as unpaid leaves for their employees. In this context, the lack of employment of new personnel has created a job finding problem for people oriented toward this field. The fact that some countries do not accept visitors from foreign countries, due to the virus variables, has also caused this situation to create bigger problems in the sector. The pandemic period has created a crisis not only for airline companies and their employees, but also for food, fuel, luggage, accommodation, cleaning companies, and ticket selling websites. The impact of the pandemic on the production and supply link in the sectors where airline companies receive service has created a problem in the way of transferring services, even in the number of flights that are in critical condition (Maneenop & Kotcharin, 2020).

In order to evaluate the impact of the pandemic process on the aviation industry through production resources, businesses that produce aircrafts and parts, fuel businesses, and catering businesses are at the forefront. Aircraft manufacturing companies contribute to the formation of the fuselage by integrating many parts of the aircraft, such as engine, tire, and flight equipment. On the other hand, we can consider the extraction of the fuel as raw material and processing it as the production process. Subsequently, fuel is presented to air transport companies as a product source. Finally, catering businesses produce food and allow these foods to reach flight personnel, passengers, and ground services in air transport companies. The problems experienced by all these enterprises in the process of providing production resources include cargo, information exchange, purchasing power, coordinated work, and decrease in customer potential.

The hesitation of cargo transportation by land, sea, and air, at the beginning of the pandemic period, created an important resource transportation barrier. Although cargo transportation was not affected as much as passenger transportation, the initial gap entailed great costs. The fact that the companies producing aircrafts and their parts are in different countries and even in other continents negatively affected the product sharing between each other during the pandemic period. Restrictions and measures between countries have greatly reduced transport. This situation caused delays in production. Fuel production enterprises were directly affected by the restrictions of the pandemic between countries, as they usually transport fuel from the main centers by sea. The process of bringing together the products of companies providing catering services was impacted by the negative effects present in the cargo segment.

Information exchange has become one of the concepts that had a negative impact during the pandemic process. Highly qualified employees of aircraft, fuel, and catering businesses or their environment experienced health problems, thus decreasing the productive human capacity. Interdisciplinary studies at the point of information exchange fell to lower levels due to the measures taken. While the businesses exchanged information to find a common solution against the pandemic, they could not share information relevant to the production of their own product resources. It was a production process overshadowed by the impact of the pandemic and the desire to eliminate it or adapt as soon as possible. Innovations were made on the basis of how we live with the pandemic, not on production materials.

Another topic to be considered is purchasing power. The pandemic causes production companies to suffer a great deal of loss as they cannot provide customer financing. Since companies with a lot of short-term foreign resources cannot find customers for the products and services they produce in this process, they become unable to repay the foreign resources they use in their investments. To pay companies, they took their positions in the market with a low purchasing power due to both the lack of customer potential and the insufficient working capital.

The pandemic period paved the way for remote or hybrid work in aviation, as in every field. Although the works are managed remotely, contact with the products should be in cooperation with production. Therefore, companies are forced to work face to face in a coordinated manner. By taking the necessary precautions, the working potential of the companies has decreased compared to the past, with reductions in working time. For this reason, the employees of the company that manufactured the aircraft could not come together and be in the production phase of the product, which led to a lack of coordination. Although the fuel and catering production did not encounter this problem as much as the aircraft production process, the problems in the production of the aircraft burdened them with a chain effect.

"Slow and Uncertain Recovery (ACI)"

ACI predicts a slow and uncertain recovery. Moreover, according to ACI, fundamentals are changing with market structure in aviation industry in the following ways:

- Airlines are implementing reductions in frequencies in their fleets and routes.
- There are job losses, companies are going through a sharp contraction in human resources.
- Due to the decrease in passenger density, the demand for wide body aircraft has decreased and the production line of Airbus A-380 and Boeing B-747 aircraft may soon be terminated.
- Due to reductions in aircraft orders, manufacturers are planning to close some of their factories.
- Operations (duty free, etc.) at airports are either closing down or going for volume reduction.
- Demand for catering services is falling sharply due to the bans on board.

The pandemic causes the aviation industry to experience the aforementioned and considerably more service problems and seems to continue to do so.

Rolls-Royce, one of the world's leading engine manufacturers, announced that it plans to lay off at least 9000 people in the aviation industry due to the economic contraction caused by the Coronavirus outbreak. The company, which produces the engines of aircraft such as Boeing 787 and Airbus 380, also stated that it may close some of its factories if the contraction in the aviation sector continues (VOA, 2020).

9.9 Conclusion

This chapter points to industry qualifications with their business environment, challenges, and types of risks in the aviation industry that could pose a threat to the efficiency of the supply chain. Furthermore, a contemporary approach to managing supply chain risks within new model is presented.

In order to manage supply risks in the aviation industry, a supply chain with appropriate capacity and competence must be established and maintained. Suppliers should continuously improve their risk management systems and establish cost leadership strategy collaborations in cooperation with aviation companies. Awareness of supply chain engineers and managers at all levels should be increased on flight safety certification, one of the basic requirements of aviation. In this context, systematic training should be given to the entire sector.

The availability of reliable air transport services provides people with access to what they need: better living standards, food, healthcare, education, safe communities and spaces, etc. Aviation is by far the world's safest and most efficient mode of long-range transportation (ICAO, Aviation Benefits Report 2019, https://www.icao.int/sustainability/Documents/AVIATION-BENEFITS-2019-web.pdf).

The aviation industry is also one of the hardest hit sectors, with an 80% drop in both passenger transport and cargo aircraft. In aviation, which is a controversial sector due to its effects on climate change, post-crisis financial support and market incentives need to be aligned with the long-term goals of reducing the impact of climate change and increasing contribution to social welfare. Although the International Civil Aviation Organization (ICAO) states that efforts to recover from the financial losses of the pandemic will not override targets such as carbon offsetting and transition to sustainable aviation fuels, there is a long way to go for the flight industry to be environmentally friendly and sustainable (Akkoc and Genc, 2020 https://www.iklimhaber.org/surdurulebilir-ulasim-covid-19-sonrasi-trendler-sorunlar-ve-cozumler/).

The aviation industry has dramatically reduced its usage capacity in both passenger transport and cargo aircraft. Occasionally, national restrictions have halted aviation operations. In addition, aviation has been the focus of criticism due to its negative environmental effects and within the scope of global warming. As a result, the sustainability index has also been created for aviation companies and its economic and environmental impacts have begun to be compared. Considering the pandemic as an opportunity for developments in the field of sustainable growth, it is deemed important to increase the relevant efforts in aviation, to increase financial support and market incentives for post-pandemic recovery.

The aviation sector is one of the sectors most affected by the COVID-19 pandemic, which has a global impact. During the quarantines in April and May, it was observed that the number of passengers served plummeted due to the complete closure of the borders between countries. As of July 2020, TAV Airports' airports in Turkey, Tunisia, and North Macedonia have been reopened for international flights; the full opening of Georgia, which was opened in a very controlled manner, has been postponed throughout the year. The scope of opening of Medina, which was opened limitedly in September, is gradually expanding. Zagreb Airport remained open during the epidemic. After the reopening of the borders, the countries including each other on a mutual "safe countries" list is the most important factor determining the traffic at the airports. Each country accepts passengers without the requirement for self-isolation from the countries included in the "safe countries" list determined by them. Therefore, with the two countries listing each other on the "safe country" list, a significant increase in commercial travel traffic between the two countries began (TAV Airports Holding, 2021, https://webcmstavairports.tav.aero/files/1615449193_Faaliyet%20Raporu%202020%20TR.pdf).

Until the COVID-19 pandemic restricted and heavily paused our lives and aviation activities, the aviation industry achieved a remarkable growth momentum. This growth diversifies various investment areas in the areas of social, operational, and human factors. Many projects carried out to increase mobility create an environment that indirectly supports the development of aviation, as these mobility-based projects increase the number of customers and their diversity in aviation. In this respect, aviation contributes to the creation of new business areas. Moreover, aviation, a global industry, contributes to cultural change and interaction by providing a supportive environment. The development of aviation in both developed and developing countries helps economic, social, and environmental developments. Tourism, education, airport cities, integration of modes of transport are just a few examples. The concept of airport cities has started to spread worldwide, leading to an increase in the revenues of airports. Therefore, aviation acts as a catalyst, bringing together all the dynamics of the economy in a good pace. We are predicting that, after the pandemic is constrained and eliminated, aviation will gain this growth and development momentum again. Furthermore, aviation will contribute to the recovery of other economic sectors.

Until the pandemic constraints began, the number of aircrafts operating in the industry, in the airline, airport, ground service providers, maintenance companies, training academies, flight schools, and airline fleets increased. Consequently, the developing and growing fleets increased the need for flight crew, maintenance team, and qualified personnel. Sadly, pandemic-based restrictions and airspace closures have abruptly interrupted this remarkable momentum of growth and development in aviation.

This situation tests the industry's resilience against all risks triggered by the pandemic. It is predicted that the quantity and quality of cooperation in the sector will change until and after the pandemic is taken under control. There will also be significant changes in the number and ownership structures of organizations operating in the aviation sector. Likewise, we are predicting that stakeholders will experience radical changes in their fields and these changes will be reflected directly or indirectly to the aviation industry.

AviSCRM—supply chain risk management in aviation—is a system that connects businesses with each other and with supply stakeholders. In this system, the company that manages the chain is at the center, and the performance of the supplier businesses around the chain directly affects the success of the system. In order for the system to be successful, it is important for the business to establish a strong, long-term, cooperative, and trust-based relationship with its suppliers. Since the performance of each business that makes up the supply chain affects the whole chain, businesses and their suppliers should view each other as stakeholders and partners and continue the course of their relations in this perspective.

Corporations in the aviation sector will be able to manage their risks optimally by working with supply chains that have a high ability to adapt to situational conditions, are open to innovations, and have a flexible business model that can easily adapt to changes and can make sustainable decisions dynamically (KPMG Turkey, 2021, https://assets.kpmg/content/dam/kpmg/tr/pdf/2020/03/covid-19-tedarik-zinciri.pdf).

9.10 Case Study: TAV Airports Holding: Risk Management in the Supply Chain and Growth Strategy-Based Approach

TAV follows a different growth strategy by shifting from the supplier to the supply provider position in supply chain management. Thus, it gains a competitive advantage as a service provider by strengthening its position as an outsourcing provider in different areas such as "duty free sales, food and beverage, ground services, passenger lounge management and services in the fields of information technology." TAV implements a growth strategy focused on increasing its service businesses in terms of quantity and quality. By becoming one of the important supply sources in the fields of duty-free sales, food and beverage, ground services, passenger lounge operations, and information technologies in the supply chain, it manages the supply risks by turning the risks into opportunities at the airports it operates. It includes these areas within the scope of self-abilities by eliminating external resource dependency.

TAV Airports Holding provides services in the fields of duty-free sales, food and beverage, ground services, passenger lounge operations and information technologies at 91 airports in 26 countries. TAV Airports follows three different growth strategies: organic growth, inorganic growth, and growth of service companies (https://webcmstavairports.tav.aero/files/1615449193_Faaliyet%20Raporu%202020%20TR.pdf).

With the increase in the number of countries mutually declaring each other with Turkey as "safe countries," a meaningful recovery has started in the airports in Turkey as of August 2020. A very rapid recovery was observed especially in Antalya and Bodrum. In September, the last month of the high season, Antalya international flights reached 45% of 2019 passengers on a monthly basis. Accordingly, the number of Bodrum international passengers reached 59% of the number of international passengers in the same period of 2019. Clearly, this rapid recovery, which took place in a short period of 8 weeks and while the epidemic conditions continued, shows the existence of the accumulated travel demand for short-distance economic holiday destinations. In this context, it is seen that the recovery in TAV's airports can be very rapid when normalization begins. According to the data of the State Airports Authority (DHMİ) for the year 2020, the total number of passengers using airports in Turkey decreased by 61% compared to the previous year and reached 81.6 million. The ratio of the total number of passengers of Ankara Esenboğa, İzmir Adnan Menderes, MilasBodrum, GazipaşaAlanya, and Antalya Airports operated by TAV Airports in Turkey to the total number of passengers of the airports in Turkey was 27% in 2020 due to the negative impact of the pandemic on the tourism sector. Last year, this rate was around 40%. According to the data announced by the State Airports Authority (DHMİ), the total number of commercial aircraft using the airports in Turkey decreased by 53% in 2020 and reached 621 thousand. The ratio of the total number of commercial aircraft landing and taking off at Ankara Esenboğa, İzmir Adnan Menderes, MilasBodrum, GazipaşaAlanya, and Antalya

Airports, operated by TAV Airports in Turkey, was 27% in 2020. This rate was around 40% in 2019 (TAV, 2021, https://webcmstavairports.tav.aero/files/1615449193_Faaliyet%20Raporu%202020%20TR.pdf).

References

AIRBUs. (2021). Be an Airbus Supplier, https://www.airbus.com/en/be-an-airbus-supplier

Akkoç, S., & Genc, B. (2020). Sustainable transport: Post-COVID-19 trends, problems and solutions, *Climate News*. https://www.iklimhaber.org/surdurulebilir-ulasim-covid-19-sonrasi-trendler-sorunlar-ve-cozumler/

COSO. (2017). *ERM inegrating with strategy and performance*. Retrieved at 30 April 2021 from https://www.coso.org/Documents/2017-COSO-ERM-Integrating-with-Strategy-and-Performance-Executive-Summary.pdf

Esposito, E., & Raffa, L. (2007). Global reorganisation in a high-technology industry: The aircraft industry. *International Journal of Globalisation and Small Business., 2*. https://doi.org/10.1504/IJGSB.2007.015480

Foster, Courtney. (2016). Airline Industry Supply Chain Threats, The British Standards Institution (BSI),December 7, 2016 Retrieved at April 2021 from https://www.bsigroup.com/en-US/blog/supply-chain-blog/security/airline-industry-supply-chain-threats/

GE Turkey Blog. https://geturkiyeblog.com/havacilik-endustrisinin-daha-hizli-toparlanmasina-yardimci-olabilecek-uygulama/

ICAO. (2019). Aviation benefits, https://www.icao.int/sustainability/Documents/AVIATION-BENEFITS-2019-web.pdf).

IEA International Energy Agency. (2020). *Changes in transport behaviour during the Covid-19 crisis*, Jeremy Sung and Yannick Monschauer, https://www.iea.org/articles/changes-in-transport-behaviour-during-the-covid-19-crisis).

ISO 31000:2009(en)Risk management — Principles and guidelines https://www.iso.org/obp/ui/#iso:std:iso:31000:ed-1:v1:en

IATA (2018), Future of Aviation Industry 2035, The International Air Transport Association (IATA) and School of International Futures (SOIF), Accessed by https://www.iata.org/contentassets/690df4ddf39b47b5a075bb5dff30e1d8/iata-future-airline-industry-pdf.pdf

KoçaK, D. (2016). Economic features of Airline companies. Airline transportation (pp. 1–19), Erzurum: Atatürk University Deneyim Açıköğretim Publishing House, Turkey.

KPMG Turkey 2021. https://assets.kpmg/content/dam/kpmg/tr/pdf/2020/03/covid-19-tedarik-zinciri.pdf

Maneenop, S., & Kotcharin, S. (2020). The impacts of COVID-19 on the global airline industry: An event study approach. *Journal of Air Transport Management, 89*, 101920. https://doi.org/10.1016/j.jairtraman.2020.101920

Oçlu, B. (2015). Establishment of efficient and efficient supply chains in the Turkish Defense Aviation Industry. *Buying Journal*, Retrieved at May 05, 2021 from https://satinalmadergisi.com/turk-savunma-havacilik-sanayiinde-etkin-ve-verimli-tedarik-zincirlerinin-kurulmasi-2/

OECD. (2021). Keys to resilient supply chains, Risk management tools: Anticipate risks, https://www.oecd.org/trade/resilient-supply-chains/

Republic of Turkey Presidency, Strategy and Budget Directorate. (2020). Aircraft Production and Maintenance Working Group Report, Eleventh Development Plan Specialization Commissions Handbook, 11-Eleventh Development Plan (2019-2023) Special Expertise Commission Reports, Retrieved at April 02, 2021 from developed from https://www.sbb.gov.tr/wp-content/uploads/2020/04/HavaAraclariUretimi_ve_BakimOnarimiCalismaGrubuRaporu.pdf.

SATAIR. (2020). *The top 10 risks the aviation industry is facing*, Jan 1, 2020. https://blog.satair.com/ten-risk-in-aviation-industry.

SATAIR. (2021). Ten Risk in Aviation Industry,https://blog.satair.com/ten-risk-in-aviation-industry

TAV Airports Holding. (2021). https://webcmstavairports.tav.aero/files/1615449193_Faaliyet%20Raporu%202020%20TR.pdf

Turkish Airlines. (2021). TÜRK HAVA YOLLARI A.O. CDP Climate Change Program 2021 Report FY 2020, https://investor.turkishairlines.com/documents/surdurulebilirlik/turk-havayollari-a_o.pdf

VOA. (2020). International, Aircraft Engine Manufacturer British Rolls-Royce to Lay off 9,000 People. https://www.amerikaninsesi.com/a/ucak-motoru-ureticisi-ingiliz-rolls-royce-9-bin-kisiyi-isten-cikaracak/5427589.html. May 2020.

Yont, M., & Bugdayci, H. (1998). *Organizational problems in airline companies and its importance for Turkey*, 4th Transport Congress Denizli, pp. 169–175.

http://www.oecd.org/coronavirus/policy-responses/covid-19-and-the-aviation-industry-impact-and-policy-responses-26d521c1/

https://armacsystems.com/optimizing-component-availability-sourcing-post-covid-19/

https://www.airbus.com/aircraft/market/orders-deliveries.html#results

https://www.boeing.com/commercial/

https://www.oliverwyman.com/our-expertise/insights/2021/jan/global-fleet-and-mro-maket-forecast-2021-2031.html?utm_source=forbes&utm_medium=referral&utm_campaign=mro-forecast&utm_content=2021-jan&utm_id=cmp-10984-x9y4v0

https://www.oliverwyman.com/our-expertise/insights/2020/nov/covid-19-closures-in-aerospace-supply-chain.html

https://www.pwc.ie/reports/aviation-industry-outlook-2021.html

http://s2.q4cdn.com/661678649/files/doc_financials/annual/2016/2016-Annual-Report.pdf. Oliwer Wyman, Global Fleet & MRO Market Forecast 2017-2027, 2017a (oline).

http://aviationweek.com/january-2018. Boeing, The Boeing Company 2016 Annual Report, 2016 (online).

http://s2.q4cdn.com/661678649/files/doc_financials/annual/2016/2016-Annual-Report.pdf. Oliwer Wyman, Global Fleet & MRO Market Forecast 2017-2027, 2017b (online).

https://investor-relations.lufthansagroup.com/fileadmin/downloads/en/financial-reports/annual-reports/LH-AR-2020-e.pdf

https://thinktech.stm.com.tr/uploads/raporlar/pdf/21202091831971_stm_sivil_havacilikta_buyuk_veri.pdf

https://webcmstavairports.tav.aero/files/1615449193_Faaliyet%20Raporu%202020%20TR.pdf

SCRM in the Automotive Industry: AutoSCRM 10

One of the only ways to get out of a tight box is to invent your way out

—*Jeff Bezos*

10.1 Automotive Industry Supply Chain Risk Management "Driver Industry"

Transportation, health, and economy are integral parts of a whole for sustainable development. The environment of high uncertainty hinders the development and implementation of strategies by vision and risk management systems for transportation sectors and their supply chains, as applied in other sectors. Thus, optimized management of risk factors that impact operational, environmental—especially health, nowadays—and economy areas in the transportation sector is pivotal to evaluate corporate performances in a wider perspective. Furthermore, it is a key requirement for the creation of both added value and sustainable development. This much sought-after managerial optimization can be approached by developing risk management systems and applying them in supply chain management, by reshaping them for industries and/or businesses.

Business models are being shaped dynamically by the business environment, due to the COVID-19 pandemic. In the context of this new transforming process, managing risks, namely mitigating threats and seizing opportunities, sustainable use of economic resources, and decision-making on their allocations, are fundamental elements for both sustainable automotive industry and all its stakeholders. The best practices of selected companies in the automotive sector will be presented at the end of this chapter, by interpreting them in terms of risk management and in relation with strategies (see Fig. 10.1). The supply network of these companies is set according to corporate risk strategy. Clearly, it is of primordial importance that

M. Helmold et al., *Supply Chain Risk Management*,
Management for Professionals, https://doi.org/10.1007/978-3-030-90800-3_10

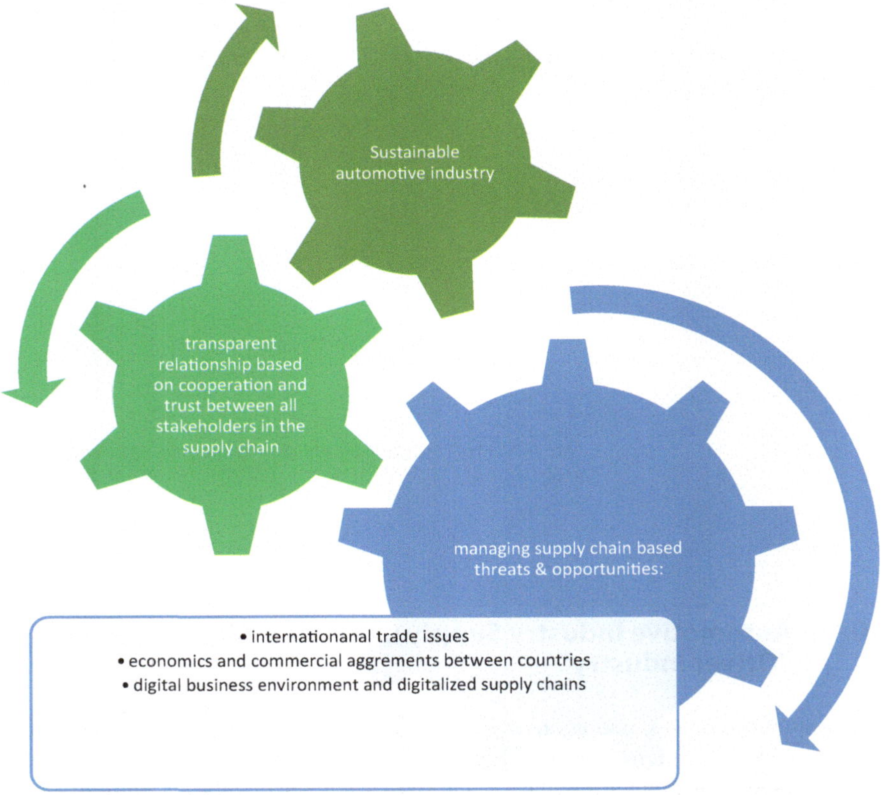

Fig. 10.1 Economic and risk wheels of sustainable growth in automotive industry. (Source: Author)

relationships in this network should be both transparent and based on cooperation and trust between all stakeholders in the supply chain. Indeed, stakeholder relations have an impact on supply chain sustainability.

The automotive industry is a decisive and guiding industry that supports many sectors and directly affects their development. In fact, the automotive sector is considered a sector that reflects countries' development and economic resilience. Thus, supply chain risk management is particularly vital, as the automotive industry has the most complex supply chain system. Managing the risks of this constantly changing environment is therefore essential for the sustainable automotive industry. The reason is that optimization in adapting to these changes can be achieved with the flexibility gained thanks to risk management. Suppliers certainly play a critical role in protecting brands and building trust. Moreover, risk management creates an infrastructure to be agile and capable of overcoming unexpected situations.

The automotive sector has a driving and determining effect on economies in industrialized countries. The driving power the sector has on the economy and its driving effect on other sectors is due to its interaction and relationship with other branches of industry and other sectors of the economy. The automotive sector, with all its elements, creates remarkable effects on the national economy. Therefore, developments and changes in all functions such as production, R&D, and marketing in the automotive sector create results that affect economies as well as other industries.

Furthermore, the obligation for the goods and services produced in today's business environment and framework to be produced in the geography where they are consumed no longer exists.

Different stages of automotive production are scattered across different countries. Global automotive companies consider criteria such as proximity to the market, investment climate availability, and easy access to raw materials, while deciding on the countries they will manufacture (ODD, 2013). Moreover, business models in the automotive sector are developed and being shaped according to the needs and demands of today's business world with the contingency approach. As a result of these developments and changes, businesses constantly try to adapt by working with different business practices. Within the framework of these new conditions emerging in the business and competition environment, it is required that all managerial and operational processes in the automotive industry be managed in a cost-effective and holistic manner. Within this context, a strategy is developed, considering all risks, in view of both threats and opportunities. It is aimed to improve performance by implementing activities, in accordance with the developed strategy at all stages, from suppliers to customers. The system that supports the achievement of this goal is defined as AutoSCRM (Automotive Industry Supply Chain Risk Management).

The automotive sector, with its contribution to employment, exports, and technology, has determinative impact on both other business sectors and also the countries. The automotive sector creates high added value for their economies and provides high levels of employment. Being an international cooperation and trade area, the automotive industry has a determining and driving effect in subsectors of engine, electronics, and software, as well as in primary sectors, such as iron and steel, petrochemicals, glass, and tires.

The automotive industry is one that exceeds $ 250 billion worldwide, with the acceleration of production in the direction of efficiency and sustainability. A unique automobile culture exists all over the world, and the automotive industry perfectly caters to the needs of that culture. The industry covers not only the sale of cars and other motor vehicles, but also their design, manufacture, and repair. In addition, the umbrella of the automotive industry includes services such as the sale of various accessories and auto parts that are important to keeping a car running efficiently within its systems (World Atlas, 2017).

Moreover, the automotive sector is directly related to and in interrelation with the energy, tourism, and service sectors. The automotive sector largely contributes to making the energy sector one of the leading industries in the world. In terms of service sectors, it makes significant contributions to the development of many service sectors while creating opportunities for their local in the countries in view of employment, subsectors.

10.2 Electric-Influenced Supply Chains with New Competitive Strategies in the Automotive Industry

The current supply business environment is rapidly changing owing to electric vehicles industry. New trategies are developed from new industry dynamics. Determiners in doing business in the automotive industry are changing. Therefore, supply chain risk management becomes more vital for automotive industry, since risks are transforming in parallel to the change.

A worldwide shift away from internal combustion engine (ICE) vehicles with increasingly electrified powertrains is underway, and with it the formation of burgeoning electric vehicle supply chains (Monnet, 2021).

"From Traditional Automotive Supply Chain to Electric: EVs and Supply Chain"

New technologies, changing consumer preferences, and intensifying regulation will help reshape the automotive industry in the years ahead. Adoption of electric vehicles (EVs) will have a profound impact on the automotive supply chain. Key differences between the makeup of EVs and ICE vehicles reveal which supplier subsectors are most at risk (PWC United States, 2021). In this respect, AutoSCRM will help managing these arising risks.

Automakers and suppliers are cutting costs so they can invest in new technology (Ewing, 2019). Global car sales are declining at the same time that companies are pouring billions of dollars into new technologies like autonomous driving and electric cars, which are easier to assemble and require fewer workers and fewer parts. Due to changes such as in parts, spare parts, materials, equipment, hardware,and accessories used in the production of electric vehicles, the number of suppliers has been dramatically decreasing and changing (https://www.nytimes.com/2019/12/31/business/electric-cars-germany-economy.html).

Thus far, sales of electric cars make up a small share of the overall auto market; yet, they are growing fast. If the trend continues, it spells trouble for the hundreds of suppliers that make parts for internal combustion engines. Supply chain management systems, risks, and their components are changing since there is a transition toward more electric vehicles that have far fewer components and are easier to manufacture (Adapted from Ewing, 2019). With nearly all major original equipment manufacturers (OEMs) looking to expand their output of EVs, demand for new parts has presented new challenges for suppliers and risks for manufacturers (Smith, 2021).

In the traditional supply chain, many parts, products, materials, and equipment are supplied from different geographies. In recent years, procurement strategies have developed in the direction of outsourcing all their needs, except self-talent, by focusing on capabilities. However, business environments are transforming. When we look at digital and technology-oriented enterprises, the development of the scope of the core capabilities of new strategies focuses on the production of all parts, accessories, equipment, and spare parts by the main manufacturer as much as possible, then shifting the role of supplier for other businesses and gaining strategic advantage. The current supply chain environment is rapidly changing owing to electric vehicles industry.

The rise of EVs poses a particular risk for auto suppliers. Major systems that are essential to vehicles with internal combustion engines are absent from EVs. Manufacturers of exhaust systems, fuel systems, and transmissions face the prospect of disruption, as EVs become more mainstream. Those lacking financial flexibility and digital wherewithal are likely to struggle the most. Although PwC expects that adoption will grow at a modest pace for the time being, EVs' share of the automobile market will likely begin to expand more rapidly in the medium term. OEMs and suppliers alike should start preparing for that future today (PWC United States, 2021).

The Tesla example strongly shows that supply chain management in the automotive industry will change sharply with its suppliers and risks. Tesla impresses all of us as a successful example that gives strong signals of the spread of electric cars and related technology with its transforming works and showing the new direction of acceleration.

Requiring relatively fewer traditional automotive parts, modern cars are dependent on semiconductors, microchips, sensors, batteries, and numerous other electronic components that provide technological advantages (Smith, 2021).

Automakers outsource many of the parts they need. Tesla, on the other hand, manufactures 80% of the parts of the car, as a deflecting strategy. This is important as a production strategy that drastically changes the supply structure and number of suppliers. Following a similar strategy for sales, Tesla directly sells the cars instead of using dealers, and even sells online without having a physical dealer in many places. At the same time, Tesla, foreseeing the effect of digitalization and its opportunities in both production and business models, invests in autonomous driving technologies.

In addition, Tesla changes the dynamics of the automotive industry, production technologies, vehicle features, used parts, equipment, and in-vehicle technology with innovations, such as the continuous connection of the cars it produces to the Internet and remote software updates.

The implementation of such strategies has made Tesla one of the three largest automobile companies in the world by market value. These strategies, moreover, shape the future of supply chains, starting from today. Technological developments and the direction of production should be carefully followed for the current application of supply chain risk management.

The engineering complexity of automotive manufacturing has created different tiers of suppliers. For example, first-tier global suppliers produce systems design and specialized systems supplies, such as heating and cooling devices and brake systems. These suppliers are then supported by second and third tiers of suppliers (Khan, 2011, p. 111).

The automotive sector is in the position of purchaser of products produced by sectors such as iron-steel, petro-chemistry, plastic, glass, textile and electronics, and supplies motor vehicles needed by sectors such as agriculture, tourism, construction, infrastructure, transportation, and defense. The automotive sector is also closely connected with the marketing, dealer, after-sales service, fuel, finance, and insurance sectors, which enable raw materials and subindustry and final products to reach the consumer (Piskin, 2017, http://www.osd.org.tr/sites/1/upload/files/otomotiv_sektor_raporu_tskb-2208.pdf.

It is widely accepted that the automotive industry is one of the sectors most affected by globalization. The merger that goes hand in hand with globalization is an important feature of the sector. The sector has been united around a small number of brands and companies. The share taken from the total vehicle production is considered to be an indicator of the merger (Altay, 2019). In the automotive industry, digitalization in both production and service, the volatile operating environment, globalization, new business models, and new technologies produce a sharp and noticeable transformation vis-a-vis suppliers.

Suppliers that are not prepared to meet the challenges brought about by rising EV adoption could pose a risk to automobile manufacturers at the same time, as their own business is evolving. It would be wise for original equipment manufacturers (OEMs) to future-proof their supply chains, to determine if key suppliers are taking the necessary steps to hold their position as valuable partners in a changing world (PWC United States, 2021).

In addition to the employment and added value created directly by the sector, a wide range of sales and after-sales services is also provided, such as receiving input from many other sectors and advertising and marketing activities for automotive products, financial institutions for automobile finance, repair, maintenance and spare parts sales, and insurance sector. Considering these, it appears to be an indirectly serious source of employment (Baskak and Mihcioglu, 2019, http://www1.mmo.org.tr/resimler/dosya_ekler/1e567798fc9ccd2_ek.pdf.

10.3 Risk Management Means for the Automobile Industry

Risk management is a vital system in automotive industry. Leading sector players have risk management systems which are strong, sound, and shaped according to their objectives. One of the best samples is presented below.

> Volkswagen Group's risk management system (RMS) and internal control system (ICS) based on assumption that Only by promptly identifying, accurately assessing and effectively and efficiently managing the risks and opportunities arising from their business activities can they ensure the Volkswagen Group's long-term success. The aim of the RMS/ICS is to identify potential risks at an early stage so that suitable countermeasures can be taken to avert the threat of loss to the Company, and any risks that might jeopardize its continued existence can be ruled out. (Volkswagen, 2020)

> Also, The point they emphasize, promptly identifying the risks and opportunities arising from their operating activities and taking a forward-looking approach to managing them is crucial to their Company's long-term success. A comprehensive risk management and an internal control system help the Volkswagen Group deal with risks in a responsible manner. Assessing the likelihood of occurrence and extent of future events and developments is, by its nature, subject to uncertainty. important point that, they are therefore aware that even the

best RMS cannot foresee all potential risks and even the best ICS can never completely prevent irregular acts."

Source: Volkswagen (2020), Annual Report, Report on Risks and Opportunities, https://annualreport2020.volkswagenag.com/group-management-report/report-on-risks-and-opportunities.html

Supply chains in automotive industry play a decisive and determinative role in increasing and sustaining profit in the industry.

The purpose of supply chains, which includes activities in all processes from raw material to the consumer, is to implement a sustainable global competitive production in line with the consumer demands. Quality, cost, logistics, and design / technology management are common in the supply chain. Especially since vehicle production and raw material and spare parts must be in full harmony, it is necessary to establish a long-term strategic cooperation between the companies that produce motor vehicles and spare parts in every field (TÜSİAD-Sabancı University Competition Forum (REF) and the Federation of Sectoral Associations (SEDEFED), 2010).

In the automotive industry, the main manufacturers, procurement, industry, sales and after-sales, electronics industry, software industry, enterprises, and service companies are included in both production and value chains (see Fig. 10.1). Managing the supply chain requires risk management-based coordination across all stakeholders in the sector. In Europe and Latin America, the automotive industry value chain is organized according to these tiers of suppliers. The lead firm-assembler concentrates and deals directly with the first-tier suppliers, that is, Toyota and Denso. Auto assemblers and these global first-tier suppliers have formed relationships which cut across the globe. These global first-tier suppliers are then responsible for coordinating activities with the second and third tiers of suppliers. This work organization saves time and creates close collaborations and knowledge exchange between the lead assembler/s and its first-tier suppliers, and therefore gives access to unique network resources (Khan, 2011).

So Who Are the Stakeholders in Supply Chain Risk Management? "AutoSCRM Stakeholders"

Supply chain is both threat and opportunity for automotive sector players, since suppliers have a determinative role in sustainability in production. Due to COVID-19, global manufacturers such as Ford, Toyota, Fiat Chrysler Automobiles (FCA), Nissan, and Honda announced that they were suspending their production due to supply problems. The production completely halted in the factories of some brands. Moreover, there are brands that suspended the production of certain models. The difficulties experienced in the supply of chips and other electronic parts affect the production, and this is considered to be the main reason for the interruption of production (see details from https://otomobil.haber7.com/otomobil/haber/3056882-mercedes-ford-fiat-toyota-nissan-subaru-ve-hondada-tedarik-sorunu).

Automotive industry is directly related to specific fields such as, principally, Electronics and Software, Software Security and Block Chain, Regulations and

Smart Vehicles, Adaptive Platform for Smart Vehicles, Emerging Technologies on the Automotive Ecosystem, 5G and Inter-Vehicle Communication, Electronics in Vehicles, Artificial Intelligence, Technology, and Ethics, as these issues are the areas that have potential to both directly and indirect improvements and changes in the automotive industry and determine the direction of the transformation in the sector.

Due to the intense competition in the automotive supply industry, there have been many partnerships and mergers in the course of time. In the automotive sector, the globalization of the market and capital intensity were also very high, compared to other sectors. Moreover, automotive suppliers are merging. The share of the top 20 suppliers is approximately 85% of world production. Among these companies, those who are referred to as a group are the ones that incorporate more than one automotive company and appear to have completed their mergers in the past. These 20 companies are mainly distributed in six countries such as Japan, Germany, South Korea, the USA, China, and France. They are included in the same list with the Italian FCA Group. They develop and implement strategies to transform companies' products and production in line with their sustainability strategies (adapted and commented from Altay, 2019) (Fig. 10.2).

Today, increasing competition requires companies to focus on every step, from planning to purchasing and reaching the customer, with the aim of increasing their profits by minimizing their expenses; therefore, this necessity brings about conceptual changes. Even in the TS 16949 standard, which is based on the automotive sector, where competition is most intensely experienced, this concept is included as one of the aims of the standard, with the expression "emphasizing the change and reducing losses in the supply chain."

What is Iso 16949?

It is a standard designed for continuous improvement and prevention of errors, waste reduction, and supply chain for the automotive industry. It is published in March 2002 by the International Automotive Task Force (IATF) and the International Organization for Standardization ISO. This standard complies with country-specific regulations. The ISO Ts 16949 standard is a standard applicable to all industries related to automotive design, application, manufacturing, assembly, service, and automotive. It seeks Iso 16949 funds throughout the standard supply chain. Iso 19949 has gathered automotive standards such as EAQF France, VDA6 Germany, AVSQ Italy, and QS 9000 America under a single standard. (http://www.eurocert.com.tr/iso-16949.aspx)

The globalized business environment has caused that everybody could be each other's customer or supplier, regardless of geographic location. It has combined efforts toward both purchasing and sales with the goal of both accessing and delivering products and services, in a time-effective and cost-effective manner. The realization of this goal will be possible with the correct determination of cost strategies and

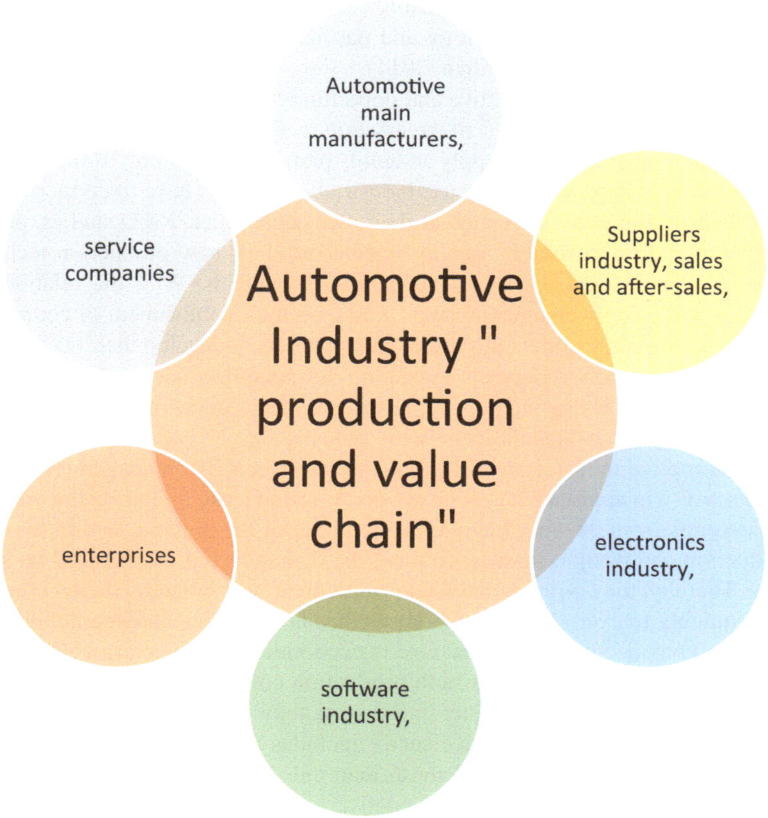

Fig. 10.2 Automotive production and value chain. (Source: Author)

the performance of management systems in accordance with the strategies. Therefore, the most critical point is the development of the cost leadership strategy in alignment with the technology-oriented development and competition strategy.

The automotive industry has the power to create a dynamic impact for all economies. In effect, the automotive sector creates added value; contributes, directly and indirectly, to employment; and leads and inspires technological developments. Due to these aspects, the automotive industry is a determinant affecting the development of countries and of the sector per se. Thus, it is important to improve risk management and risk assessment and mitigation capabilities at both organizational and corporate levels, in order to maintain the current resilience and sustainability of the industry. Volkswagen Group management concept considers sustainable relations with their suppliers.

The global automotive industry is largely dependent upon radical innovations, such as fuel efficient and electrical cars, which can create a sustainable competitive advantage for these auto firms. It is, therefore, reasonable for the automotive suppliers to examine their industry position and partnerships with key automotive firms to acquire access to technology and partner resources thus filling important strategic and operational gaps (Khan, 2011).

Within the scope of cost-effective and opportunity-based risk management implementations in the production parts of the aviation sector, comprehensive strategies are developed and implemented to supply assembly parts that are getting from the subsidiary industry. This is primarily because industrial companies have the opportunity to allocate their resources to areas such as their own capabilities, R&D studies, product development and improvement, quality-oriented studies, new production technologies, creating new segments, and developing new models. With the relationships established with supply chain companies, based on the establishment of cooperation and trust, sector manufacturers also help their suppliers to develop their business.

AutoSCRM actually represents managing sustainability across the entire automotive value chain. Managing the supply chain requires coordination based on risk management among all stakeholders in the industry.

The automotive industry should have a supply chain risk management that has adopted a win-win approach based on cooperation and trust, including the assembly and spare parts from the very beginning to the end of the process, within the scope of production and design, in order to meet the demands and needs of all its stakeholders. Thereby, they will be enabled to implement new business models that will respond quickly to ever-changing market demands, and to establish a flexible, sustainable, and balanced structure that covers economic-social-operational areas.

Timely access to resources for both production components and customers and production stands out as key points in the sustainability of the automotive sector. The supply chain in the automotive sector includes the supply of materials to be used in production, the transfer of these materials to semi and complete product production and their production, and the delivery of finished products to consumers. The timing of the supply of materials to be used in production is of primordial importance for the automotive industry. For the sector waiting for semi-finished products, late supply of materials disrupts production, while early supply increases stock and storage costs.

The automotive industry is the determiner industry in the economic development of the countries and its sustainability. We have entitled it as *"Driver industry"* (Fig. 10.3).

In this respect, network design is of strategic importance as multi-criteria decision-making problem for managers. It is essential to review the network design in the supply chains after the changes in business models, changes in market structure, company mergers, or changes in factor costs, and make the necessary improvements with the contingency approach. In line with the competitive strategy of the company, projections are made with a visionary perspective, and market forecasts are made based on the analysis and analysis results related to the development of the business environment and economic conditions. The procurement strategy is developed by taking into account all the resources of the business, including human, economic, technological, equipment, abilities, and capacity. As a result, managers

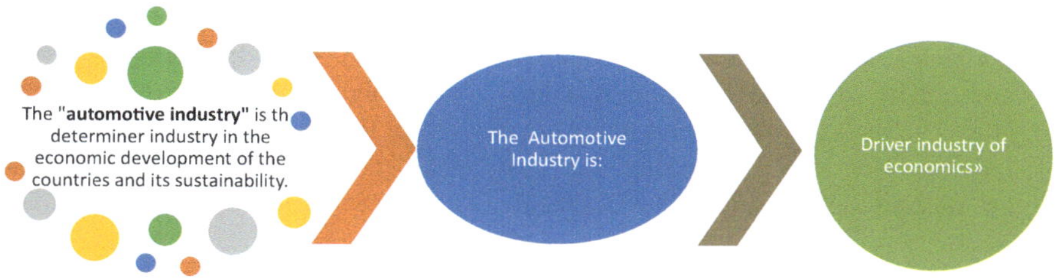

Fig. 10.3 Automotive as driver industry. (Source: Author)

decisions are made on their supply chain network according to corporate strategy and resources with their competence fields.

AutoSCRM is a system that timely guarantees the needs of the automotive industry. By managing risks and risk resources, timely and accurate shipments and activities in the sector can be carried out as may be needed. According the Metzner et al. (2001), supply chain management is defined as the systemic, strategic coordination of the traditional business functions and the tactics across these business functions within a particular company and across businesses within the supply chain, for the purposes of improving the long-term performance of the individual companies and the supply chain as a whole. A supply chain is defined as a set of three or more entities (organizations or individuals) directly involved in the upstream and downstream flows of products, services, finances, and/or information from a source to a customer (Metzner et al., 2001). Supply chain risk management improves supply chain flexibility, as well as supports strengthening cooperation for production and sales.

The automotive industry has one of the most complex supply chains. The sector plays a pivotal role to the economies of newly industrialized countries. This mainly applies as in Turkey, for instance, where the further development and growth of this sector, which makes huge contributions to tax revenues, employment, and balance of payments, is critical for the growth of the Turkish economy.

The automotive industry has a major impact on other sectors, due to its structure. Consequently, the automotive industry has a major impact on the economy of the country where it is located. Therefore, changes in the sector directly affect the entire economy. Apart from its own structure, the automotive sector is also closely related to the marketing, dealer, service, fuel, finance, and insurance sectors that enable raw materials, subindustry, and final products to reach the consumer, and it is the industry branch that provides the most important support to the development of the defense industry. High environmental and safety standards and consumer demands in developed markets lead to an intensive technological development in the automotive industry (T.R. Ministry of Science, Industry and Technology (2020), https://www.sanayi.gov.tr/plan-program-raporlar-ve-yayinlar/sektor-raporlari/mu2007011621).

Having a strong and recognizable brand in the industry means maintaining the brands' competitive power by providing continuous development, creating and applying technology. In this respect, companies should be able to use the value-added chain and e-commerce concepts included in the "New Economy" concept, which is one step ahead of globalization, at every stage from raw material procurement to sales and distribution stages. In the globalization process, while the target was an activity strategy on domestic markets at the beginning, today this target has moved toward optimizing the positions of the supply-production-market regions around the world (TAYSAD, 2020).

10.4 Risk Sources in the Automotive Sector

Main risk fields in automotive sector are identified in following topics:

- Container shortage and risk of losing customers
- Electric vehicle technology
  - Development of digital technologies
- Financing risks
- Trade wars and slowdown imports
- Semiconductors and chips
- Operational risks and resources
- Digitalization in supply chains

Risk of container shortage: *The change in the import-export balance and the problem of* container supply in global trade.

There is a very serious trade contraction in the world. Businesses encounter difficulties finding empty containers for export. The COVID-19 pandemic has greatly affected many sectors and business areas from healthcare to automotive and from tourism to aviation. Supply chains are one of the pandemic impact areas in the world economy. Currently, the use of containers in international maritime transportation has increased the need for empty containers due to the deterioration of the supply-demand balance during the pandemic. However, numerous countries cannot find empty containers to export.

Recent transportation problems in global markets create problems especially in food and agricultural products. The container crisis has been ongoing for months, especially due to the intense demand from China, and the effects of the crisis have begun to emerge in the exports of the countries. Along with the pandemic, there was an "empty container" crisis on the seaway, where nearly 90 percent of world trade was carried out. Due to the deterioration of the supply-demand balance, most of the vessels and containers are diverted to trade between China and the USA. This risk creates a situation where exporters in many countries face difficulty in finding empty containers. Likewise, due to the pandemic, the vessels waiting at the port for days and the change in the import-export balance created a shortage of container supply in global trade. Especially since the vessels moving from China to the USA could not unload their cargo, they could not return in a short time, thus creating a

Fig. 10.4 Fundamental risk sources in the automotive supply chain risk management

supply problem. The crisis experienced also witnessed historical rises in freight. Container freight between Europe and the Far East increased by 300 percent in the last year, exceeding 10 thousand dollars. Container price also rose almost twice. This situation experienced in global maritime trade also dealt a heavy blow to the exports of many industrialized countries (Yucel, 2021) (Fig. 10.4).

10.4.1 Container Shortage Creates Operational Risks

In addition to the slowdown in imports, the increase in exports has accordingly increased the empty container shortage, resulting in orders to remain in warehouses. With the decrease in imports, due to the high exchange rate, the number of ships and containers arriving in the country decreased. For this reason, many goods remain in warehouses due to the shortage of containers for sea freight. Furthermore, the increase in freight in this process significantly increased the costs.

Companies across the globe are faced with the risk of finding containers in the operational field due to these decisions of the countries, as well as the current risk in terms of international trade in their supply chains. International relations and bilateral trade restrictions are currently changing the business environment, and, therefore, supply chains are also being restructured.

Political risks have always been a particularly emphasized risk area in risk management. Since both countries and relations between countries are affected, they have a high potential to affect the activities and sustainability of companies. For example, trade and economic relations between the USA and China, which are on the agenda of managers today, are one of the risks that affect the uninterrupted operation of the supply chain. Decisions taken regarding international trade have the power to change the results of global business activities in terms of both production and supply.

Automotive supply chain needs effective management in risky areas such as sustainability, collaborations, networks, cost containment, customer demands, and new business models.

According to Deloitte Turkey Report, the automotive industry needs to manage its risks in line with the resources in order to act to reduce the risk during the epidemic. Human, finance, and resources are at the center of the current risk and the measures to be taken against it (Deloitte, 2020):

(i) Human: Focusing on customer demand, creation, and improvement of customer contact points; focusing on employee care, protection, health and safety assurance, and career development.
(ii) Financing: Focusing on cash flow risk, especially in retail channels that are directly affected by the market.
(iii) Resources: Strengthening production and sales cooperation; improving supply chain flexibility.

According to statistical information of International Organization of Motor Vehicle Manufacturers, 84 million motor vehicles were produced worldwide in 2020 (see Fig. 10.3) (OICA, 2021), but 2021 statistics will be different from past ones, due to the extreme conditions of the pandemic (Fig. 10.5).

10.4.2 Risks of Electrical Vehicle Technology

Apparently, another risk is arising from electric vehicles' battery. This is because the global demand for electric vehicles is growing while questions still exist about the viability of the EV battery supply chain. Demand might increase so quickly in the near term that the supply chain could face difficulties keeping abreast (Perryman, 2021). Therefore, capacity problem may appear in supply chain in this respect (Perryman, 2021).

Another risk in complex and transforming industry environment, information flow, is one of the main determinative risks to productivity on the automotive supply chain.

Batteries present an additional risk source to automotive suppliers. They are the heaviest component in an EV and difficult to transport, thus providing battery suppliers geographically closer to a vehicle's final point of manufacture, with an advantage in competitive contracts. Most batteries are currently produced in Asia; hence, other regions may need to invest in battery manufacturing to maintain current automotive production (Smith, 2021).

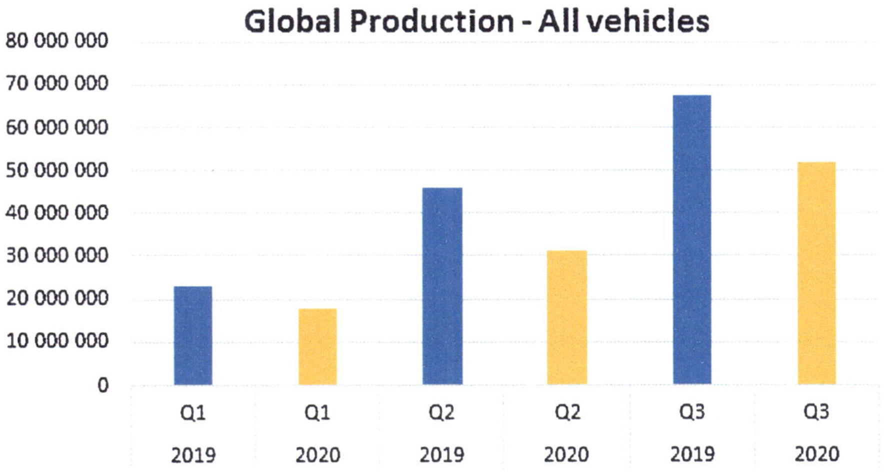

Fig. 10.5 Global production numbers, all vehicles, OICA, 2020. (Source: https://www.oica.net/2020-statistics/)

Production and demand management optimization can be achieved with risk-based planning in supply chain processes. Through this supply chain, operational processes are decided. After planning the product segment and its types, studies are carried out on demand forecasts. Moreover, analyses are carried out by including risk scenarios. The results of these analyses are used in purchasing and ordering decisions. Production process time plans are prepared with the integration of demand and order. Furthermore, risk scenarios are prepared for the quotas of the local and regional dealers. Subsequently, similar predictive analyses are made for spare parts, equipment, and related accessories. Different risk scenarios are prepared and efforts are made to minimize downtime by determining alternatives for all kinds of demand changes and production disruptions. Therefore, supply chain optimization is required to achieve successful results of all these plans and risk management practices. (adapted from SlideShare of "Toyota Supply Chain Management: A Strategic Approach to Toyota's Renowned System." Ananth Iyer, Sridhar Seshadri & Roy Vasher. McGraw-Hill, 2009. sf: 40).

10.4.3 Risks of Chips and Semiconductors

10.4.3.1 Chips: The Oil of the Digital Age[1]

The pandemic changed consumer behavior, resulting in shortages. Consumers keep buying new phones, computers, new tablets, and Xboxes in order to work remotely

[1] In this section, DW, 2021 source has been used extensively. DW (2021), How microchips became the 'oil of the digital age', Top Stories, Business, Video, https://www.dw.com/en/how-microchips-became-the-oil-of-the-digital-age/av-56699977

and to cope with the lockdowns. In this context, companies upgrade their digital infrastructure to enable remote working. As a result, these companies and all these purchases are driving up the demand for chips. An economic downturn was estimated at the outbreak of the pandemic. Industries such as the automakers reduced chip purchases. However, the economy in East Asia bounced back sooner than expected, with more demand for cars.

As the coronavirus crisis reshaped supply and demand, chip companies are scrambling. Clearly, if there is one industry that cannot simply quickly ramp up production or ask its clients to do without its products for a while or shift its manufacturing elsewhere rapidly, it is the chip industry. Supply chains have been spread across countries, as the cost of communication has been reduced along with the cost of transportation. Therefore, it was largely considered beneficial to spread the production of semiconductors out of their high-tech components across countries. It is theoretically possible, based on some fundamental theories of economics, that, by doing so, production cost could be reduced, thereby increasing efficiency. However, in the past years, as concerns over technology and technological sovereignty have grown, this has been viewed as geopolitical risk rather than economic benefit. It should certainly be considered that geopolitical complexity is to play a key role in this. Therefore, one should run through the basics (DW, 2021).

(i) Every country in the world needs chips.
(ii) Chips are complicated to produce.
(iii) The world economy runs on chips.

Who makes chips and who is enabled to buy them goes a long way toward defining who stagnates and who progresses. One expert likens it to one other commodity that has seen its own share of geopolitical contentiousness. In this respect, chips have been called "*the new oil in the digital age!*" Everything, from phones to air conditioning, and everything in between, uses chips. Clearly, as technology becomes more central, chips become more important. And most importantly, what is absolutely critical, is the ability to manufacture smaller and smaller chips with more features.

As chips get smaller, their power increases. The performance of computers is improved. As next-generation 5G connectivity becomes more common, the Internet continues to expand, and AI-powered technology evolves, the demand for more powerful chips of various kinds will grow accordingly. The more powerful the chips, the more specialized their production becomes and the fewer the manufacturers that are able to produce them. The three companies below are considered to produce the most advanced chips in the world. The three major chip manufacturers, which are Top three leading semiconductor companies, are as follows (by sales revenue 2020):

(i) Intel $73.09bn
(ii) Samsung &60.48bn
(iii) TSMC &45.52 bn

Importantly, these companies are not of the same type. Samsung and Intel are considered to be integrated device manufacturers, namely, companies that design, manufacture, and sell the chips from start to finish, whereas TSMC is considered to be a foundry, namely, a company that makes chips for companies without factories themselves or "fabs" as they are known in the industry jargon.

Meanwhile, the set-up cost for factories that produce these chips increases in value with each generation of chips produced. The minimum cost of setting up a factory with a 5 nanometer (nm) chip production line is $5.4 billion. An example of this is the iPhone A14 chip considered to be, currently, the fastest chip in a phone. This chip is found in iPhone 12 and is produced by TSMC. Consumers may not realize this, consumers may not know about TSMC; however, it is TSMC that enables Apple to produce iPhone 12.

TSMC and its home country, Taiwan, is in a unique position; this is all part of the geopolitical complexity. In a nutshell, this hugely important industry is located in Taiwan, thus putting Taiwan in the center of this geopolitical complexity. It appears that the semiconductor industry was the real flash point on whether or not China successfully invaded Taiwan. The global supply chains would be disrupted by this. Furthermore, there as some concerns whether China would take over Taiwan's manufacturing industry or the semiconductor industry. Moreover, because of Taiwan's critical role in manufacturing these chips, that could be relatively problematic for the companies that use TSMC.

Chips being as important as they are, they figure prominently in the often intertwined discussions of security and technological advancement. Suppose the USA comes up with its special kind of list. In this view, human rights violation and IP theft will be issues for future. Therefore, chips are the new economic security and geopolitical flashpoint. The question on what should be done now arises. Clearly, global coordination is important at this point.

Countries appear to want to gain a competitive advantage in the chip race, whereas semiconductors are an important part of this race. Furthermore, restrictions of countries against each other create risks for countries, and countries develop their own strategies on this. As a result, new supply chains are established within the scope of value chains. Indeed, trust is one of the most critical elements in supply chain management. Therefore, companies that can be within the scope of chain of trust are likely to create value by managing their risks. In the light of the above, chips are the new economic, security, and geopolitical flashpoint.

10.4.3.2 Semiconductor and Chip Significance for the Automotive Industry

Semiconductor and chips are vital risk sources to supply chain in automotive industry. Chips are main part to production in many industries today. Semiconductors are a main element of chips. As demonstrated, production elements are shaping semiconductors and chips and their producers. The biggest obstacle for the world's largest manufacturers to increase car production has been the failure of chip manufacturers to meet the incoming demand. Many factories experienced disruptions due to problems in chip supply (https://www.bloomberght.com/otomotivde-cip-krizi-2272228).

"Chip Crises Biggest Risk in Sustainable Supply Chains"

COVID-19 pandemic has affected all areas of life. In addition to the social and economic effects, the technological effects of the pandemic have been on the agenda for a while. The chip crisis is shaking the automotive industry on a global scale. Subsequently, the automotive sector leads these technological effects. Moreover, estimates are made by many companies.

The semiconductor chip crisis experienced by the automotive industry stands out among the sectoral crises with a pandemic effect. While the giants of the industry underline that the supply crisis has disrupted production, semiconductor chip manufacturers also face the risk of not being able to respond to increasing demands.

Due to the increasing demand in the technology sector, automobile manufacturers cannot adequately access the semiconductor chips they need. While many brands are affected by the ongoing crisis, it is stated that production has come to a half, at some points.

Speaking to Reuters, GM spokesperson, David Barnas, said, "Despite our efforts to reduce the effects, the shortage of semiconductors will affect GM production, especially in 2021." It appears that Fiat Chrysler Automobiles (FCA), Ford, Honda, Mercedes-Benz, Nissan, Subaru, Toyota, and Volkswagen stand out as manufacturers negatively affected by the supply shortage. In addition, according to Reuters, Volkswagen China operations head, Stephan Wollenstein, stated that there was a global chip supply shortage and the German manufacturer's production in December was seriously affected. The brand said it lost tens of thousands of cars' sales due to this production shortage.

Car manufacturers such as Daimler, Nissan, and Honda faced the risk of reducing production due to shortages in chip supply. According to Volkswagen, last year chip manufacturers said that they allocated a large part of their production capacity to fast-consuming electronics and were caught off guard by the surprisingly strong automobile demand (Bloomberght, 2021 https://www.bloomberght.com/otomotivde-cip-krizi-2272228).

Semiconductor chips may be tiny; yet, the role they play in the global economy is huge. Approximately a trillion are made per year, and they are critical components in the digital devices and products daily used by billions of people worldwide. However, the global upheaval of the pandemic has prompted a supply chain crisis in the sector. The car industry, which is increasingly reliant on chips as it ramps up electric car production, has been by far the worst hit. The severe semiconductor shortage has forced the world's biggest carmakers to drastic production cuts in the early months of 2021. Last week, Ford said it could miss out on up to $2.5 billion (€2.06 billion) of earnings this year, due to the crisis. Volkswagen, Nissan, and Honda have also announced major production cuts. The sector, as a whole, could lose more than $60 billion as a result of the problem, which was caused primarily by a pandemic double whammy in March 2020. When car manufacturing plummeted back then, demand for consumer electronics of all kinds soared, as populations across the world were forced to stay at home (DWb, 2021).

As stated in DWb (2021), chip crisis raises questions for car sector, with complications likely to continue (Top Stories, Business, Accessed April 03, 2021 by https://www.dw.com/en/chip-crisis-raises-questions-for-car-sector-with-complications-likely-to-continue/a-56538970).

According to an article in the *Wall Street Journal*, the demand for technological devices during the pandemic has a share in the crisis. As the demand for many electronic devices such as personal computers and game consoles has increased, global chip manufacturers have also flooded semiconductor manufacturers with demand. When conditions such as remote work were added to this supply-demand imbalance, the scale collapsed, or it is about to collapse. This is what makes semiconductor chips harder to find and increases their cost to manufacturers (Shepardson, 2021).

Auto companies have become major buyers of semiconductors in recent years, and they have used semiconductors everywhere, from motor control units and transmissions to large tablet-like displays embedded in the dashboard. According to experts, the transition to electric vehicles also requires more software-based systems.

Automotive production has been heavily affected, with auto companies around the world halting production. This is apparent not only to them, but also to machine and well-known device manufacturers. Moreover, the chip shortage feeds the current international relations problems. Demand for future uses does not seem likely to actually slow down. To understand the repercussions of the chip shortage in our lives, one should look at the big picture. This may be the reason why it has been rather difficult to find a PS5 or VW Passat to buy lately. Approximately 1 trillion chips are produced annually (DW, 2021):

So, an annual chip production of 1,000,000,000,000 chips, means approximately 128 chips per person in the world. Suffice to say the world runs on chips/semiconductors.

The automotive industry must have a strong supply chain management, from design to spare parts, to meet the expectations of its external stakeholders, especially its customers globally. Only by doing so will it be able to establish a flexible, stable, and balanced structure that will respond quickly to the ever-changing market demands. The pandemic has changed market conditions and limited access to parts needed for production.

Clearly, timing is of primordial importance for the automotive industry. The supply chain in the automotive sector includes the supply of materials to be used in production, the transfer of these materials to semi and full product production and their production, and the delivery of finished products to consumers. The timing of the supply of materials to be used in production is very important for the automotive industry. For the sector waiting for semi-finished products, late supply of materials hinders production, and early supply increases stock and storage costs.

Changes in manufacturing processes, consumer demands, and new, disruptive trends, all impact on the vehicle supply chain network for raw materials, parts, and finished automobiles. Both internal and external factors require automotive supply chain managers to minimize costs, optimize manufacturing and distribution, and ensure that parts and products get to the right organizations at the right time (Blume Global, 2021).

The COVID-19 crisis caused many automakers to pull back from production in early 2020, then lower their forecast for the rest of the year. But since those days, demand for cars and trucks has grown faster than expected, and the supply and production problem has arisen in certain critical parts, including computer chips (WSJ, Reuters, https://www.sozcu.com.tr/2021/ekonomi/cip-krizi-otomotiv-sektorunu-global-olcekte-salliyor-iste-krizin-nedenleri-6249705/).

> General Motors Co on Feb. 9 said the global chip shortage could shave up to $2 billion from 2021 profits and extended production cuts at three North American plants. It also said it would partially build and later finish assembling vehicles at two other factories because of the chip shortage.
>
> No. 2 U.S. automaker Ford Motor Co warned this month the chip shortage could lead to a 10% to 20% loss in first-quarter production, resulting in a potential hit to operating earnings of $1 billion to $2.5 billion. It had said it lost some production of its top-selling F-150 pickup truck.
>
> A shortage of auto chips could affect nearly 1 million units of global light vehicle production in the first quarter, data firm IHS Markit said Tuesday, adding that it still expects most of the volume to be recovered in the remainder of 2021.
>
> In a Jan. 19 letter to Deese first reported by Reuters, the United Auto Workers union and auto trade groups asked the Biden administration to consider "urging major silicon wafer foundries to ramp up production of automotive grade wafers."
>
> The chip shortage has affected many other automakers, including Toyota Motor Corp, Volkswagen AG, Stellantis NV, Renault, Subaru, Nissan Motor, Honda Motor and Mazda Motor Co.

Reporting by David Shepardson; Editing by Clarence Fernandez and Gerry Doyle

In Germany, Volkswagen has pointed the finger at suppliers, saying it gave them timely warning last April—when much global car production was idled due to the coronavirus pandemic—that it expected demand to recover strongly in the second half of the year. The auto industry spends approximately $40 billion a year on chips—about a tenth of the global market (Busvine & Steitz, 2021).

Worldwide, Volkswagen has more than 120 plants that build components or complete vehicles. It sources material from roughly 8500 first-tier suppliers. Within Europe alone, Volkswagen manages around 18,000 truckloads every day, and transports more than 75 million cubic meters of material each year. To add to the challenge, Volkswagen gives individual plants and business units significant autonomy in the operation of their logistics processes, with the group logistics function responsible for overall strategy, setting standards, and assuring synergies (https://www.dhl.com/global-en/home/about-us/delivered-magazine/articles/2019/issue-5-2019/building-the-digital-automotive-supply-chain.html).

These are turbulent times for the auto-mobility sector. Sector stakeholders are trying to sustain supply chain efficiency. Huge global growth, especially in emerging markets, coupled with increasing government regulations to meet emissions targets; rising consumer expectations for personalization; and decreasing product cycle times are all adding up to a volatile environment (DHL, 2021).

In order to survive, manufacturers must adapt and rethink their current supply chains. Production is moving closer to consumption, new players are entering the market to support an emerging era of vehicles that are becoming technology on wheels, and OEMs are heavily investing in mega-plants in emerging markets (Ibid).

10.5 Best Practices: Case Samples from the VW Group

This sample company was selected as it has high levels of transparency in strategic terms, an objective information sharing approach, and advanced supply chain risk management systems besides its improved internal control systems. Their AutoSCRM are both shaped according to their objectives and strategies and implemented with high performance.

The selected company uses best practices in its risk management systems as a sustainable method to create added value. In these companies, the application performance of corporate-wide risk management systems and the success of obtaining the advantages of enterprise risk management is very high. All the abovementioned reasons are the preference reasons of this company as a case study.

Another important reason for choosing this company is that both high-level risk management systems have been developed in these countries, and these systems are being implemented with high performance. In this company, the application performance of corporate risk management systems and the success of obtaining the advantages of risk management is very high.

As is known, enterprise risk management provides reasonable assurance to achieving corporate goals. In addition, risk management is vital in the successful development and implementation of the corporate strategies at all organizations. It is predicted that companies with high performance in risk management system implementation will achieve their goals in the implementation of strategies during and after COVID-19, as well. Therefore, VW Group is the selected company in this respect. In general, the goal is the same in risk management system-based implementations, but the scope of each system varies from company to company. Their common point is that they minimize threats and provide reasonable assurance in seizing opportunities.

10.5.1 Best Practice from the VW Group

Volkswagen Group Companies: Volkswagen, Audi, SEAT, ŠKODA, Bentley, Bugatti, Lamborghini, Porsche, Ducati, Volkswagen Commercial Vehicles, Scania, and MAN[2] (https://www.volkswagenag.com/en/group.html).

Automotive supply chain requires sophisticated management techniques, information technology and close coordination of all parties involved, directly or indirectly, in fulfilling a customer request. A supply chain is dynamic and involves the constant flow of information, product, and funds between different stages that includes not only the manufacturer and suppliers, but also transporters, warehouses, retailers, and even customers themselves (Curovac, 2021). Strategy development is essential to managing and mitigating risks in the transportation sector. Furthermore, as the risk management emphasizes, another plan is needed for the possibility of failure of the strategy taken and implemented. Successful companies develop different strategies for different scenarios and improve their preparedness for every situation.

Automotive is a necessary and indispensable element of trade, economy, and social life in selected companies among others. The best practices of selected companies in the automotive sector will be presented by interpreting them in terms of risk management and in relation with the strategies adopted (Fig. 10.6).

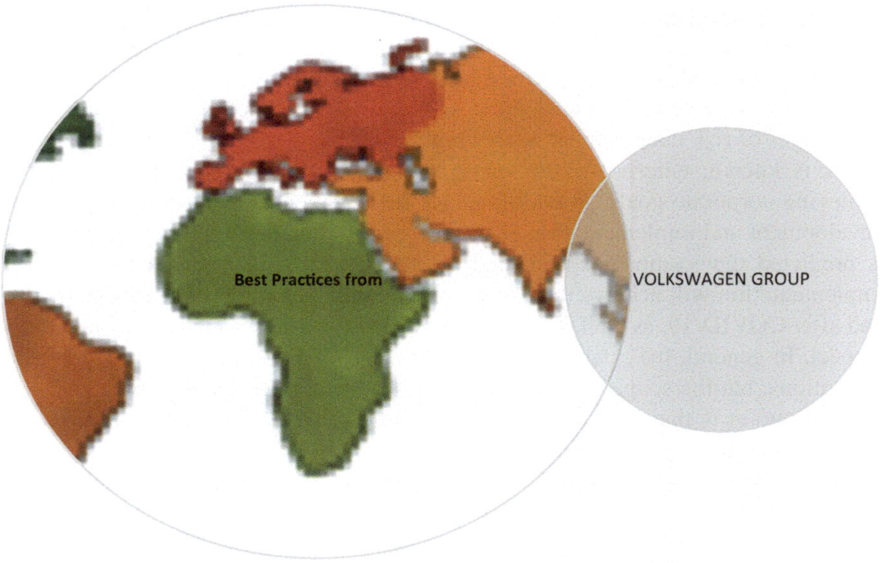

Fig. 10.6 Best practices sample: Volkswagen Group

[2] https://www.volkswagenag.com/en/group.html

The implementation of successful and effective risk management has considerable potential to result in the reduction of future risks and the high success of the transportation sector in the short term. When the current conditions and studies are followed, it can be seen that risk management has already been determined and started to be implemented by the companies that have been the pioneers of the automotive sector in their continents. In this part, examples from selected best practices will be presented in detail to serve as a guide to other companies. These best practices will help other companies develop their own strategies and risk management systems and successfully implement these systems.

10.5.2 The Volkswagen Group

The Group comprises 12 brands from seven European countries: Volkswagen, Audi, SEAT, ŠKODA, Bentley, Bugatti, Lamborghini, Porsche, Ducati, Volkswagen Commercial Vehicles, Scania, and MAN. In addition, the Volkswagen Group offers a wide range of financial services, including dealer and customer financing, leasing, banking and insurance activities, and fleet management (Volkswagen, 2021).

"Sustainability in Supplier Relations"

Volkswagen Group management concept considers sustainable relations with their suppliers. The Volkswagen Group want to fulfill their responsibility in their business relationships on a global level and act proactively beyond fulfilling legal requirements. In procurement, they follow a three-pronged approach to establishing sustainable supply chains with the focuses of decarbonization, human rights, responsible procurement of raw materials, and combating corruption. The approach of Volkswagen Group requires transparency in supplier relationships that go beyond the first tier (tier 1), as follows (Volkswagen, 2021):

1. *Prevent:* Sustainability requirements are enshrined in contracts and specifications, particularly the Code of Conduct for Business Partners. Suppliers are trained and sustainability awareness is raised.
2. *Detect:* Sustainability risks in the supply chain are systematically analyzed and prioritized. Sustainability is anchored in the material contract award decisions across the Group and a rating of potential suppliers' sustainability performance (S-Rating) is used. The basis for this is a self-assessment tool and on-site checks conducted on a risk-based approach.
3. *React:* Various measures are available to react to the risks and impacts identified. These include a standardized internal process to review breaches by individual suppliers and action plans from on-site checks. The key objective is to rectify and prevent breaches and to actively and effectively improve suppliers' sustainability performance.

As part of their sustainable supplier management measures, they pay particular attention to protecting those groups of people who, along their supply chain, are at particularly high risk of human rights abuses. In line with the requirements of a risk-based approach, they concentrate the measures on the supply chains that are associated with particularly high risks for negative impacts, according to their analyses. These particularly include their raw material supply chains. The way Volkswagen Group organizes the responsible sourcing of raw materials is driven by the requirements of the OECD Due Diligence Guidance for Responsible Supply Chains of Minerals from Conflict-Affected and High-Risk Areas, which contains guidelines for management approaches, for risk identification and prevention, for checking smelters and for communication and reporting instruments.

VW Group assumes that their responsibility for ensuring a sustainable and fair supply chain—they established sustainability criteria for their suppliers on a contractual basis as long ago as 2014. Since 2019, VW Group has checked compliance with their standards as part of the award process. BVG has considerable tools to uncover and investigate potential violations, thereby improving social and environmental conditions at their suppliers' production sites (Wilson, 2021).

Suppliers and Sustainability: State-of-the-Art Monitoring with AI (Volkswagen Group Italia S.p.A., 2021)

Volkswagen, Porsche, and Audi harness artificial intelligence (AI) to identify sustainability risks in the supply chain (https://theindustrialtimes.com/volkswagen-reduces-supply-chain-sustainability-risk-with-ai/).

Audi, Porsche, and Volkswagen are working on a joint project to monitor all levels of their supply chain using artificial intelligence, helping them to identify potential sustainability risks involving their suppliers. Environmental pollution, human rights abuses, and corruption are among the risk factors at an early stage of the supply chain—not only from direct business partners but also at the lower levels. The basis for this innovative monitoring system is an intelligent algorithm developed by the Austrian start-up Prewave (Volkswagen, 2021).

The Volkswagen Group is already using artificial intelligence to analyze texts for semantic relevance in more than 50 local and wider-ranging risk categories. This covers a broad spectrum. In the case of criteria from the "Social" category, for example, the focus is on labor law developments, unrest among the workforce, child labor, and discrimination in the workplace. Relevant criteria from the "Environment" category use public data for aspects such as air pollution, water pollution, and consumption or waste problems. With regard to issues such as cyber risks, the AI analyzes reports indicating suspected cyber-attacks, computer fraud, or data theft. Audi is automatically informed whenever a potential sustainability risk begins to develop. The matter is scrutinized in detail within the company, and action is taken as appropriate (AUDI, 2021) (Fig. 10.7).

In VW supply chain risk management, the technology can identify and analyze supplier-related news from publicly available media and social networks in more than 50 languages and in over 150 countries. If the algorithm finds any indication of

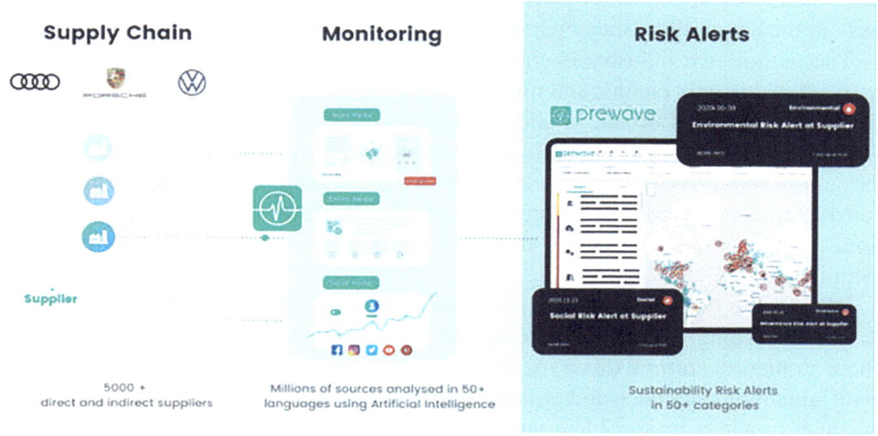

Fig. 10.7 VW supply chain risk management. (Source: Volkswagen Group Italia S.p.A. (2021). https://modo.volkswagengroup.it/en/lab/suppliers-and-sustainability-state-of-the-art-monitoring-with-ai)

a sustainability risk in the supply chain, the brands are notified. The relevant department then looks into the facts and considers initiating countermeasures against the supplier. In doing so, artificial intelligence provides a proactive early warning system for breaches of the Volkswagen Group's sustainability requirements. It therefore supplements traditional reactive complaint channels such as mailboxes and Ombudspersons. Since the pilot project began in October 2020, the brands have analyzed more than 5000 keywords and have monitored over 4000 suppliers (Volkswagen Group Italia S.p.A., 2021).

Monitoring supply chains is an extremely complex undertaking. Constant change is the rule. The status quo with regard to suppliers and their upstream partners is constantly changing, with some companies departing and others joining, which means that complete control is impossible. That makes it all the more important to understand the potential risks and make connections early on. Audi therefore operates a comprehensive risk monitoring that combines various methods and systems (AUDI, 2021).

The sustainability in Supplier Relations concept is based on the "Volkswagen Group requirements regarding sustainability in its relationship with business partners" (Code of Conduct for Business Partners). The latter embeds VW AG expectations of business partners' conduct with respect to key environmental, social, and compliance standards in contractual agreements. Tier-one suppliers are expected to pass those requirements down along the supply chain. Before taking into consideration to work with a potential supplier, VW AG uses a country risk analysis and other data to obtain a clearer picture of the social, environmental, and human-right risks in the areas where they operate (Curovac, 2021).

The automotive industry is characterized by low margins, high volumes, high costs, global supply chains, and multilayer suppliers. In general, automotive supply chains are deep and broad. In addition, cost reduction efforts such as JIT, single-sourcing, outsourcing, and globalization add to the network complexity and increase the supply chain risks in the automotive industry. The automotive supply chain risks considered here include the different risks that come from sourcing, supply, production, storage, logistics, and distribution in the automotive supply chain (Shiping, 2018).

We assume that AutoSCRM (Automotive Supply Chain Risk Management) is shaped according to the objectives of the enterprises, corporate structure, supply chain strategies, cultural diversity, legal requirements, and geographical conditions. With situational approach and organization-specific shaping, supply chain risk management provides reasonable assurance in achieving the goals of the organization, saving resources, allocating resources accurately and on time, and increasing corporate performance. Moreover, a supply chain risk management increases organizational resilience. Developing resilience and reducing complexity through supply chain risk management in the automotive industry is the strategic approach that supports competition in all supply chain-related activities. It is, therefore, important to analyze the current situation with a situational approach and to implement the optimum risk management handling strategy. As an exemplary situational risk management decision, VW Group has decided to slow down production at its home base due to the risk of supply shortages.

10.6 Case Study: TOFAŞ

TOFAŞ, a Turkish company, appears to have a sufficient infrastructure to apply AutoSCRM. TOFAŞ has set the development-oriented supply chain. TOFAŞ seems to have the infrastructure to implement risk management. TOFAŞ seems to have recognized the importance of the supply relations risk management.

Founded in 1968, TOFAŞ is the only company in Turkey that manufactures both passenger cars and light commercial vehicles. TOFAŞ is a Koç Holding and Fiat Chrysler Automobiles (FCA) partnership in which each controls an equal stake. With 24.3% of its capital publicly traded, TOFAŞ's shares are included in both the Borsa İstanbul BIST 30 and BIST 100 indexes as well as in the exchange's Corporate Governance Index and Sustainability indexes. TOFAŞ is foremost among Fiat Chrysler Automobiles' strategically important production centers. TOFAŞ is also a distributor, handling the domestic sales of six brands in Turkey, namely, Fiat, Fiat Professional, Alfa Romeo, Jeep, Maserati, and Ferrari.

TOFAŞ appears to have determined its corporate objectives as maintaining competitive power, optimizing product and purchasing costs, obtaining the best quality and delivery performance in purchased products and services, and ensuring their sustainability. In this direction, the company seems to contribute to the continuous development of its employees and its suppliers, one of the most important elements of the value chain, to increasing their business success and productivity. TOFAŞ believes that forming a continual development-oriented supply chain that adopts business ethics and norms synonymous with itself is one of the tenets of the sustainability of its success (adapted TOFAŞ, 2021) http://ir.tofas.com.tr/en/m-4-6.html).

TOFAŞ's procurements fall under three main headings defined as: Direct Materials, Spare Parts, Services & Industrial Procurement. In 2019, TOFAŞ's total procurements budget amounted to EUR 3.4 billion in value. The company purchases its direct materials from 149 suppliers located in 14 cities across the country.

In TOFAŞ, Just in Time and Just in Sequence applications are extensively used for both domestic and imported suppliers, in order to minimize material stock levels, reduce material movements in production, and ensure operational efficiency in factories. In addition, Milk Run system is used in purchasing materials from suppliers in Turkey. Case Optimization has been successfully implemented by the company for many years in order to take environmental factors into consideration in logistics processes and to standardize material movements, and joint studies are carried out with subindustry companies for continuous improvement. Despite working with a high percentage of domestic suppliers, TOFAŞ does not have a supplier park (Adapted from Ergene, 2017).

In the conduct of all of its procurements operations, TOFAŞ focuses on establishing and maintaining business-partner relationships while making efforts to help its suppliers enhance their performance in many different areas, such as product design, organizational and technical improvements, quality, cost improvement, physical and financial risk mitigation, manufacturing process improvement, collective procurement, and sustainability. In the conduct of its supplier development activities, TOFAŞ's primary goal is to create a proactive and autonomous procurements process that completely replaces previously existing business practices that are merely reactive and focused on "problem fixing." Throughout the year, TOFAŞ organizes a variety of special training and other activities for its suppliers, in order to share its own technical knowledge and experience with them and to support suppliers' efforts to improve and perfect their own human resources, management, and production processes.

While TOFAŞ selects the ones that will be supplying inputs for its assembly line operations, based on their access to submanufacturing capacity, there are certain basic criteria that it expects every potential supplier to satisfy. Specifically, all suppliers must adhere to the following (https://ir.tofas.com.tr/en/m-4-6.html):

- Possess both the technical (quality/cost competitiveness, delivery performance, project management, production capacity, co-design) and the organizational competencies capable of satisfying the automotive industry's expectations
- Be financially robust

- Hold ISO/TS 16949 (quality) and ISO 14001 (environment) certifications
- Possess advanced design, manufacturing, and testing competencies
- Have successfully passed TOFAŞ-conducted Supplier Eligibility Assessment and Process Audit inspections
- Be able to contribute favorably to TOFAŞ's own competitiveness by supporting improvements in its quality and cost-effectiveness
- Have demonstrated an ability to consistently improve themselves and increase their competitive strength by keeping a close watch on what its domestic and international competitors do
- Demonstrate a willingness and an ability to engage in a transparent and mutual-trust-based business-partner relationship in their dealings with TOFAŞ

In conducting all of its procurement processes, TOFAŞ ensures that its relationships with suppliers are transparent, mutually trust-based, and competitively sustainable within the overall framework of a long-term business relationship. Whenever TOFAŞ considers the procurement aspects of its new projects, it gives particular attention to acquiring the latest technological abilities for the Turkish automotive industry, on the one hand, and to boosting its own competitive strength, on the other hand. In line with this, TOFAŞ encourages international firms that are global manufacturers of automotive components to invest in Turkey or to enter into joint ventures with local suppliers. While taking measures to reduce its actual procurement costs, TOFAŞ also engages in an ongoing effort to streamline its business processes, through the use of advanced procurement methods and digitalization (TOFAŞ (2018), Annual Report, supply Chain Management, https://ir.tofas.com.tr/en/m-4-6.html). According to TOFAŞ's approach and implementations, TOFAŞ has infrastructure to implement AutoSCRM in more systematic way.

Best practices are useful to design corporate-specific management system setting, according to corporate objectives and strategy. In effect, best practices examples are guiding and inspiring for companies.

10.7 Conclusion and Remarks

Transport is a necessary and indispensable element of trade, health, economy, and social life. Health and economy are integral parts of a whole for sustainable growth.

Today, increasing competition conditions require companies to focus on every step from planning to purchasing and reaching the customer with the aim of increasing their profits by minimizing their expenses, and this necessity brings about conceptual changes.

Although planning, purchasing, stock management, storage, transportation, and distribution of raw materials or finished products were seen as secondary and separate works in the past, these links of the chain are interconnected processes from "Customer to Customer" within the concept of "Supply Chain" formed in recent past.

Even in the TS 16949 standard, which is based on the automotive sector, where competition is most intensely experienced, this concept is included as one of the aims of the standard with the expression "emphasizing the change and reducing losses in the supply chain."

Due to COVID-19, behavior and business practices in transportation modes have begun to change, similarly to all our applications in both business and social life. Some of these changes in transport are likely to be permanent. In line with these changes, presentation of transportation services and business style of supply chains in transportation sector are reshaping with risk management-based strategies. In this context, successful applications of these transport services are important, as they will guide other countries in the best use of resources and in optimized managing of the threats posed on the sectors by pandemic conditions.

As already demonstrated, supply chain networks are another channel through which COVID-19 negatively impacts the global economy. After the COVID-19 pandemic, the functioning of global procurement has been disrupted, which has created spillover effects at different levels in supplier networks. Specifically, automotive companies have halted their production due to a lack of parts, as in many different industrial sectors. Even with luxury items such as Swiss watches, manufacturers have faced a short supply of parts. Consequently, disruption in supply chains has increased the cost of work for manufacturing companies. As a result, manufacturers that supply almost 70% of their products from China are on the brink of bankruptcy. As factories in China closed and transportation routes collapsed, it has become increasingly difficult to market products around the world. Moreover, 75% of companies in the USA reported disruptions in their supply chain. Many US companies have doubled their lead times routine (Taylor & Schwartz, 2020).

Sound enterprise risk management implementations improve corporate performance. Leading organizations are aware that risk provides a competitive advantage. These organizations, which manage their risks more effectively, reveal their potential and add value to all their stakeholders. For this reason, our risk management-based viewpoint has reflected at supply chains (adapted from Deloitte https://www2.deloitte.com/tr/services/risk.html).

Ensuring the integration of a risk management system that covers all stakeholders of the industry's supply chain with all management systems is considered critical for an uninterrupted and effective supply chain planning cycle. Demand forecasts, stock analysis, and production planning comprise the sustainability areas of the automotive industry. The subject of inventory management is always on the agenda of managers as a source of risk in the automotive industry. The number and types of risks that need to be managed for the sustainability of the automotive industry's supply chain is high. In order to manage these risks, there is a need for a risk management system to be established to support the objectives and strategy of the enterprise. A supply chain risk management system is required to support institutional resilience against unexpected situations such as pandemics. AutoSCRM, which is presented in this book, has been developed to support the resilience of the automotive industry.

It is predicted that the pandemic will transform and shape supply chains as well as business models. At this point, it is predicted that positioning in terms of being global and regional will come to the fore. If regional supply chains come to the fore, then the risk map of suppliers will change. It is, therefore, necessary to develop a new risk map and to redefine its risks, to prioritize them and to choose management options. This points to the need for flexible risk management and information systems compatible with transformation. Therefore, with a strategic and visionary perspective, risk management systems are integrated into the managerial planning function, making it necessary to operate with an integrated and digital planning infrastructure.

The philosophy based on local optimization, in which both process in a company and various supplier's stakeholders such as suppliers, manufacturers, distributors focus only on their own best interest, leaves its place to a holistic view and integrated data-based applications to achieve this. Automotive supply chains are both differentiated and also have unique qualifications from other sectors at important points. In the automotive industry, the supply chain process, policies, rules, contracts, and standards has been defined much more specifically and clearly than in other industries. These definitions were also privatized according to the relations between the stakeholders. The process and stages of the process are clear between all stakeholders, from supplier to supplier, from supplier to manufacturer, from manufacturer to distributor. In fact, it can be said that the world's most mature supply chain structures are in the automotive industry. Despite this advantage, the automotive industry has a much more complex structure and is under time pressure compared to other sectors. In automotive, product, material, spare parts and process complexity are high. In addition, the automotive industry struggles with stock and lead time pressures without compromising the target of high customer satisfaction. Due to the volatile business environments, business conditions, providing sustainability is more challenging, and the areas of improvement that will provide advantage fields, such as digitalization and innovation, are getting harder day by day. This creates the need to implement the most important supply chain risk management function (adapted from Kaplancik, 2020).

Risk management is a dynamic and disciplined system that ensures that risks that prevent organizations from reaching their goals and opportunities that facilitate achievement of goals are recognized and managed in advance. The system, which started with private sector applications, has also been adopted by public institutions. The main purpose of enterprise risk management is to support profit-increasing practices in the private sector and to help improve the benefit factor in public institutions.

Clearly, the travel and transportation sector has been one of the sectors that suffered the most damage from the pandemic. With the COVID-19 pandemic, hopes for a more sustainable order have flourished, both positive and negative results have emerged in terms of sustainable transportation, and different trends have been observed in many cities. On the one hand, the demand for private vehicle use increases and confidence in public transport decreases, and, on the other hand, cycling and walking options also become more attractive. For example, in Istanbul, there was a 50% decrease (more than two million passengers) in the number of public transport passengers in the first 3 weeks of March. As vehicle sales boomed in Istanbul, bicycle projects started with the encouragement of the municipality in many cities, such as Paris. UK Transport Secretary, Grant Shapps, says the time is right for the green transport revolution. In fact, the COVID-19 crisis has revealed the importance of building stronger infrastructure systems in the transportation sector. In this context, automation is a good option to create transport systems that are more resistant to crises (PWC, 2021).

The automotive industry is a truly global sector and the level of interaction with other production sectors is high, and its contributions to sustainable growth in social and economic areas are also great. In addition, it has a strategic meaning and determining power as a dynamo for the world economy with its added value, innovation, employment, and driving structure. The automotive industry is a sector that is developing more and more rapidly and technology intensively, and its impact on the national economy is increasing. Factors such as the productivity increase needed in this sector, effective use of resources, administrative and technical organization, and digitalization and managing the risks of the supplier network gain great importance. In this context, features such as investment in risk management-based R&D, quality management, cooperative relations between the main and subindustry, employment of qualified workforce, application of flexible production methods, and effective marketing are the determining factors in terms of sustainability.

Agenda: EVs-Based New Risks for Suppliers

Suppliers should begin considering how the mainstreaming of EVs will affect their businesses. They should develop a realistic point of view on EV adoption in key markets that takes into account the technological and regulatory landscapes and consumer preferences. Subsequently, they must take a critical look at product portfolios and determine which components could see slowing demand as EV sales increase (PWC United States, 2021).

AutoSCRM is a holistic management system that creates added value for businesses and has become one of the main building parts for businesses. In order for corporate risk management to be successfully integrated and implemented, it is important to consider it as an integral part of the current strategic planning process. In essence, AutoSCRM should be integrated into existing management tools. Establishing a risk culture and creating a common risk perception in the organization is critical for the effective application of AutoSCRM and to obtain the benefits it will provide.

Apparently, there should be a relationship between management and approach. For the effective implementation of the corporate risk management approach, a healthy exchange of information should be ensured between the corporate risk management approach and the tools that support governance processes such as internal control, internal audit, and external audit. The information produced within the framework of each management tool should be a resource for each other, so that the benefit of each management tool for the organization and the efficiency of the processes in question should be increased. Corporate risk management should be established flexibly with a contingency approach, kept up to date, and supported by technological infrastructure.

Business models are changing in the business world, whose momentum of change is high and affected by external factors. While businesses try to gain competitive advantage by developing appropriate strategies, they also try to optimize their short delivery time, flexible organization, cost-effective applications and operations, high quality, and customer satisfaction. Moreover, enterprises in the sector create products and services for this purpose. Under these conditions, companies are now trying to manage their risks and to be sustainable in fierce competition by joining forces as a supply chain, not alone.

Supply chain management focuses on being cost-effective today. It is anticipated that cost-effective strategies will continue to be effective in the future. It should not be forgotten that pioneer examples, such as Tesla, will also change and reshape the supply chain management.

It is anticipated that both manufacturers and suppliers should invest in technology in order to manage risks in supply chain management. The market is gradually shrinking. The producers' aims to be cost-effective in the shrinking market shape their activities and collaborations in terms of number and quality, as access to limited resources becomes difficult and resources are gradually decreasing. Collaborations and partnerships come to the fore in managing the risks arising from these reasons. Thus, leading manufacturers in the world have many collaborations in different geographies. As a result, the competitive environment and approach to competition are also transforming. In this context, the ability to act in accordance with these developments and changes is considered critical for suppliers to manage their risks.

References

AUDI. (2021). *How digitalization is improving sustainability in the supply chain, Value Creation & Production, Core Topics, Sustainability, Company*, April 22, 2021. https://www.audi.com/en/company/sustainability/core-topics/value-creation-and-production/supply-chain-digitalization.html

Altay, T. A. (2019). *What's happening in the automotive sector? Chapter 1, engineer and machine*, February 2019. https://www.mmo.org.tr/sites/default/files/14_0.pdf

Baskak and Mihcioglu. 2019. *Main company-supplier relations in automotive industry and a survey application*. http://www1.mmo.org.tr/resimler/dosya_ekler/1e567798fc9ccd2_ek.pdf

Blume Global. (2021). *Top 4 automotive supply chain challenges and solutions*. https://www.blumeglobal.com/learning/automotive-supply-chain/

Busvine, D., &Steitz, C. (2021). *Analysis: Carmakers wake up to new pecking order as chip crunch intensifies, CHANGE SUITE Reuters*, Feb 19, 2021. https://www.reuters.com/article/us-autos-chips-analysis/analysis-carmakers-wake-up-to-new-pecking-order-as-chip-crunch-intensifies-idUSKBN2AJ0LD

Curovac. (2021). *Sustainable supply chain Management in Automotive Industry, obstacles and challenges: The case of Volkswagen Sarajevo, Faculty of Civil and Industrial Engineering Master in transport systems engineering*, Sapienza University of Rome, 2019.

Deloitte. (2020). *How the automotive industry moves to reduce risk during the pandemic*, Deloitte Turkey. https://www2.deloitte.com/tr/tr/pages/manufacturing/articles/otomotiv-endustrisi-salgin-sirasinda-riski-azaltma-yonunde-nasil-hareket-ediyor.html

Deloitte. https://www2.deloitte.com/tr/services/risk.html

DHL (2021). *Auto mobility, driving supply chain efficiency*. https://www.dhl.com/tr-en/home/our-divisions/supply-chain/sectors-overview/automotive.html

DW. (2021). *How microchips became the 'oil of the digital age'*, Top Stories, Business, Video. https://www.dw.com/en/how-microchips-became-the-oil-of-the-digital-age/av-56699977

DWb. (2021). *Chip crisis raises questions for car sector, with complications likely to continue*, Top Stories, Business. Accessed April 03, 2021 by https://www.dw.com/en/chip-crisis-raises-questions-for-car-sector-with-complications-likely-to-continue/a-56538970

Ergene, M. R. (2017), Supply chain restructuring in the automative sector, Unpublished Master Thesis, Department of International Trade and Logistics, Logistics and Supply Chain Management Program, Social Science Institute, Maltepe University, İstanbul. https://openaccess.maltepe.edu.tr/xmlui/bitstream/handle/20.500.12415/3878/486372.pdf?sequence=1&isAllowed=y

Ewing, J. (2019). Electric cars threaten the heart of Germany's economy. *The NewYork Times*. https://www.nytimes.com/2019/12/31/business/electric-cars-germany-economy.html

Kaplancik, O. (2020). *Digitalization way opened by pandemic in automotive supply chain*, Turkish Automotive Industrialists' Magazine TAYSAD, November December 2020 No: 117. http://www.taysadmag.com/haber/otomotiv-tedarik-zincirinde-pandeminin-actigi-dijitallesme-yolu

Khan, Z. A. (2011). *Technology transfer effectiveness through international joint ventures to their component suppliers: a study of the automotive industry of Pakistan*, Doctor of Phılosophy, Birmingham Business School College of Social Sciences University of Birmingham, UK June 2011.

Metzner, J. T., DeWitt, W., Keebler, J. S., Min, S., Nix, N. W., Smith, C. D., & Zacharia, Z. G. (2001). Defining supply chain management. *Journal of Business Logistics, 22*(2), 2001. http://www.aui.ma/personal/~A.Berrado/MGT5309/DEFINING%20SUPPLYCHAIN%20MANAGEMENT_Metzner%20et%20al.%202001.pdf

Monnet, F. (2021). *The electric vehicle supply chain: Manage risk*, Accelerate Production, JABIL. https://www.jabil.com/blog/electric-vehicle-supply-chain.html. Accessed by May 26, 2021.

ODD. (2013). *World and Turkey Authomovie Sector*. http://www.odd.org.tr/folders/2837/categorial1docs/821/ic%20dokumanlar.pdf

OICA. (2021). *2020 Statistics*. Retrieved at February 20, 2021 from https://www.oica.net/2020-statistics/

Perryman, A. (2021). *A growing appetite for EVs tasks the supply chain to scale*, Supply Chain Dive. Retrieved from https://www.supplychaindive.com/news/electric-vehicle-battery-sourcing-material-manufacturing/596148/. June, 2021.

Piskin, S. (2017). *Automotive sector report, 2020 domestic market expectations in the perspective of Turkish automotive industry competitiveness and demand dynamics*, January 2017. Retrieved at April 2021 from http://www.osd.org.tr/sites/1/upload/files/otomotiv_sektor_raporu_tskb-2208.pdf

PWC Turkey. (2021). *New Coronavirus (COVID-19): Roadmap in tackling the crisis*. https://www.pwc.com.tr/covid-19-ile-mucadele

PWC United States. (2021). *Electric vehicles and the impact on the automotive supply chain*. https://www.pwc.com/us/en/industries/industrial-products/library/electric-vehicles-supply-chain.html

Shepardson, D. (2021). *White house ramps up effort to tackle automotive chip shortage*, Technology News, Reuters. https://www.reuters.com/article/us-autos-semiconductors-biden/white-house-ramps-up-effort-to-tackle-automotive-chip-shortage-idUSKBN2AI0C4

Shiping, Z. (2018). *Supply chain risk management in automotive industry*. University of Windsor (Canada). ProQuest Dissertations Publishing, 2018. 10975942.

Smith, N. (2021). *Electric vehicles are disrupting automotive supply chains*, Assent Compliance Blog. https://blog.assentcompliance.com/index.php/automotive-supply-chain-disruption/

T.R. Ministry of Science, Industry and Technology. (2020). *Automotive Sector Report*, General Directorate of Industry, Sectoral Reports and Analysis Series, 2020. https://www.sanayi.gov.tr/plan-program-raporlar-ve-yayinlar/sektor-raporlari/mu2007011621

Taylor, D., & Schwartz, J. (2020). *Volkswagen suspends production as coronavirus hits sales*. Reuters. Available at: https://www.reuters.com/article/us-volkswagen-results2019/volkswagen-suspends-production-as-coronavirus-hits-sales-idUSKBN2140OF. Accessed 15 March 2020.

TAYSAD Association of Motor Vehicle Manufacturers. How Do Suppliers Take Part in New Projects? March-April 2020 Issue 113 Year: 22. http://www.taysadmag.com/uploads/tedarikciler-yeni-projelerde-nasil-yer-aliyor16052020220501.pdf

TÜSİAD-Sabancı University Competition Forum (REF) and the Federation of Sectoral Associations (SEDEFED). (2010). *Automotive sector, Series of Sectoral Competitiveness Reports*, Competitiveness Report, Federation of Sectoral Associations, ISBN: 978-605-88308-1-3, 2010.

Volkswagen, A. G. (2021). *Sustainability in the Supply Chain, Sustainability in supplier relations – Volkswagen Group management concept*. https://www.volkswagenag.com/en/sustainability/sustainability-in-the-supply-chain.html; and *Group*. https://www.volkswagenag.com/en/group.html. Accessed 25 May 2021.

Volkswagen Group Italia S.p.A. (2021). *VW Supply chain risk management*. https://modo.volkswagengroup.it/en/lab/suppliers-and-sustainability-state-of-the-art-monitoring-with-ai

Wilson, G. (2021). *Volkswagen reduces supply chain sustainability risk with AI*, Supply Chain Digital, https://supplychaindigital.com/procurement/ey-and-harvard-law-discuss-barriers-contract-management. May 30, 2021.

World Atlas. (2017). *Everything about Automotivbe Industry*. Retrieved April 2021, from https://www.dunyaatlasi.com/otomotiv-endustrisi-hakkinda-her-sey/

WSJ, Reuters. https://www.sozcu.com.tr/2021/ekonomi/cip-krizi-otomotiv-sektorunu-global-olcekte-salliyor-iste-krizin-nedenleri-6249705/

Yucel, A. (2021). *Container crisis created VIP class*, Logistic, Dunya Newspaper, 2021.

Sustainability and Corporate Social Responsibility (CSR) in SCRM

11

It takes 20 years to build a reputation and five minutes to ruin it.

– Benjamin Franklin (1706–1790)

11.1 Sustainability in SCRM

The term "corporate social responsibility" (CSR) was used by Howard R. Bowen in his book *Social Responsibility of the Entrepreneur* in 1953.. Bowen preaches in his book for greater consideration of society by the big corporations in the USA (Corporate America), as these corporations have considerable power and, with their economic endeavors, have a great impact on the lives of citizens. In the decades that followed, the concept of corporate social responsibility (CSR) continued to develop, initially through the zeitgeist of the social movements in the 1960s, for example through the civil rights movement, the consumer movement, the environmental movement, and the women's movements (Helmold 2020). Figure 11.1 depicts the elements of sustainability.

11.2 Corporate Social Responsibility (CSR)

Sustainability and corporate social responsibility (CSR) are essential factors for achieving competitive advantages and for employee satisfaction. Employees want to work for companies with social standards and rules (Stibbe, 2019). For a successful sustainable development, actors from politics, companies, non-profit organizations, science, and education deal with the topic of sustainable management. Examples show that CSR is not just a question of multinational companies (MNC),

M. Helmold et al., *Supply Chain Risk Management*,
Management for Professionals, https://doi.org/10.1007/978-3-030-90800-3_11

Fig. 11.1 Sustainability elements in SCRM. (Source: Author)

but also of other organizations from various industries such as start-ups, companies in metropolitan areas, small and medium-sized enterprises (SMEs) in rural areas—from high-tech to organic agriculture (Wunder, 2017). CSR is also known by a number of other definition names. These include corporate responsibility, corporate responsibility, business ethics, corporate citizenship or stewardship, business ethics, responsible entrepreneurship, and triple bottom line, to name just a few (Helmold 2020). As CSR issues are increasingly integrated into modern business practices, there is a trend to refer to them as "responsible competitiveness" or "corporate sustainability." CSR is the way companies integrate social, environmental, and economic concerns into their values, culture, decision-making, strategy, and business operations in a transparent and accountable manner, thereby establishing better practices within the company, creating wealth and improving society (Wunder, 2017).

An important point to note is that CSR is an evolving concept that does not currently have a generally accepted definition. In general, CSR is the way companies integrate social, environmental, and economic concerns into their values, culture, decision-making, strategy, and business operations in a transparent and accountable way, thereby establishing better practices within the company, creating wealth and society improve. As sustainable development issues become increasingly important, how the corporate sector addresses them becomes an element of CSR. The World

Business Council for Sustainable Development has described CSR as the business contribution to sustainable economic development. Building on compliance with laws and regulations, CSR usually includes "beyond the law" obligations and activities related to the following:

- Corporate governance and ethics
- Health and safety
- Environmental stewardship
- Human rights (including core labor rights)
- Sustainable development
- Conditions of work (including safety and health, hours of work, wages)
- Industrial relations
- Community involvement, development, and investment
- Involvement of and respect for diverse cultures and disadvantaged peoples
- Corporate philanthropy and employee volunteering
- Customer satisfaction and adherence to principles of fair competition
- Anti-bribery and anti-corruption measures
- Accountability, transparency, and performance reporting
- Supplier relations, for both domestic and international supply chains

SCRM concepts focus primarily on improvements of the operational processes and efficiency (Helmold & Samara 2019). Another goal is to reduce waste and thus to reduce operating costs. In the last years, sustainability has become more and more important, so that any organization must deploy sustainability elements alongside a lean organization. Sustainability or corporate social responsibility (CSR) has the following elements as shown in Fig. 11.2. The figure shows that there is a strong need to align the supply chain implementation process with the sustainability strategy in order to avoid the negative impacts that lean production could have on the environmental and social components of sustainability. Although the concept of corporate social responsibility (CSR) has been advocated for decades and is commonly employed by corporations globally, agreement on how

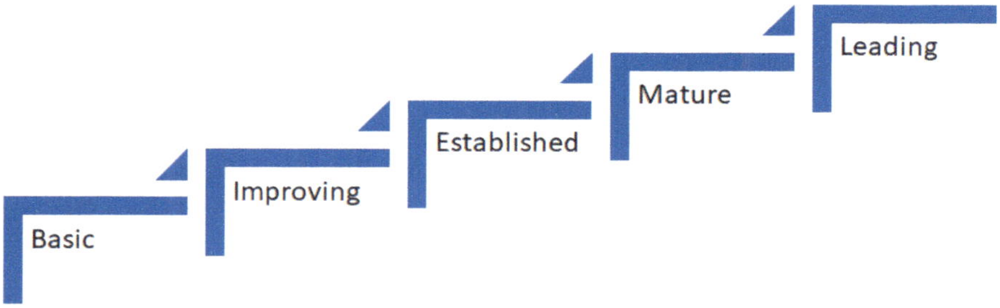

Fig. 11.2 CSR maturity levels. (Helmold 2020)

CSR should be defined and implemented remains a contentious debate among academia, businesses, and society. This gap is problematic for corporations because they are increasingly being required to align with societal norms while generating financial returns (Stibbe, 2019). In order to remedy this problem, the following definition is presented: corporate social responsibility is a business system that enables the production and distribution of wealth for the betterment of its stakeholders through the implementation and integration of ethical systems and sustainable management practices. Many of the concepts in the proposed definition are commonplace among CSR practitioners and organizations, the validations for the key segments—production and distribution of wealth, stakeholder management, ethical systems, sustainable management practices—coupled with the application of a systems approach and other business practices make the definition unique and conclusive.

11.3 CSR Maturity Levels

Maturity is a measurement of the ability of an organization for continuous improvement in CSR as shown in Fig. 11.2. The higher the maturity, the higher will be the chances that incidents or errors will lead to improvements either in the quality or in the use of the resources of the discipline as implemented by the organization.

11.4 Global Compact Principles

Corporate sustainability starts with a company's value system and a principles-based approach to doing business. This means operating in ways that, at a minimum, meet fundamental responsibilities in the areas of human rights, labor, environment, and anti-corruption. Responsible businesses enact the same values and principles wherever they have a presence, and know that good practices in one area do not offset harm in another (Helmold & Terry, 2016). By incorporating the Ten Principles of the UN Global Compact into strategies, policies, and procedures, and establishing a culture of integrity, companies are not only upholding their basic responsibilities to people and planet, but also setting the stage for long-term success. The UN Global Compact is a principle-based framework for businesses, stating ten principles in the areas of human rights, labor, the environment, and anti-corruption. Under the Global Compact, companies are brought together with UN agencies, labor groups, and civil society (Fig. 11.3). The framework provides a universal language for corporate responsibility and a framework to guide all businesses regardless of size, complexity, or location. Joining the UN Global Compact means to take an important, public step to transform our world through principled business. Participation makes a statement about values, and it benefits both society and companies' long-term success.

Fig. 11.3 Global Compact principles. (Source: United Nations)

Corporate sustainability starts with a company's value system and a principled approach to doing business. This means operating in ways that, at a minimum, meet fundamental responsibilities in the areas of human rights, labor, environment, and anti-corruption. Responsible businesses enact the same values and principles wherever they have a presence, and know that good practices in one area do not offset harm in another. By incorporating the Global Compact principles into strategies, policies, and procedures, and establishing a culture of integrity, companies are not only upholding their basic responsibilities to people and planet, but also setting the stage for long-term success.

11.5 Case Study: Volkswagen's Lean and Green Award

The Volkswagen Wolfsburg plant receives the "Lean & Green Management Award 2019" in the "Automotive OEM" category for its efficient and sustainable production. More than 250 works from more than ten countries and 20 different industries participated in the competition. "We are proud that our persistent work has been successful in saving resources and that we have been awarded the prestigious

'Lean & Green Management Award' for this," said Stefan Loth, Head of Volkswagen's Wolfsburg plant. At the Wolfsburg location, we prove that efficient vehicle production while at the same time conserving resources is not only possible, but makes sense. Because the production also carries an ecological responsibility. The deliberate use of raw materials and energy plays a key role in our environmental commitment. In terms of production efficiency, Volkswagen's parent plant focuses on its "PQM" strategy—productivity, quality, and crew. Every year more than 400 workshops take place, with which the Wolfsburg workforce improves the processes and thus reduces the production costs per vehicle. The plant consistently uses the Volkswagen Production system that describes the basics, standards, and methods by which the manufacturing processes are designed, executed, and constantly developed. The Volkswagen parent plant is also on course for sustainability and the implementation of the "Zero Impact Factory" environmental program. An important building block for protecting the environment and promoting biodiversity are, for example, the process water basins located on the plant site. Thanks to the internal operating water cycle, every drop of water passes through the site about four to six times, helping to keep water consumption per vehicle very low. The "Lean & Green Management Award" is awarded annually by the consultants Growth Consulting Europe and Quadriga Consult and the trade publication AUTOMOBIL INDUSTRIE. The award was recently ranked as one of the highest rated sustainability awards in Germany in a study by the University of Hohenheim (Fig. 11.4).

Fig. 11.4 Volkswagen Lean and Green Award 2019. (Source: Volkswagen)

References

Helmold, M., & Terry, B. (2016). *Global sourcing and supply management excellence in China. Procurement guide for supply experts*. Springer.

Helmold, M., & Samara, W. (2019). *Progress in performance management. Industry insights and case studies on principles, application tools, and practice*. Springer.

Helmold, M. (2020). Lean Management and Kaizen Fundamentals from Cases and Examples in Operations and Supply Chain Management. Springer Cham.

Stibbe, R. (2019). CSR-Erfolgssteuerung. Den Reformprozess verstehen, Reporting und Risikomanagement effizient gestalten. Springer Wiesbaden.

Wunder, R. (2017). CSR und Strategisches Management. Wie man mit Nachhaltigkeit langfristig im Wettbewerb gewinnt. Springer Wiesbaden.Volkswagen (2019). Volkswagen Werk Wolfsburg erhält den Umweltpreis „Lean and Green Man-agement Award". Retrieved 20.11.2019. https://lean-and-green.de/de/award-gewinner.Volkswagen (2019). Volkswagen Werk Wolfsburg erhält den Umweltpreis „Lean and Green Management Award". Retrieved 20.11.2019. https://lean-and-green.de/de/award-gewinner.

12 Supply Chain Audits and Quality Management Systems (QMS)

Quality is everyone's responsibility.

—*W. Edwards Deming*

12.1 Supply Chain Audit Definition

An audit is a systematic and structured evaluation of a system, process, product, or other area with the aim of identifying deviations from the target state. Audits can be carried out internally or externally and are based on standardized audit questions and audit checklists. Audits should lead to constant improvements and are a fundamental part of every management system (Tritschler, 2014). As a result of an audit, the need for action and corrective measures (Corrective Action Requests; CARs; Open Items) are identified and set down in a scheduled action plan. The type of audit used depends on the type of goals that a company wants to have identified as "achieved." If it wants to know—possibly in the course of preparing for certification—what status it is at with regard to the fulfilment of the respective standard requirements, it will first carry out internal audits, then (optionally) a pre-audit can be carried out by the certification company; this would make it clear whether the management system in question is already ready for a certification audit, which then ultimately decides on certification. For the sake of completeness, it should be mentioned that two annual monitoring audits are pending between the issuing of a certificate and the 3 years later following audit for recertification. Table 12.1 shows the five types of audits and their respective descriptions.

M. Helmold et al., *Supply Chain Risk Management*,
Management for Professionals, https://doi.org/10.1007/978-3-030-90800-3_12

Table 12.1 Audit types

1.	Systems audit	Evaluation of a Quality Management
2.	Process audit	Evaluation of a Process from Input (via Transformation) to Output
3.	Product audit	Evaluation of a Product
4.	Control audit	Evaluation of the Progress
5.	Other audits	Finance, Environmental or other Audit

Source: Helmold (2021)

12.2 Systems Audit

The system audit evaluates the standard requirements for quality management system (QMS). The term system audit refers to the evaluation of a quality management system. The auditing of a management system, for example, according to DIN EN ISO 9001: 2015, is called a system audit. This can also be a combination of several management systems such as environment, quality, and occupational safety, which are then referred to as an integrated management system (Adam, 2020). DIN EN ISO 9001 defines the minimum requirements for a quality management system for the manufacture of products or services (QM system; QMS) that an organization must meet in order to be able to provide products and services that meet customer expectations and any official requirements. At the same time, the management system should be subject to a continuous improvement process (Brugger-Gebhardt, 2016). Although the process-oriented approach was introduced with the 2000 revision, there were considerable problems in its implementation. This should be made easier by the revision. In addition, the standard calls for a more risk-based approach. A formal QM manual will no longer be necessary if the organization provides appropriate documentation in another way. There will also no longer have to be a "top management representative" in the formal sense. The current version of ISO 9001 was last revised in 2015. Building on EN ISO 9001, IATF 16949 exists for series production in the automotive industry. Compared to EN ISO 9001, it places more extensive requirements on the quality management system. The basic idea of ISO 9001: 2015 is that companies must consider the requirements of their stakeholders for long-term success. That is why the standard has emphasized the interested parties as an independent point. In contrast to ISO 9001: 2008, the focus is no longer just on the customer, but on the interest groups (interested parties). In addition to the customer, this includes also the suppliers, owners, employees, authorities, business partners, or even competitors. ISO 9001 continues the approach of planning (plan), performing (do), checking (checking), and acting (act), in short PDCA cycle, in order to continuously improve the quality management system as a whole and its processes. The 10 elements of DIN EN ISO 9001: 2015 are listed in Fig. 12.1. In point 10, elements of lean management are anchored through the evaluation of improvement processes.

No.	DIN EN ISO 9001:2015	PDCA/Deming-Cycle
0.	Introduction	
1.	Scope	
2.	Normative References	
3.	Definitions	
4.	Context of the Organisation	PLAN
5.	Leadership	
6.	Planning	
7.	Support	Do
8.	Operations	
9.	Performance Evaluation	Check
10.	Continuous Improvement	Act

Fig. 12.1 Audit elements of the DIN EN ISO 9001:2015. (Source: Author)

12.3 Process Audits

Process audits evaluate process chains in companies from input through transformation to output. Due to the process-oriented approach, the standard is easy to apply and independent of the size of the company and the company's purpose. The effectiveness and efficiency of the organization in achieving the set goals is improved and customer satisfaction is also increased by meeting expectations. A process is a set of interrelated or interacting activities that convert inputs into results. The process audit approach enables an organization to:

- Understanding requirements better and meet them more consistently (improved, consistent, and predictable results)
- Focusing on added value (lower costs and shorter cycle times through the effective use of resources)
- Establishing effective process performance indicators
- Improving processes based on the evaluation of data and information
- Encouraging employee participation and clear responsibilities

Process audits are described in Fig. 12.2.

12.4 Product Audits

As part of the examination of a defined number of products, the product audit confirms the quality capability of the production process based on the quality characteristics of a product. It is checked whether the product complies with the specified specifications and special customer and supplier agreements. A product audit is the

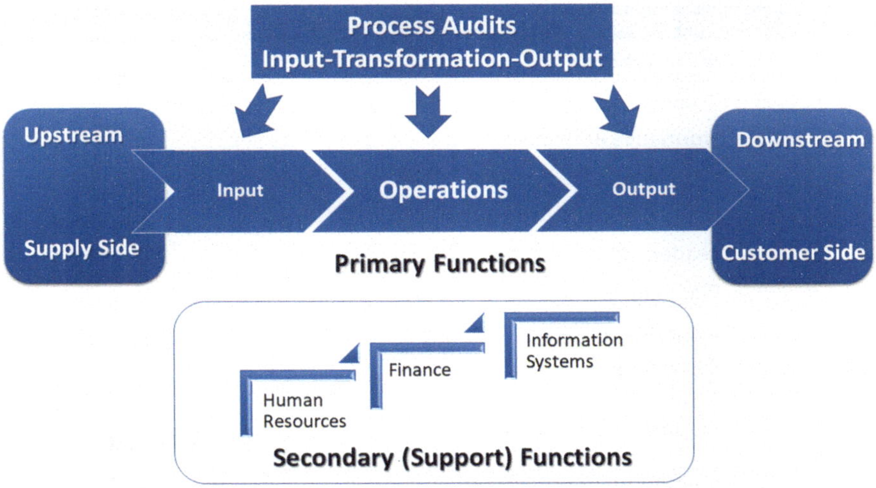

Fig. 12.2 Process audits. (Source: Audit)

planning, implementation, evaluation, and documentation of tests, namely (Helmold, 2021):

- Of quantitative and qualitative characteristics.
- In material products.
- After completion of a production step.
- And before passing it on to the next customer (internal / external).
- On the basis of target specifications.
- By an independent audit.

A product audit is used to assess compliance with the company's own quality requirements. In addition, it aims to assess the compliance with the expressed and unspoken customer requirements (with the "eyes of a very critical customer"). The product audit represents a measure to check the effectiveness of the quality tests and control measures carried out and leads directly and at short notice to process and product improvements. Finally, it creates an internal basis of trust with regard to the requirements of product liability and checks the conformity of the products, including the legal requirements. Within the automotive industry, the PPAP process is a common process for product qualification (Helmold, 2021). The production part acceptance process PPAP (Production Part Approval Process (PPAP)) is a procedure from the QS 9000, which has now been replaced by ISO / TS 16949 (Helmold & Samara, 2019). This procedure comes from the automotive industry and has been successfully implemented there for years it is primarily about the quality of the parts supplied, which means that the parts from the series tools or series processes must correspond to the drawings. In addition to the parts delivered for inspection, the sampling (Part Submission Warrant; PSW) is a central element in the sampling process.

12.5 Control Audits

Control audits are special audits outside of the regular audit plan within the value chain to verify the progress of audits and can have the following reasons:

- Progress control.
- Special process audits, for example, for processes such as gluing, painting, and welding.
- Escalation audit.
- Audits based on customer requirements.

Control audits are normally done between 3 and 6 months after the initial audit in order to validate the closure of corrective actions and to confirm the necessary implementations for improvements (Helmold & Terry, 2016).

12.6 Specials Audits

Special audits are audits with a special focus, for example, safety audit, tax audit, special process audits, or 5S audits. The International Organization for Standardization—ISO for short (from Greek ἴσος isos, German "equal" is the international association of standardization organizations and develops international standards in all areas with the exception of electrics and electronics, for which the International Electrotechnical Commission (IEC) is responsible, and with the exception of telecommunications, for which the International Telecommunication Union (ITU) is responsible. Together these three organizations form the WSC (World Standards Cooperation) (Heras-Saizarbitoria, 2018). The ISO umbrella has many audits and audit types, which are internationally applied. Two important ISO norms are the ISO 14001 and 27,001. The international environmental management standard ISO 14001 defines globally recognized requirements for an environmental management system and is part of a family of standards (Helmold & Terry, 2021). The international standard ISO 27001 for Information technology (IT Security techniques, IT security management systems, IT requirements) specifies the requirements for the establishment, implementation, maintenance, and continuous improvement of a documented information security management system, taking into account the context of an organization. In addition, the standard contains requirements for the assessment and treatment of information security risks according to the individual needs of the organization (Helmold, 2021). Figure 12.3 shows Dr. Helmold and Mrs. Lee during an audit at Mitsubishi Heavy Industries in Nagasaki-Japan.

Fig. 12.3 Audit at Mitsubishi Heavy Industries by Dr. Helmold. (Source: Author)

12.7 Case Study: 5S Audits at Berliner Kindl Schultheiss Brewery (BKSB)

As the examples given above for the effects of the 5S method already show, the 5S method has its greatest effect on the types of waste "waiting," "transport," and "movement". This is primarily due to the fact that search times and distances can be reduced significantly with the 5S method by sorting out, systematizing, and standardizing. Another, albeit mostly minor, effect is the reduction of scrap and rework. For example, damage to the product caused by dirt, such as scratches on the surface, can be reduced or even prevented by regular cleaning of the workplace. Processing

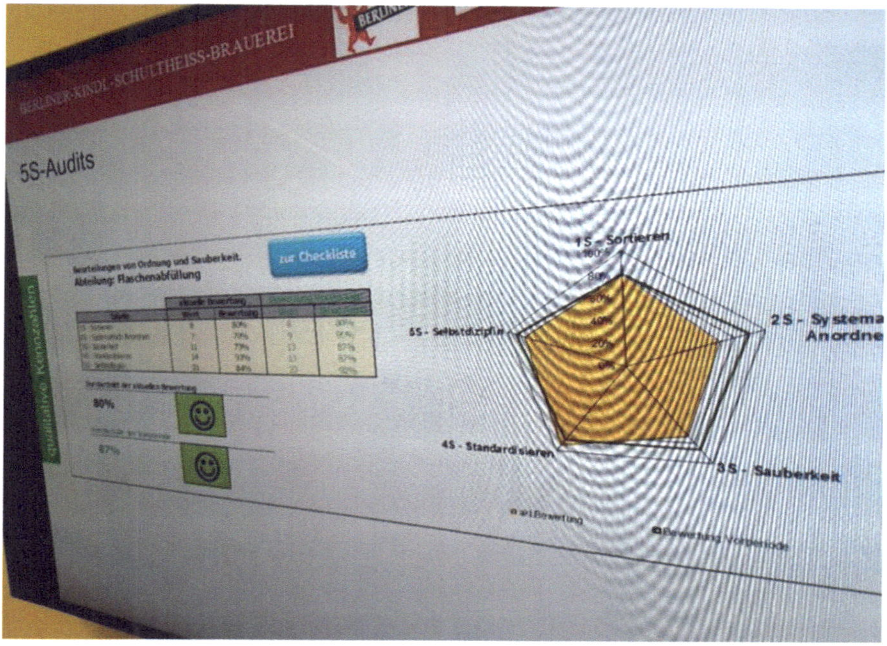

Fig. 12.4 5S Audits at Berliner Kindl Schultheiss Brewery (BKSB). (Source: Author)

machines can also lead to rejects or defects due to heavy soiling, which can be avoided with regular cleaning. The Berliner Kindl Schultheiss Brewery in Berlin carries out regular 5S audits as shown in Fig. 12.4. The audits are carried out in bottling and other areas. If needs for action are identified, these are put into an action plan with responsibilities and a target date. This action plan can be viewed by all employees.

References

Adam, P. (2020). *Agil in der ISO 9001. Wie Sie agile Prozesse in Ihr Qualitätsmanagement integrieren*. Springer Wiesbaden.

Brugger-Gebhardt, S. (2016). *Die DIN EN ISO 9001:2015 verstehen. Die Norm sicher interpretieren und sinnvoll umsetzen*. Springer Wiesbaden.

Helmold, M. (2021). *Kaizen, Lean Management und Digitalisierung. Mit den japanischen Konzepten Wettbewerbsvorteile für das Unternehmen erzielen*. Springer Wiesbaden.

Helmold, M., & Samara, W. (2019). *Progress in performance management. Industry insights and case studies on principles, application tools, and practice*. Springer.

Helmold, M., & Terry, B. (2016). *Global sourcing and supply management excellence in China. Procurement guide for supply experts*. Springer Singapore.

Helmold, M. & Terry, B. (2021). Operations and supply management 4.0. Industry insights, case studies and best practices. .

Heras-Saizarbitoria, I. (2018). ISO 9001, ISO 14001, and new management standards. .

Tritschler, J. (2014). Audit quality. Association between published reporting errors and audit firm characteristics. .

Outlook to SCRM 2030 13

Simplicity is the ultimate sophistication.

—Leonardo da Vinci (1452–1519)

13.1 Trends in Global Supply Chains and Supply Chain Risk Mitigation

13.1.1 Transformation Toward Circular and Flexible Value Chains

Experts have recently addressed the importance of the need to transform the linear value chain and convey new approaches to modern value and SCRM. The focus is on the vision of a responsibly designed global supply chain in the form of the regenerative circular supply chain. The importance of globalization and technical progress for the economic and social future is shown (Lehmacher, 2016). In the next years, SCM and SCRM will become more strategically, emphasizing some of the main issues and problems of SCM and logistics, including distribution network configuration, supply chain strategy, supply chain integration, strategic partnering, and inventory control. Additionally, SCRM will add items like SCRM tools, SCRM methodologies, problem-solving approaches, including network flow optimization, enterprise resource planning (ERP), outsourcing vs. buying, statistical process control, and lean and total quality management (Rehman et al., 2019).

13.1.2 Flexible Sensors and Software Across Supply Chains

Manufacturers want flexible operations and supply chains that allow them to use one production line to make multiple products. However, the benefits of flexibility are hard to capture because time-consuming changeovers are required to prepare

M. Helmold et al., *Supply Chain Risk Management*,
Management for Professionals, https://doi.org/10.1007/978-3-030-90800-3_13

machinery to manufacture different products. By implementing lean tools, such as single-minute exchange of dies, manufacturers can remove non-value-adding activities from the changeover, thus significantly accelerating the process. Companies that implemented smart SCRM tools, lean methods, and modern operations management will be able to benefit from these technologies (Küpper et al., 2017). New sensors and software make it possible for machines to automatically identify products and load the appropriate program and tools without manual intervention. Because the changeover is automated, operators can focus on performing value-adding activities.

13.1.3 Predictive Algorithms and Virtual Maintenance

SCRM in 2030 will include algorithms and virtual tools. In many manufacturing industries, equipment breakdowns and failures lead to high inventory levels, significant working capital cost, and low efficiency (Küpper et al., 2017). Companies can use lean methods, such as autonomous or preventive maintenance, to significantly increase the overall equipment effectiveness (OEE). By using autonomous maintenance, for example, companies assign responsibility for specific do-it-yourself maintenance activities to their operators, significantly reducing the downtime required to correct minor issues. Leading manufacturers are making the most of these lean methods by using advanced analytics algorithms and machine-learning techniques to analyze the huge amounts of data collected by sensors. The output identifies the potential for breakdowns before they occur. Such predictive insights prepare operators to perform autonomous maintenance at the optimal time, thereby reducing disruptions and minimizing unnecessary downtime and replacement costs.

13.1.4 Digital Quality Systems and Error Prevention in Supply Chains

SCRM 2030 methodologies will use digital error prevention appliances. Production capacity is wasted if products do not meet specifications. Even worse, if a company ships poor-quality products to customers, they will incur higher costs and likely lose trust in that supplier. Many lean management tools, such as self-inspection, poka yoke, and jidoka, have been developed to reduce the probability of mistakes and increase the rate and speed of error detection. For example, the analysis by Boston Consulting Group shows that self-inspections improve the process of providing feedback to engineers and operators, thereby accelerating error detection and reducing the number of defects by 50 percent to 70 percent. However, to achieve zero defects, manufacturers must support self-inspections by using a data-driven analytics approach to identify the root causes of errors. Operations Management 4.0 technologies and innovative lean methods allow such support by providing reliable context data and the ability to conduct detailed tracking. The analysis of errors is enhanced through, for example, camera-based visual inspection, correlation models, and real-time monitoring of process parameters (Küpper et al., 2017).

13.1.5 Digital Human Resources and Automated Training

Elements of health, safety, and environment (HSE) are among the most important production paradigms. To ensure operator safety, one lean approach uses signs to tell operators where they may walk. Another supply chain and lean approach uses detailed tracking of incidents and near misses to identify areas for improvement. Companies can use low-cost wireless sensors to improve the effectiveness of such efforts. For example, they can fit operators with sensors that will alert them to the presence of dangerous gases or the possibility of a clash with nearby forklifts or trucks. Companies can further improve safety by using virtual reality to train workers. Offsite training in a virtual environment is more efficient and effective than training in an actual work environment, and the approach appeals to the younger generation of workers. Seeking to reduce the high accident rate among new hires, a provider of service rigs developed immersive-training sessions in which workers practice often-dangerous tasks in a virtual simulation of the work site (Küpper et al., 2017).

13.1.6 Digital Resource Planning and Sustainability

Future ERP systems will be integrated into the entire value chain from raw material makers to the final the end customers. Digitalization will enable a transparent and sustainable supply chain including departments like procurement, operations, marketing, planning, logistics, finance, human resources, and distribution (Helmold & Terry, 2016).

13.2 Supply Chain and Lean Management Integration

When it comes to the outlook of SCRM for the future 10 years, one can say that tools and processes will become more digitalized, virtual, and autonomous. After digitization as a megatrend has long been in the foreground, artificial intelligence (AI) is increasingly becoming the focus of technically induced social change. AI or KI (German: Künstliche Intelligenz) stands for a group of technologies and applications that implement intelligent and IT-based solutions based on digital infrastructures and often using mass or big data. At present, the focus is on user behavior when shopping, in social media or in media consumption. Examples from everyday life are image and speech recognition, navigation and driver assistance systems, customized advertising, dating services, or translation programs, the results of which have become virtually error-free. Automated emergency detection, control of energy consumption, or remote control of household appliances are summarized under the term "Smart Home." However, the applications of AI will have a significant impact on lean management and the digital synchronization of supply network systems. The use of artificial intelligence also extends into the artistic sphere and space. It is reported by machines that make images in the style of famous artists

(Siebenmorgen, 2016), or recognize composers. Where mass data is available on the Internet, which can be statistically analyzed, patterned, computed, and used predictively by high-performance computers, the use of artificial intelligence is more likely than in areas where mass data is not available. Although the term AI was invented by John McCarthy at the Dartmouth Conference back in 1956 (Helmold & Samara, 2019), it is only now, with the ever-increasing amount of available data and the development of computers, that it is unimaginable to reach unimaginable masses perform o. There is a distinction between "weak AI" and "strong AI." Weak AI refers to technologies with strong application relevance and the goal of developing a very concrete solution in clearly defined, given problem contexts. All of today's AI systems fall into the category of this weak AI. The strong AI, in contrast, has a much wider and more ambitious goal: it attempts to mimic or even surpass the full intellectual ability of humans, regardless of a concrete problem context. It can be seen that AI and related technologies, on the one hand, are subject to high expectations, on the other hand, but also to defensive responses. The idea that machines can behave like humans and that all expressions of life as well as machines are connected to each other via the Internet leads to a new boom in dystopian expectations of the future. The discomfort of losing the idea of the uniqueness of human consciousness and control over the machines is supported by impresarios such as Stephen Hawking and Elon Musk, who see tremendous momentum in AI, capitalist monopolists dominating the market, and warnings speak out against abuse. In addition to the still unclear developments in society as a whole, sector-specific solutions are formulated and tested in concrete terms, for example, in the working world (Smart Factory, Smart Office, Ambient Environment), in leisure time (chess computer, gaming, navigation), and in the health sector (smart devices for rehabilitation, diagnoses). Operations in ever smaller devices, in every day life must configured and be aligned to the optimum process and supply chain. This raises the question of how and by what means new employment opportunities can be created. Major shifts are indicated in the industrial sector (Industry 4.0), in trade, but also in the media, jurisdiction, agriculture, or insurance (Siebenmorgen, 2016). New professions are expected in the service, IT, and media sectors. Changes in favor of both low and high skilled occupations and elimination of intermediate skills are likely. As a necessary consequence of the expected job loss, a far-reaching restructuring of the social system in the direction of the unconditional basic income and a robot tax is discussed. Terms such as Smart Home, Smart Cities, Smart Region, and Smart Health summarize developments aimed at further developing technical and social infrastructures. Smart City comprises a city development in which the "large technical systems" are to be optimized, integrated, and monitored on the basis of digital networking. The processes of the municipalities are to be accelerated, made more transparent and more inclusive by digital techniques, whereby participatory processes are modified. At the supra-local level, it is expected that the digital infrastructure will enable companies and workers to be kept or won. Cooperations and voting could be made easier, including mobility offers and mobility platforms.

Smart and lean factory of the future will be able to produce the required amount of product, while spending fewer resources than at present. One of the important aspects of the new industrial revolution is the ability to work with and to react on-real-time demands in a systematic end-to-end supply chain process, which will direct the production of a significant reduction in the time form of instant just-in-time pull production. Data and virtual simulations will affect the optimization of ordering, planning, and production times significantly (Helmold & Samara, 2019). In the Lean Management concept 2050, it is forecasted that flexible manufacturing facilities will occupy an integral part of the whole value chain and will be equipped with cyber-physical systems, which is a single whole of the Internet and the real physical objects. Such integration has significant advantages: the interaction with the environment, adapting a rapidly changing environment, rapid reconfiguration, self-optimizing will lead to shorter lead times, and the reduction of waste by a more resourceful process. Using a variety of sensors and built-in mechanisms have a significant impact on the structure optimization of the company, as well as it can lead to a substantial conservation of resources of the enterprise. This approach can further convert the production system into an environmentally safe, efficient advanced manufacturing.

13.3 Case Study: Lean and Safe Supply in Airbus Through AirSupply

Airbus SE, formerly Airbus Group SE, is a company based in the Netherlands that is active in the aerospace and defense industry. The company operates through three segments: Airbus Commercial Aircraft, Airbus Helicopters, and Airbus Defence and Space. The Airbus Commercial Aircraft segment focuses on the development, manufacturing, marketing, and sale of commercial jet aircraft and aircraft components, as well as on aircraft conversion and related services. The Airbus Helicopters segment specializes in the development, manufacturing, marketing, and sale of civil and military helicopters, as well as on the provision of helicopter-related services. The Airbus Defence and Space segment produces military combat aircraft and training aircraft, provides defense electronics and global security market solutions, and manufacturers and markets missiles. For the commercial side, more than 75 percent of the value creation is done by suppliers. The suppliers are supplying components and systems, which are assembled to subsystems by Airbus operational sites. These subassemblies are produced in four different countries and then shipped downstream to the final assembly as shown in Fig. 13.1. The subassemblies are delivered from different national sites to the final assembly lines. Airbus uses the AirSupply system, which integrates ERP systems on the downstream side. AirSupply is a single supply chain solution for direct deliveries to Airbus by its suppliers in the downstream supply chain (Siebenmorgen, 2016). The integration of ERP systems makes the supply or value chain very transparent, so that actions for improvements can be allocated quickly to shortcomings. Additionally, the model enables to synchronize companies's manufacturing and logistics systems digitally and physically through the application of lean management tools (Helmold & Samara, 2019). The portal is shared by the main European aerospace companies within the BoostAeroSpace hub.

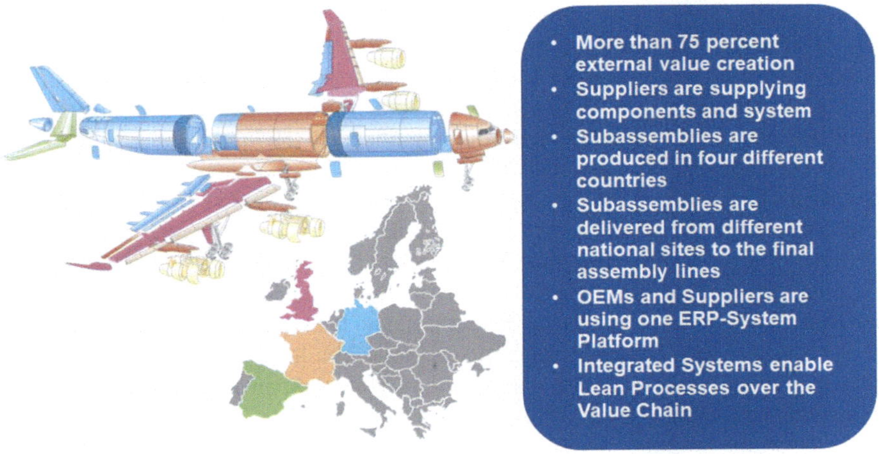

Fig. 13.1 AirSupply network. (Source: Author's own figure, adapted from SupplyOn)

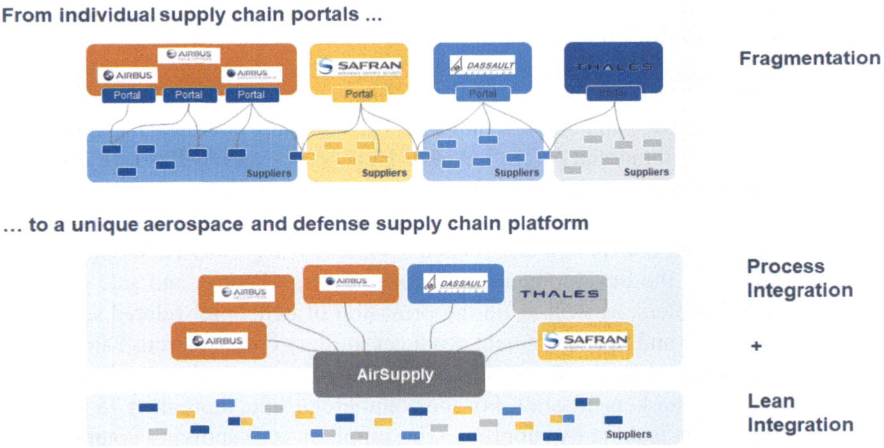

Fig. 13.2 AirSupply. (Source: Author's own figure, adapted from SupplyOn)

The AirSupply collaborative hub helps manufacturers and suppliers to gain visibility, as well as ensure control and integration for critical business processes. This common secured platform for European aerospace and defense industry players results from the BoostAeroSpace cooperation led by Airbus, Dassault Aviation, Safran, and Thales as shown in Fig. 13.2. It provides a single solution for the aerospace community connecting original equipment manufacturers (OEMs) and suppliers, standardized supply chain collaboration processes and shared formats for data exchange, and one platform for a single supply chain process collaboration via the internet (Software-as-a-Service provided by SupplyOn, with worldwide service).

References

Helmold, M. & Terry, B. (2016). Lieferantenmangement 2030. Wertschöpfung und Sicherung der Wettbewerbsfähigkeit in digitalen und globalen Märkten. Springer Wiesbaden.

Helmold, M., & Samara, W. (2019). *Progress in performance management. Industry insights and case studies on principles, application tools, and practice.* Springer.

Küpper, D., et al. (2017). Boston Consulting Group. When Lean Meets Industry 4.0. The Next Level of Operational Excellence. Retrieved 28.11.2019. https://www.bcg.com/publications/2017/lean-meets-industry-4.0.aspx.

Lehmacher, W. (2016). *Globale supply chain. Technischer Fortschritt, transformation und circular economy.* Springer Wiesbaden.

Rehman, K., Syed, A. and Zhang, Y. (2019). Strategic supply chain management. .

Siebenmorgen, F. (2016). Industrie 4.0. Das Potenzial schon heute nutzen. Retrieved 28.11.2019. https://www.supplyon.com/wp-content/uploads/import/DE_SCM%20Magazin_Industrie%20 4.0.pdf.

SupplyOn (2020). SupplyOn - The Supply Chain Business Network. www.supplyon.com/de.

The manufacturer's authorised representative in the EU is Springer Nature Customer Service Centre GmbH, Europaplatz 3, 69115 Heidelberg, Germany. If you have any concerns regarding our products, please contact ProductSafety@springernature.com

Printed and bound by CPI Group (UK) Ltd, Croydon, CR0 4YY
30/09/2026
02225462-0010